THE CRISIS OF THE
STANDING ORDER

THE
CRISIS OF THE
STANDING ORDER

*Clerical Intellectuals and Cultural Authority
in Massachusetts, 1780–1833*

Peter S. Field

University of Massachusetts Press

AMHERST

Copyright © 1998 by

The University of Massachusetts Press

ALL RIGHTS RESERVED

Printed in the United States of America

LC 98-10818

ISBN 1-55849-143-0

Designed by Steve Dyer
Set in Adobe Minion by Graphic Composition, Inc
Printed and bound by BookCrafters

Library of Congress Cataloging-in-Publication Data

Field, Peter S., 1962–
The crisis of the standing order : clerical intellectuals and
cultural authority in Massachusetts, 1780–1833 / Peter S. Field
p.   cm.
Includes bibliographic references and index.
ISBN 1-55849-143-0 (cloth : alk. paper)
1. Massachusetts—Intellectual life—18th century.
2. Massachusetts—Intellectual life—19th century   3. Elite
(Social sciences)—Massachusetts—History—18th century.
4. Elite—(Social sciences)—Massachusetts—History—19th century.
5. Congregational churches—Massachusetts—Clergy—History—
18th century.   6. Congregational churches—Massachusetts—Clergy—
History—19th century.   7. Social conflict—Massachusetts—
History—18th century.   8. Social conflict—Massachusetts—
History—19th century.   I. Title
F69.F48   1998
305.5′2′097446109033—dc21   98-10818
                                                                              CIP

British Library Cataloguing in Publication data are available.

For Helen

"Do you consider love the strongest emotion?" Leverkühn asked.

"Do you know a stronger?"

"Yes, interest."

—DR. FAUSTUS

Contents

PREFACE

G OETHE ONCE REMARKED rather modestly that "every one of my writings has been furnished to me by a thousand different persons." In writing my slender volume I too have profited from the council, critique, suggestions, and support of myriad persons. I trust they will discover something of themselves in the ensuing pages.

This project began over a decade ago when as a sophomore at Columbia University I was fortunate to enroll in James P. Shenton's year-long seminar on nineteenth-century American history. Out of that college course I gained two close friends. The first, Jim Shenton, remains an original. His catholic tastes, broad knowledge of history, intellectual generosity, and devotion to his students serve as a constant reminder of what it means to be a teacher. The consummate sage adviser, Jim read the manuscript at several stages, painstakingly edited many sections, and helped me steer it through the dissertation process. His support has been critical at every step.

Darren Staloff was a fellow student in that college class. Chess enthusiast, friend, coconspirator, and himself a historian, Darren uniquely combines a razor-sharp analytic mind with a furtive imagination. Far more than an academic, Darren is an intellectual in the best sense of the word. His sociohistorical musings about a "thinking class" were the genesis of my work. He has my great thanks for reading numerous versions of the manuscript and generously sharing his thoughts on early American history.

Two other graduate students played important roles in the development of my thinking. From Plato to pragmatism to pike fishing, Michael Sugrue and John Recchiuti have helped me hash and rehash my thoughts about far more than New England intellectuals. Generously taking time out from their own projects, they bear responsibility for much that is worthwhile in this book.

I gratefully acknowledge the support of Eric Foner and Richard Bushman. The most recent in a distinguished line of Columbia historians, they eloquently illustrate how learning about the past continues to teach us valuable lessons about the present. Dick Bushman came to Morningside Heights in time to offer a hopeful ABD much helpful advice. Reading successive drafts of my chapters, he demonstrated his unique gift for criticizing by positive reinforcement. His ability to draw attention to just the better parts of my work made that much more pleasurable the process of completing a thesis.

Eric Foner sponsored my doctoral dissertation. One of the best classroom teachers I know, he is an exceptional writer whose style I have tried to emulate. Between thrashings on the tennis court, he shared with me his keen insights, trenchant criticisms, as well as his encyclopedic knowledge of the secondary literature. Multitudes of mistakes, inaccuracies, and gaffes were thus eliminated from the final product. I continue to enjoy his friendship and contagious passion for American history.

Andrew Delbanco and Randall Balmer, in addition to teaching me about topics from Herman Melville to religious revivals, read several drafts of my manuscript while serving on my dissertation committee. A few blocks uptown, Jim Watts and Judy Stein made me feel like a welcome colleague for the several years I taught at the City College of New York. Their constant good cheer and encouragement created a congenial atmosphere for an adjunct instructor whose mind was more often than not on the nineteenth century.

Thanks are also due to a number of scholars with no Columbia affiliation, as far as I know, whom I was fortunate enough to meet upon my arrival in Tennessee. They include Paul Conkin, who read the entire manuscript, Lewis Perry, Ted McAllister, and my colleagues at Tennessee Tech. Special thanks are due Bill Brinker, Helen Deese, the late B. F. Jones, Kriste Lindenmeyer, Jeff Roberts, Katherine Osburn, George Webb, and Michael Birdwell. My colleagues eloquently exemplify the fact that accomplished scholarship is produced at so-called teaching universities.

Mary Kupiec Cayton and Judy Field read the entire manuscript and offered many invaluable suggestions, while William Barney, Nancy Field, Dean Grodzins, Daniel Walker Howe, and Jean Matthews read various chapters and graciously shared their insights. Clark Dougan, author and

now senior editor at the University of Massachusetts Press, greatly facilitated the final stages of publication. Heather Atkins, Monica Phillips, and
Pam Wilkinson helped to prepare the index, notes, and bibliography.

I gratefully acknowledge the institutional and financial support of a Columbia University Presidential Fellowship, a Center for American Cultural
Studies Fellowship, and three successive years of Faculty Release-time research grants from Tennessee Technological University. Thanks too for the
assiduous assistance of the staffs of the Andover-Harvard Library, Harvard's Houghton, Pusey, and Widener libraries, the Massachusetts Historical Society, Yale's Beinecke Rare Book Library, and the Columbia University library system. The editors of the *Journal of the Early Republic* have
granted me permission to reproduce portions of chapters 3 and 5, which
appeared in the *Journal of the Early Republic* under the title "The Birth of
Secular High Culture in America: The *Monthly Anthology and Boston Review* and Its Critics."

Finally, I am indebted to the members of my family, who have been a
continuous source of support during the long gestation of this book. I
could not have finished it without them and their encouragement. Again,
many thanks to all.

THE CRISIS OF THE
STANDING ORDER

Introduction

For two centuries the Standing Order comprised the Congregational ministers of Massachusetts.[1] A remarkable coterie of learned men, the Congregational clergy commanded the respect, deference, and, for the most part, allegiance of magistrate and citizen alike. While never a theocracy—Puritan practice forbade clerics from holding political office—the members of the Standing Order enjoyed a unique social status. Boasting neither political power nor great wealth, such famous figures as Increase and Cotton Mather, Henry Wise, Jonathan Edwards, Solomon Stoddard, and Charles Chauncy dominated their society as much as any other social class before American independence.

Ministers, as the intellectual stratum of Massachusetts, secured their station by means of cultural virtuosity. In a society in which only a tiny fraction of the public had the benefit of any schooling, virtually all the clergy had the benefit of several years of higher education. Most ministers had graduated from college. Their vocation required the assimilation, dissemination, and, for a minority, the production of high culture—traits that

---

1. The Standing Order was the name long ago adopted by the Bay State's Congregational ministers in large measure because they shepherded the established religion of the colony. This term reflected both the dominance and the unity of the Massachusetts ministers. Noted Harvard University church historian William Wallace Fenn used the term extensively in his own work. See, for example, Fenn, "The Revolt against the Standing Order," in *A Religious History of New England—The King's Chapel Lectures* (Boston, 1917), 96–113. More recently, Conrad Wright defined the Standing Order as the "traditional" term "used to designate the special relationship between church and state in the Puritan colonies of New England." See Conrad Wright, "From Standing Order to Secularism," in *The Liberal Christians* (Boston, 1970), 110–23.

virtually guaranteed public authority.[2] From a materialist perspective, the ministerial stratum's relatively formal and abstract manipulation of cultural symbols set it apart from others.[3] Specifically, ministerial alacrity in utilizing biblical exegesis to reveal the "deep structural" meaning of the sacred texts enabled the clergy to command deference and position in colonial society.[4] Members of the Standing Order gained cultural authority in direct proportion to society's uncoerced adoption of their symbolic systems. For two hundred years, the people of Massachusetts supported their ministers through public taxes in exchange for their compelling explanation of the nature of the world and the individual's place within it.

In recent years, a great deal of innovative scholarship on Puritan New England has focused on the Congregational clergy and the transmission of culture. Historians from Harry Stout and Darren Staloff to Peter Williams and David Hall have focused on the myriad means, far beyond written treatises, that ministers utilized to create and transmit culture. Ironically, while these scholars have consciously steered clear of the type of close textual analysis so brilliantly elaborated by Perry Miller, their studies if anything magnify the importance of the minister in the "aural" culture of colonial New England.[5] Building on this recent scholarship, the present work explores several aspects of the Congregational clergy's complex relationship with the various classes in society in the course of the final fifty years

---

2. I define intellectuals as those whose vocation requires some combination of assimilation and production of high culture, with fewer producing than disseminating it. High culture is the abstract and formal use of symbols within a given culture. As such, it is, by definition, historicist and contextual in nature.

3. The seminal work on legitimate domination is that of Max Weber, whose two-volume *Economy and Society* (Berkeley, 1978) was my starting point. In volume 1, chapter 3, Weber sets out his three types of legitimate authority: legal, traditional, and charismatic. None of these applies precisely to the ministers of the Standing Order, whose legitimation stemmed more from what might be called "cultural domination."

4. Typology was the most common hermeneutic device at the time. See Arthur Danto, "Deep Interpretation," *Journal of Philosophy* 78 (November 1981): 691–706, for a compelling discussion of "deep interpretation."

5. David Hall, *The Faithful Shepherd: A History of the New England Ministry in the Seventeenth Century* (New York, 1972); Harry S. Stout, *The New England Soul: Preaching and Religious Culture in Colonial New England* (New York, 1986); Darren Marcus Staloff, *The Making of an American Thinking Class: Intellectuals and Intelligentsia in Puritan Massachusetts* (New York, 1997); and Peter Williams, *Popular Religion in America: Symbolic Change and the Modernization Process in Historical Perspective* (Chicago, 1989).

of the Standing Order. While the principals of the narrative—William Emerson, Jedidiah Morse, John Thornton Kirkland, Jeremiah Evarts, Joseph Stevens Buckminster, Lyman Beecher, and their colleagues—proved less central to their times than their illustrious Puritan predecessors, they nonetheless figured prominently in the formation of Massachusetts culture in the early republic.[6] Emerson, Morse, Kirkland, and the other ministers of the Standing Order bear close examination because they produced and disseminated high culture at a turning point in American cultural development. As the Standing Order split apart, one group of ministers proved instrumental in the movement away from religion as the virtually exclusive expression of high culture. These Boston-area ministers, whom I called the Brahmins, created a secular high culture, while their opponents sought to revitalize traditional Congregational piety.

I characterize my work as a social history of intellectuals. Unlike traditional intellectual history, it neither examines nor explains the ideas behind or "informing" the cultural output of the clergy. I consciously avoid a close analysis of their doctrinal, ideological disagreements and disputations, as this is not my purpose. Many scholars have written compelling works on Congregational theology, ideology, ideas, and mentalité.[7] It goes without saying that we know a great deal about Congregationalists' beliefs and the nuances in the differing faiths of liberals, orthodox, strict Calvinists, Hopkinsians, and so on. Instead, I offer what I believe to be an important complement to the "history of ideas" approach in which the ministers of the Standing Order emerge as an intellectual stratum with their own interests, both material and ideal. My approach is materialist insofar as it does not

---

6. Two of the best recent studies of the impact on American culture of the Congregational clergy are Donald Scott, *From Office to Profession: The New England Ministry, 1750–1850* (Philadelphia, 1978) and Harry Stout, "Rhetoric and Reality in the Early Republic: The Case of the Federalist Clergy," in *Religion and American Politics*, ed. Mark A. Noll (New York, 1990), 62–76.

7. See, for example, Daniel Walker Howe, *The Unitarian Conscience: Harvard Moral Philosophy, 1805–1861* (Cambridge, Mass., 1970); Perry Miller, *The Life of the Mind in America from the Revolution to the Civil War* (New York, 1965); Andrew Delbanco, *William Ellery Channing: An Essay on the Liberal Spirit in America* (Cambridge, Mass., 1981); and Lewis P. Simpson, ed., *The Federalist Literary Mind: Selections from the* Monthly Anthology and Boston Review, *1803–1811* (Baton Rouge, 1962). I self-consciously eschew discussing minds, spirits, or conscience. See Darren Marcus Staloff, "Intellectual History Naturalized," *William and Mary Quarterly*, 3d ser., 50 (1993):406–17.

"fall back on the old-time mentalistic semantics," as the linguistic philosopher Willard Quine states.[8] It construes cultural symbols as tools, created and utilized by human beings. These Congregational clerics of the Standing Order did not so much adopt, or fall back on, ideologies as create them. They produced culture for specific purposes.[9] As a social historian of intellectuals, I seek to elaborate the mundane issues of self-interest, class alliances, power, and prestige that influenced, if often in occluded ways, the actions and decisions of the ministers of the Standing Order.[10]

As the dialectical adversary of idealist history, the present work is informed by a thoroughgoing materialism.[11] While it may have some similarities to the Progressives' scholarship of the early twentieth century, it is not simply a reconstitution of Beardian materialism. The Progressives creatively employed class analysis, to be sure, but they never really subjected intellectuals to the same type of materialist scrutiny as the bourgeoisie or proletariat. My topic is a posited collective agent, a class or stratum, with identifiable united interests. While a materialist history, it nonetheless

---

8. Willard Van Orman Quine, *The Roots of Reference* (La Salle, Ill., 1974), 36.

9. Church historian and Harvard professor emeritus Conrad Wright has called for more attention to "institutional restructuring, ... the part of the story that historians have treated least adequately." See his introductory essay in Conrad Wright, ed., *American Unitarianism, 1805–1865* (Boston, 1989), 4. Wright's fine work sets the standard for going beyond traditional ideological explanations for the conflicts among the Congregationalists.

10. The social historian of intellectuals offers a hybrid of two trends in the historical profession. She applies the skeptical stance of the social historian to intellectuals, the stratum generally studied by intellectual historians, and she looks suspiciously at agents' professed intentions and explanations. Like the bourgeoisie and the proletariat, the intellectual stratum must be studied in terms of its interests. The social historian of intellectuals contends, with candid cynicism, that intellectuals produce and disseminate ideologies frequently for self-serving reasons. Like others in society, they seek money, power, and prestige as often as the "truth." Other historians have called for some sort of synthesis; see Jane H. Pease, "Can This Old Union Be Restored? Some Questions About Social and Intellectual History," *Journal of the Early Republic* 11, no. 1(spring 1991): 1–18, and Thomas Bender, *New York Intellect* (Baltimore, 1987).

11. Materialism is the doctrine that the world is made of material entities. Historical materialists, like Marx and Engels in the nineteenth century, argued that human society and history ought to be analyzed in a similar mechanistic fashion as the so-called natural world, as opposed to the teleological, non-naturalistic interpretations of human history and behavior offered by idealists. Opposition to idealism in its many guises unifies the materialists.

differs in several fundamental ways from the "dialectical materialism" that forms the basis of most so-called Marxist studies. When writing about intellectuals, Marxist historians have relied overwhelmingly on the notion of hegemony as articulated by twentieth-century Hegelian Marxists Antonio Gramsci and Georg Lukács. Accordingly, they portray thinkers in a subsidiary role, as "organic intellectuals" in service to the real constituent classes of capitalist society, the bourgeoisie and the proletariat.[12] To offer a class history of intellectuals is not to argue that ideas, religious or otherwise, are irrelevant to individuals' lives. Ideas do play an important, even critical, role in historical figures' lives, just as they do in ours. Indeed, it is the multiple functions that ideology serves that make the study of intellectuals as the creators of culture so compelling.[13] The basic intuition of the social historian of intellectuals, then, is that it would make no sense, to the point of disfunctionality, for individuals to believe what was contrary to their basic self-interest.[14]

Following the work of Max Weber and "new-class" theorists, I argue that ownership of the means of production is not the sole measure of the social division of labor.[15] From the earliest hydraulic societies of the ancient

---

12. See Antonio Gramsci, "The Formation of Intellectuals," in *The Modern Prince and Other Writings* (New York, 1957), 118–25, and Georg Lukács, *History and Class Consciousness: Studies in Marxist Dialectics* (Cambridge, Mass., 1971).

13. This is not to suggest that intellectuals somehow controlled or brainwashed society. Reception theorists and postmodern literary critics have demonstrated that, as Mary Cayton points out, the impact of culture may well have less to do with the speaker than the listener. See Mary Kupiec Cayton, "The Making of an American Prophet: Emerson, His Audiences, and the Rise of the Culture Industry in Nineteenth-Century America," *American Historical Review* 92 (1987): 597–620.

14. There are at least three minimum attributes characteristic of any ideology: to explain the basic features of the world; to elaborate what is "right" behavior based on its description of the world; and to go beyond believability, to become virtually assumed as true. For other definitions, see John Thompson's two works: *Studies in the Theory of Ideology* (Stanford, 1990) and *Ideology and Modern Culture* (Berkeley, 1984); see also, Alvin Gouldner, *The Dialectic of Ideology and Technology: The Origins, Grammar and Future of Ideology* (New York, 1976).

15. A number of sociologists have built on the seminal work of Max Weber. They include Milovan Djilas, *The New Class: An Analysis of the Communist System* (New York, 1957); George Konrad and Ivan Szelenyi, *The Intellectuals on the Road to Class Power: A Sociological Study of the Role of the Intelligentsia in Socialism* (New York, 1979); and Alvin Gouldner's *Dark Side of the Dialectic* trilogy: *The Dialectic of Ideology and Technology;*

Near East, as Marx himself understood when describing the Asiatic mode of production, intellectuals as medicine men, priests, and keepers of the temple held tremendous power, yet owned nothing.[16] From directing irrigation systems to creating ideologies that give meaning to individual existence, the intellectual class has commanded great respect, privilege, power, and prestige throughout history.

In the case of early American history, when they have written about the intellectual stratum, Marxist historians have portrayed their subjects as the toadies of the nascent capitalist class.[17] Without their own interests, the ministers of the Standing Order proved relevant only insofar as they helped the upper class secure its dominant position in society. Needless to say, I find this account overly reductive. The Congregational clergy's distinct interests demand analysis. The alliances the ministers forged, the benefits they accrued from them, and their cultural innovations bear close examination, as do the often unforeseen consequences of their actions. The social history of this intellectual stratum, then, examines the social sources of high cultural production by Congregational clerics at the end of the eighteenth and beginning of the nineteenth century.

Staking out a middle ground at once neither traditional intellectual history nor exactly Marxian, I have sought to occupy fairly new, if not uncharted, territory. By forgoing a history-of-ideas approach to my subject,

---

The Future of Intellectuals and the Rise of the New Class (New York, 1979); and *The Two Marxisms: Contradictions and Anomalies in the Development of Theory* (New York, 1980).

16. Why Marx did not discuss intellectuals as a class is an intriguing question.

17. Several recent works focus on the role of culture vis-à-vis the Boston upper class, arguing that intellectuals are merely the servants of the wealthy. In contrast, my focus is on the intellectuals of the Standing Order and their class alliances. As this work will make apparent, I believe the relationship between intellectuals and the bourgeoisie is far more complex than these authors suggest. In the case of early nineteenth-century Massachusetts, the relationship can best be described as symbiotic. The best examples of the "cultural hegemony" argument are surely Ronald Story, *Harvard and the Boston Upper Class: The Forging of an Aristocracy, 1800–1870* (Middletown, Conn., 1980); Tamara Plakins Thornton, *Cultivating Gentlemen: The Meaning of Country Life among the Boston Elite, 1785–1860* (New Haven, Conn., 1989); and, most recently, Howard M. Wach, "Unitarian Philanthropy and Cultural Hegemony in Comparative Perspective: Manchester and Boston, 1827–1848," *Journal of Social History* 26 (1992–93): 539–57. Thornton states that the ministers "functioned as cultural ornaments to mercantile society," while Wach writes that civic culture is a key means by which "civil society tests the boundaries and languages of social relations outside the realm of formal politics and establishes the sources of moral authority which define hegemonic social relationships."

some scholars may be dismayed that I somehow devalue the noble work of the intellectual. My adoption of a cultural materialist ontology undermines their belief that intellectuals are heroically engaged in the disinterested pursuit of truth. In my account, intellectuals are no more the guardians of truth than physicists merely construct a "mirror of nature." Other scholars, on the left, may be equally disturbed by my appropriation of Marxian terminology for unorthodox purposes. Marx never discussed an intellectual class, so how can you?

Prepared for the generous opprobrium of both sides, I irenically call for each to strive to find in my work that which is consistent with theirs. The social history of intellectuals may demystify the life of the mind, but only to highlight the centrality of intellectuals in society as a whole. While their motives may often be self-serving, their creations—ideologies—serve as valuable tools in a world of thinkers. Similarly, social historians should note that this work seeks to enlarge the domain of social history. It expands the use of class analysis to include that small but critical stratum of intellectuals, the "thinking class," which, like Marx himself, seemed so anomalous in Marxian history. Using the vocabulary of Marxism in new ways, I have tried to enrich it. The social history of intellectuals is the hopeful result of crossbreeding two antithetical branches of historical endeavor.

The heart of this work details the collapse of the Standing Order of Congregational ministers in eastern Massachusetts.[18] While never a monolith, the Standing Order managed to remain united until the beginning of the nineteenth century. Common interests, near universal membership in the Federalist Party, and a long-standing history of public prestige all tended to keep the clergy together. Several factors worked against these centripetal forces. Historians have demonstrated how the rise of denominationalism and the emergence of the Baptists and Methodists dramatically altered the

---

18. Of the numerous studies on this subject, the most notable are Sidney Ahlstrom and C. H. Carey, eds., *An American Reformation: A Documentary of Unitarian History* (Middletown, Conn., 1985); Glen Gaius Atkins and Frederick L. Fagley, *History of American Congregationalism* (Boston, 1942); Frank Hugh Foster, *A Genetic History of New England Theology* (New York, 1963); Frank O. Gatell, *John Gorham Palfrey and the New England Conscience* (Cambridge, Mass., 1963); Joseph Haroutunian, *Piety versus Moralism: The Passing of New England Theology* (New York, 1932); William R. Hutchinson, *The Transcendental Ministers: Church Reform in the New England Renaissance* (New Haven, Conn., 1959); William Warren Sweet, *Religion in the Development of American Culture, 1765–1840* (New York, 1952); and the many fine works of Conrad Wright.

religious landscape of postrevolutionary New England.[19] In addition, the general movement away from state-supported religion in any form doomed the religious establishment in most states in the years after independence. Americans' growing conviction that church and state should be separate would have eventually terminated the privileged position of the Standing Order in Massachusetts, if other factors had not destroyed it first.

The breakup of the Standing Order in many ways reflected the increasing diversity of New England as a whole. It was anachronistic, to say the least, for the heterogeneous citizenry that made up this emerging competitive capitalist society to privilege one religious group over others. Likewise, the ministers of the Standing Order, differing in educational and geographical background, served increasingly different constituents in such distinct ways that their differences eventually outstripped their similarities.[20] By the 1820s, the clergy had split into several camps with the polar factions of liberal, incipient Unitarians—what I call the Brahmins—and old-style orthodox Calvinists no longer speaking to each other except to exchange hostile charges and broadsides. As a result, the laity increasingly came to recognize clerics as partisans for their own, all-too-secular causes; no longer were they the sole interpreters of biblical truth, but self-serving exponents of distinct, class-based interests. With the clergy's prestige and charisma thus diminished, the disestablishment that finally came in 1833 proved only a formality. The Standing Order had destroyed itself.

After a brief chapter summarizing the first century and a half of the Standing Order, the work details the birth of what I term the Boston Brahmins, an alliance of clerical-intellectuals and prospering merchants who were united by common concerns and shared interests.[21] Unique to Bos-

---

19. See especially Nathan O. Hatch, *The Democratization of American Christianity* (New Haven, Conn., 1989).

20. A number of recent historians have discussed the east-west and Harvard-Yale distinctions. See, in particular, Wright, *American Unitarianism* and "The Controversial Career of Jedidiah Morse, *Harvard Library Bulletin* 31 (1983): 64–87.

21. The two sides of the so-called Unitarian controversy of the Congregational church have been graced with numerous names, most commonly, Unitarians and Trinitarians. Many historians have used the following terms interchangeably: Trinitarians, orthodox, Calvinists, believers in "revealed religion," and Unitarians, liberals, Arminians, and exponents of "rational religion." In this work, I opt for the terms *Brahmin* and *orthodox*, because they do not incorporate to the same extent religious, doctrinal distinctions. The term *Brahmin* denotes the alliance of Boston's liberal ministers and merchant princes.

ton, where rich parishioners had wrested control of the Congregational churches from the "confessed," the Brahmin alliance became, as Henry Adams observed, "a social hierarchy" of wealth and culture.[22] The merchants derived from this union several forms of legitimation, including an ideological defense of the existing distribution of wealth and power, as well as, in their patronage of culture, a strengthened claim to public authority. The Brahmin ministers acquired an outlet for their nascent secular aspirations as well as a vital source of patronage for their own pursuits.

In chapter 3, I examine the birth of an indigenous secular high culture. With the backing of the mercantile elite, the Brahmin ministers supplemented, and ultimately supplanted, much of their religious work with literary and artistic endeavors. Two institutions receive close examination: the *Monthly Anthology and Boston Review* and the Boston Athenaeum.[23] Brahmin ministers published the *Monthly Anthology* with moderate success for almost a decade.[24] In this unique journal and in the congenial atmosphere of the Athenaeum's meeting rooms, the Brahmins sought to imbue their high culture with many of the same functions as religion: to refine the sensibilities, to bring renown to their community, and to elevate the mind from absorption in a sordid materialism. The language of high culture, of learning and taste, became the native tongue of this new Brahmin elite flush from lucrative overseas trade and a burgeoning domestic economy. Consciously copying British examples, such as the *Edinburgh Review,* the Brahmins envisioned the *Monthly Anthology* as an entering wedge to cure America from being a cultural backwater while simultaneously securing their social position.

Both inside the private Athenaeum, which soon boasted the largest collection of books and periodicals of any library in America, and in public, the Boston mercantile elite became discriminating, conspicuous consumers of high culture. Emulating the Medici of Renaissance Florence, this republican elite funded high culture as part of its basic claim to legitimacy, establishing itself as more than merely a pack of money-mad traders.[25] Pa-

---

22. Henry Adams, *The History of the United States of America during the Administrations of Jefferson and Madison* (New York, 1921; reprint, Chicago, 1967).

23. Hereafter cited as *Monthly Anthology.*

24. The *Monthly Anthology* was, with Joseph Dennie's *Port Folio,* America's first literary periodical.

25. Frederic Cople Jaher suggests the comparison between Proper Boston and Renaissance Venice in "Nineteenth-Century Elites in Boston and New York," *Journal of Social History*

tronage of high culture distinguished Boston Brahmins from avaricious parvenus.[26]

When the Brahmins made a bold attempt to take over Harvard College, Massachusetts's most venerable cultural institution, they precipitated the first overt crisis of the Standing Order. As chapter 4 suggests, the growing resentment and animosity of those orthodox clerics outside of Boston toward their Brahmin colleagues came to a head over the future of Harvard. The jewel in the Bay State crown, as well as the main source of educated ministers, Harvard naturally attracted the interest of the mercantile elite, who shortly began sending their (male) adolescents to Cambridge almost reflexively. The Brahmins had begun to turn some of their patronage toward Harvard as early as the 1790s, but the crisis developed around filling the vacant Hollis Professorship of Divinity in 1805. Two primary consequences ensued from the fight for Harvard, both of which had important lingering effects for the concerned parties. The Brahmins gained control not only of the Hollis professorship, but also the entire institution within a decade. While in the eighteenth century the intellectual elite largely believed that science and the arts supplemented religious studies, by the second decade of the nineteenth century their actions at Harvard suggest that they now believed them to supplant religion. The cost of their victory in 1805, however, was high. The Brahmins' orthodox opponents marshaled the forces of virtually all the less established Congregational clergy as the fight for Harvard brought to a boil the simmering hostilities within the Standing Order.

After the loss of Harvard, the various anti-Brahmin elements of the Standing Order formed a united front in an attempt to preserve orthodoxy in Massachusetts. Blaming their erstwhile Boston colleagues for the general declension of religion, the orthodox sought their own class allies and created novel, partisan institutions. Chapter 5 delineates the creation and

---

6 (1973): 66. See also J. G. A. Pocock's *The Machiavellian Moment: Florentine Political Thought and the Atlantic Republican Tradition* (Princeton, 1975).

26. While criticizing the Brahmins for abandoning Romanticism, Martin Green acknowledges that those who would claim that the United States boasted no high culture at all, or that what it did have was philistine, are in error. Turning Green's title around, I would argue that Boston Brahmins are the problem, as they are creators and patrons of a genuine indigenous high culture, even if it was not Romantic. See Martin Green, *The Problem of Boston* (New York, 1966).

character of these orthodox organizations, including the doctrinal *Panoplist* magazine, the Andover Theological Seminary, and the fiercely orthodox Park Street Church in the heart of Brahmin Boston. The combative and effusive style developed through these orthodox institutions, used to such effect in the successive revivals often called the Second Great Awakening, stemmed from two social imperatives: to point up differences between orthodox and Brahmin, and simultaneously, to maintain the allegiance of Congregational laity increasingly drawn to Baptists and Methodists. By 1810, the counterattack of orthodoxy was in full swing.

In the sixth chapter I address briefly several issues of church and state in Massachusetts, as well as the growing problems between parishes and churches. I focus on two seminal events at either end of the second decade of the nineteenth century, both of which stem from the Brahmin-orthodox split: the Dorchester controversy of 1811 and the subsequent orthodox attempts to create a Presbyterian-type structure in Massachusetts. These two events—the former precipitated by the orthodox refusal to exchange pulpits with their Brahmin brethren, and the latter by the failure of ecclesiastical councils to resolve the growing disputes between the parties—shed light on the class alliances and sectarian nature of the schism in the Standing Order. The same social tensions that gave rise to the rift between Brahmin and orthodox ministers engendered a growing divergence between church communicants and parishioners. By 1820, it was only a matter of time until Massachusetts formally disestablished the Congregational church, thus ending the Standing Order.

In the final chapter, I delineate the mature orthodox and Brahmin positions vis-à-vis their class allies and social activities. With the Dedham decision, the state weighed in on the side of the parish, thus weakening further the position of the church communicants. When church militants seceded from the parish, even if they were the majority, they forfeited their rights to church property. For the orthodox, in a single blow the Dedham decision compelled them to question the value of the Standing Order. Without the prospect of continued state support, which went to the oldest Congregational church in each parish, the orthodox party changed its tactics. By the middle of the decade, the orthodox embraced the "new methods" and voluntarism of Lyman Beecher, the recently settled minister of the Hanover Street Church whose appeal was to the middle class for the most part. Beecher's methods were critical to keeping the middle-class Congregationalist. The Brahmins retreated into an increasingly conservative political

and social outlook, dominated by defense of the status quo and the interests of their wealthy patrons. By the end of the 1820s the Standing Order
had bifurcated. The Brahmins created an elitist secular high culture pa-
tronized by the mercantile elite of Boston, while the orthodox increasingly
resorted to the new measures and methods of the revivalists.[27] Out of the
remnants of the Standing Order emerged two distinct, competing cultural formations.

In sum, the first decades of the nineteenth century marked the collapse
of the Standing Order. The results proved far more profound than the dismantling of an anachronistic church establishment. Presaging the split between religious and secular culture today, the Brahmin and orthodox ministers diverged. The former gave birth to an indigenous secular high
culture, while the latter, indicting their former colleagues for the general
decline in the Congregational church, sought a revival of national piety.
While the two parties found common ground in missionary work and
eventually in antislavery politics, they failed to bridge the chasm that had
grown between them in the first decades of the nineteenth century. Lyman
Beecher and his colleagues simultaneously refashioned and reinvigorated
orthodox Congregationalism into essentially what Harold Bloom has
styled "American Religion."[28] What they sacrificed from their Calvinist Puritan heritage they gained in relevance and general appeal. As for the Brahmins, their exclusivity and elitism rapidly curbed the spread of their denomination. The Unitarian ministers who came of age in the 1830s and
1840s worried that exclusivity ultimately entailed irrelevance. This generation of ministers that included Theodore Parker, John Pierpont and, most
famously, Ralph Waldo Emerson, whose father had been one of the leading
Brahmin ministers, realized the futility of separating its high-cultural education and training from the popular appeal necessary to gain a wide audience. These young men rejected the sour grapes of their Brahmin parents
and teachers in an attempt to become the nation's first democratic intellec-

---

27. My argument incorporates some of the ideas espoused in George M. Thomas, *Revival-
    ism and Social Change* (Chicago, 1989).
28. Harold Bloom, *The American Religion: The Emergence of the Post-Christian Nation* (New
    York, 1992).

tuals.[29] They welcomed—or at least accommodated themselves to—the notion of competing for an audience in the free market of ideas.[30]

---

29. See Peter S. Field, *Ralph Waldo Emerson and the Problem of Democracy* (Baltimore, forthcoming).

30. Lawrence Buell and Mary Kupiec Cayton, following Raymond Williams, have written on the implications for American writers and artists of the emergence of a free market for the consumption of literary production. See Buell's *New England Literary Culture: From the Revolution to the Renaissance* (New York, 1984) and Kupiec Cayton's *Emerson's Emergence: Self and Society in the Transformation of New England, 1800–1845* (Chapel Hill, 1989).

CHAPTER 1

The Standing Order to 1780

An Overview

*. . . no one can doubt that her churches were to her
as the apple of her eye.*

—INCREASE MATHER

"IN NEW ENGLAND," Henry Adams once observed, "society was organized on a system—a clergy in alliance with a magistracy; a university
supporting each, and supported in turn,—a social hierarchy in which respectability, education, property and religion united to defeat the unwise
and vicious. . . . This union created what was unknown outside New England—an organized social system, capable of acting at command for
offence or defence."[1] Adams's jaundiced eye accurately assessed the closed
system that for years dominated New England. His description of the
Federalist era could as easily apply to the previous century. From the
founding of the Massachusetts Bay Colony, a special relationship between the church and state, and the preeminent position in society held
by the Congregational clergy, engendered a unique ecclesiastical and political situation. Thomas Wertenbaker derisively graced it with the epithet
"Puritan oligarchy," while Perry Miller's teacher, Herbert Schneider, erroneously referred to it as a theocracy.[2] By the eighteenth century, Massachu-

---

1. Henry Adams, *The History of the United States of America during the Administrations of
   Jefferson and Madison* (New York, 1921; reprint, Chicago, 1967), 1:76–101.
2. Thomas J. Wertenbaker, *Puritan Oligarchy* (New York, 1947) and Herbert Schneider, *The
   Puritan Mind* (Ann Arbor, 1930).

setts's Congregational ministers simply called themselves the Standing Order.

By any name, the Standing Order represented an exclusive coterie of the highly educated and culturally gifted. From John Cotton to Cotton Mather to Charles Chauncy, Congregational ministers enjoyed remarkable power and status, particularly considering that Congregational practice forbade ministers from holding office.[3] Massachusetts Bay was not a theocracy, yet ministerial social, cultural, and political domination was extensive. Harry Stout and Darren Staloff have shown that ministers used their cultural virtuosity, their status with the community, and their near monopoly on information transmission to establish an enduring position of authority over Puritan society.[4] From expounding upon sacred works to communicating the latest news, and everything in between, ministers used their knowledge as power.[5] The Congregational clergy of the Standing Order proved preeminent in far more than just the religious aspects of colonial life.[6]

Staloff has used the term cultural domination, a combination of charismatic appeal and hermeneutic skill, to describe the power situation of the first generations of the Massachusetts clergy.[7] Cultural domination re-

3. As Increase Tarbox, a noted nineteenth-century churchman and historian commented: "[W]hat we now regard as vital to the true idea of a Congregational church—the equality of all voting members in matters of government and order, making the organization a simple and strict democracy—was practically unknown in the Massachusetts Bay through all those early years." See Increase N. Tarbox, "The Congregational Churches of Boston since 1780," in *The Memorial History of Boston*, ed. Justin Winsor, (Boston, 1880–81), 3:402.

4. Harry S. Stout, *The New England Soul: Preaching and Religious Culture in Colonial New England* (New York, 1986) and Darren Marcus Staloff, *The Making of an American Thinking Class: Intellectuals and Intelligentsia in Puritan Massachusetts* (New York, 1997).

5. Pat Bonomi writes that "[c]hurches in both country and town were vital centers of community life, as government proclamations were broadcast from the pulpit and news of prices and politics was exchanged in the churchyard." See Patricia U. Bonomi, *Under the Cope of Heaven: Religion, Society and Politics in Colonial America* (New York, 1986), 88.

6. Richard D. Brown, "Spreading the Word: Rural Clergymen and the Communication Network of 18th-Century New England," *Massachusetts Historical Society Proceedings* 94 (1984): 1–14. Only in Massachusetts could one have so much as suggested that piety ought to play a greater role in society than wealth.

7. For a discussion of cultural domination, see Staloff, *American Thinking Class*, ch. 2. The most influential use of the term *hegemony* and the role of intellectuals was penned by Antonio Gramsci in the 1930s. His analysis derived in part from the work of Auguste Compte and Karl Mannheim, as well as that of Max Weber, all of whom attempted to treat intellectuals as a special case worthy of study on their own.

quired several crucial elements that the ministers incorporated into the system known as the "New England Way." Puritan ministers and magistrates demanded church attendance for all people whatever their religious persuasion or social status, enforced deference to the Congregational clergy, and taxed inhabitants for the support of their ministers as well as for building and maintaining a suitable meetinghouse for worship. At first glance, the New England Way would seem to imply that Puritan society existed for the purpose of building not a city on a hill, but a church—and it would not be far from the truth.[8]

Colonists had good reason to respect, if not revere, their ministers. In a society in which only a tiny minority had any higher education, most of the Congregational brethren had attended college. New Englanders had many an opportunity to appreciate clerical wisdom and eloquence. They heard long and learned sermons and speeches all day Sunday as well as on Thursday evening, to say nothing of special occasions, such as fast days and election days. One minister calculated that in the course of the eighteenth century, Boston ministers delivered anywhere from eight to ten thousand lectures on Thursdays alone.[9] The impact of hearing one or two ministers deliver several thousands of hours of sermons in the course of a lifetime is hard to overestimate; Harry Stout suggests that the ministers' sermons and other public pronouncements "were so powerful in shaping cultural values, meanings and a sense of corporate purpose that even television pales in comparison."[10] And the channel might not change for a generation.[11]

---

8. Literary scholar Lewis Simpson notes that "New Englanders venerated the office. They revered the pulpit as chief voice of their society. The ministry was a discipline and a government, in effect an order resembling a priesthood." Lewis P. Simpson, *The Man of Letters in New England and the South* (Baton Rouge, 1973), 4.

9. Tarbox, "Congregational Churches," 3:402.

10. Stout estimates that "sermons totaled over five million separate messages in a society whose population never exceeded one-half million and whose principal city never grew beyond seventeen thousand." Stout's interest is in the Congregational ministry's influence on culture, or ideas. Stout continues that, "in tracing the long influence of the sermon on New England culture we have seen how piety, power, and liberty represented a sacred trinity of thought and action that oriented people's identity and sense of mission over five generations." Stout, *New England Soul*, 3–4, 309.

11. Donald Weber goes so far as to claim that "recent scholarship" suggests "that the colonial sermon was the 'central ritual' of the culture, the key mode (and medium) of communication informing all levels of society." Donald Weber, *Rhetoric and History in Revolutionary New England* (New York, 1988), 150.

Another vital element of the preeminent position enjoyed by the ministry was its close relationship with the Massachusetts General Court. Magistrates leaned heavily on the ministers of the Standing Order, who proffered advice, brought information from outlying areas, and, in turn, provided a means for dispersing information from the General Court. At moments of great urgency, magistrates never failed to request counsel from the clerics, who gathered either informally, or if the matter was sufficiently important, called a synod specifically to deal with the situation.[12] The General Court and the governor rarely crossed the clergy, as both understood the vital importance of the Congregational minister to the orderly functioning of the colony.[13] For the most part, ministers and magistrates worked together toward the same ends.

The Standing Order witnessed its unique politico-theological community virtually disappear with the revocation of the Massachusetts charter in October 1684. Fortunately, shortly thereafter the Glorious Revolution toppled the king and revived the aspirations of the Puritan leadership of Massachusetts Bay. After much special pleading by the Reverend Increase Mather, the newly installed King William III granted the colony a new charter, albeit with strictures concerning toleration. As a result of novel provisions of the new charter, particularly those ensuring the rights of religious minorities, not the least of which were members of the Church of England, the Congregational clergy undertook "an innovative way to insure the clergy's influence" over the General Court; it began to hold a formal convention in Boston on the day "when the General Assembly of the Province meets, on the last Wednesday in the month of May."[14] By the beginning of the eighteenth century, "the custom of holding special or 'Occasional' meetings was continued by the clergy, particularly in connection with Election Week; this is the seed from which the annual Convention of

---

12. "The clergy in New England," writes Jacob Meyer, "were always deeply concerned in politics." See Meyer, *Church and State in Massachusetts, 1740–1833* (New York, 1933), 134.

13. As early as 1634 and John Cotton's effort to secure the reelection of John Winthrop, the clergy began to give annual "election sermons" to proclaim the "godly" candidate for office. See Lindsay Swift, "The Massachusetts Election Sermons," *Colonial Society of Massachusetts Collections* 1 (1894): 388–450.

14. Cotton Mather, *Ratio Disciplinae Fratum Nov-Angolorum* (Boston, 1726), 22. The quote continues: "Then the ministers, chusing a moderator, do propose matters of public importance, referring to the. . . ." See also David S. Lovejoy, *The Glorious Revolution in America* (New York, 1972), 143–78.

Congregational Clergy grew."[15] By means of the convention the important symbiotic relationship of ministers and magistrates matured nicely, institutionalizing the influence of the Standing Order. "Tho' they assume no *Decisive* power," wrote Cotton Mather in 1726, "yet the Advice which they [the ministers] give to the people of GOD, has proved of great Use unto the Country."[16] Ministers regularly delivered election sermons, which, while rarely involving endorsement of a candidate, informed the laity of whom they considered fit to serve as assistants to the General Court. In turn, the ministry, with whom the newly elected assistants were generally on intimate terms, held its annual convention during the opening session of the General Court. There they would enjoy a "table-fellowship . . . with members of the magistracy."[17] Samuel Mather in a 1762 convention sermon acknowledged the special relations between the ministers and magistrates of Massachusetts Bay:

> In their capacity as protectors of the Standing Order we must acknowledge, with Thankfulness to the glorious Head of the Church and Lord of the World, and at the same Time with due Honour to the Government over us, that these our Fathers have shewed their Care of these churches by enacting good Laws for their Enjoyment of their Privileges and Freedoms respecting Divine Worship, Church Order and Discipline, and for their encouragement in the peaceable and regular Profession and Practice thereof; which Laws, having received the Royal Sanction, render our churches as such as they can be the established Churches of this Province.[18]

With the Congregational clergy assembled nearby to ensure compliance, the magistrates enacted "good Laws," particularly concerning the established church. It is not hard to imagine the impact upon the duly gathered magistrates of Cotton Mather, the most famous and powerful preacher in the colony, when he addressed them with the words, *"Syres! I have a Message from GOD unto you."*[19] In sum, while ministers never served in the

---

15. An unnamed church historian in 1795 cited by Harold Field Worthley in "A Historical Essay: The Massachusetts Convention of Congregational Ministers," *Proceedings of the Unitarian Universalist Historical Society* 12 (1958): 49.

16. Mather, *Ratio Disciplinae*, 22–23.

17. Worthley, "Massachusetts Convention," 54.

18. Ibid., 57.

19. Ibid., 58 (emphasis is in the original).

government, they nevertheless made effective use of their authority to influence its actions.

The annual convention served the interests of the Standing Order in other ways as well. One minister and church historian described the role of the convention this way:

> [I]ts design has been, to promote brotherly and religious improvement; to give advice to ministers in difficult cases; to consider the best means for preserving and promoting piety; to concert measures for the propagation of religion, and to promote collections for that purpose; to act in concert, as far as suitable to the ministerial character, in all matters of general concern, respecting the interest of religion, and the order, peace, liberties, and prosperity of the Congregational Churches.[20]

The convention and the occasional special synods sought to preserve orthodoxy, as the clergy understood the importance of clerical uniformity. By definition, the Congregational church polity placed ultimate authority in the hands of the independent churches and their congregations. In fact, the ministers aired and, for the most part, resolved virtually all major doctrinal issues. Once they settled matters, the ministers of the Standing Order took great pains to ensure that the churches spoke with a single voice in matters of great import. "There is a clerical as well as a church fellowship," stated one contemporary. "Ministers belong to groups and associations, exchange pulpits, give each other right-hands-of-fellowship and the like. These are precious and vital filaments."[21] The vital importance of speaking with a singular voice was not lost on the ministers who tolerated internal discussion and even dissension but, once they declared the party line, suppressed all further debate. At least until the Great Awakening convulsed the religious landscape in the 1740s, a renegade church or minister could not long endure the collective disapprobation of his fellow ministers.

Into the eighteenth century, the official status enjoyed by the town ministers stemmed primarily from a series of acts passed by the General Court in the years immediately following the Crown's issuance of a new charter in 1692. These acts defined the precise status of the churches vis-à-vis their

---

20. Quoted in ibid., 55.
21. Quoted in Gaius Glen Atkins and Frederick L. Fagley, *History of American Congregationalism* (Boston, 1942), 127.

congregations, their parishes, and the towns of Massachusetts Bay. In addition, the General Court passed a statute providing for the permanent remuneration of the Congregational clergy by means of a tax.[22] After 1692, the state undertook the task of paying the salaries of all ministers of the Standing Order, with the exception of those of Boston.[23]

The statutes of 1692 and 1693 proved highly significant, greatly complicating later attempts to decipher the relationship of church and state in Massachusetts Bay. Previously, ministerial status was based primarily on the Cambridge Platform, which, while it carried weight in law, was concerned solely with matters of church polity. The statute of 1693 bound the church to the state by the power of the purse. It explicitly required "all the inhabitants of and rateable estates lying within [a town] or part of a town, or a place limited by law for upholding the public worship of God" to be taxed to pay for the maintenance of an "able learned orthodox minister."[24]

The new statutes, while guaranteeing ministers' salaries, dramatically changed several aspects of church polity. The most important innovation was the introduction of the inhabitants of the towns into what had been a relationship exclusively between ministers and the church communicants.[25] In deciding to tax the residents of the towns, the General Court extended to the taxpayers some privileges concerning church-related matters. If townsmen were paying their minister's salary, so the General Court held, they should have a say in his election. At first, in the statute of 1692, the town was given the exclusive right to choose its minister, thus severely limiting the power of the church communicants. The statute stated that

---

22. See *Massachusetts Acts and Resolves* (Boston, 1911), 1:103.

23. Edward Randolph wrote in "The Present State of New England" that "the ministers in Boston are paid by a collection weekly made in the several congregations by the Elders, who give the Ministers what they think fit, but in other towns they have a settled maintenance by a rate laid down upon every inhabitant." See Edward Randolph, "The Present State of New England," in *Historical Collections,* ed. Bliss Perry (Boston, 1911), 3:22.

24. See Kirk Gibson Alliman, "The Incorporation of Massachusetts Congregational Churches, 1692–1833: The Preservation of Religious Autonomy" (Ph.D. diss., University of Iowa, 1970), 13, and John D. Cushing, "Notes on Disestablishment in Massachusetts," *William and Mary Quarterly,* 3d ser., 26 (1969): 169.

25. The church communicants previously went by the name "elders," or the "elect." These were the members who experienced a conversion and professed their faith in front of the entire congregation, and they were not pleased. For the requirements of the sanctification, as it was called, see Edmund Morgan's *Visible Saints: History of a Religious Idea* (Boston, 1965).

the minister was to be elected "by the major part of the inhabitants ... at a town meeting duly warned for that purpose," and he was to be regarded as "the minister of such town."[26] The court subsequently altered the statute in favor of a rather awkward compromise, or so it would turn out to be a century later, in which the church elders elected the minister while the town's freeholders ratified the church's decision.

This innovation in church polity caused no practical problems for many years; the towns regularly deferred to the elders' judgment. From its inception, no record of any dispute on this matter between town and church had existed for over a half century. Nonetheless, the potential for conflict was not lost on the church communicants. They well understood their de jure loss of power even if it was not manifest at the moment. Their privileged status as the fathers of each congregation had already been undermined by the Half-Way Covenant, which allowed the children of communicants to enjoy all the privileges, save the Lord's Supper, of the so-called visible saints.[27] The new statutes gave the general laity, the town freeholders, the power of the purse as well as the right to veto the communicants' choice of minister. The church elders assented to such an encroachment on their power solely because the statutes of 1692–93 promised an infusion of much-needed funds. It seems likely that if so many congregations had not been in financial straits, the churches would have fought to defeat the new laws. What they gained in fiscal support they forfeited in power.

The ministers, as the architects of the 1693 laws, were of course pleased with the results. Most importantly, they had secured their salaries on what promised to be a permanent basis, while taking away one of the most powerful weapons parishes could use against a recalcitrant pastor. This was no mean achievement. Prior to 1693, the personal records of ministers contain ample complaints concerning their lack of remuneration or repeated notes concerning well-intentioned communicants failing to deliver promised salaries. Even after passage of the new statutes, the overwhelming majority of churches in Massachusetts Bay were in arrears, causing grave hardships for many ministers and their families. Indeed, pecuniary problems were virtually the only reason that ministers left their flocks.

---

26. See Cushing, "Notes on Disestablishment," 169.
27. See Staloff, *American Thinking Class,* for a discussion of the Half-Way Covenant. "The Half-Way Covenant," writes Staloff, "was one of the most brilliant ecclesiastical innovations that the Bay divines produced."

A second element of the 1693 statute proved to be even more promising for the clergy of the Standing Order. It made clear that "it was as the minister of the town, not as the minister of the church, that the clergy was supported by taxes."[28] After 1693, the minister became a public servant of sorts, no longer even nominally paid by communicants. Once in place, his salary was funded by a compulsory tax, making him far more independent than formerly. This system continued with only minor alterations throughout the eighteenth century. In 1727, Parliament insisted that parish tax collectors turn over to Anglican ministers the taxes paid by their membership. In the following years, Parliament ruled that Massachusetts grant an outright exemption to Quakers and Baptists. All the inhabitants of the parish supported the minister, whatever they thought of him or his preaching. Rumblings from disaffected parishioners, forced to support a minister whose sermons they disavowed, sounded throughout the colony virtually overnight; yet outright dissent came only much later when increasing diversity made an established church backed by compulsory taxation utterly impossible. The old system of the Standing Order required religious homogeneity.[29]

The various religious revivals and general ferment that historians call the Great Awakening posed a direct threat to the unity of the Standing Order. By the middle third of the eighteenth century, many of Massachusetts's ministers, especially those in the eastern portion of the colony, had grown rather staid. Their salaries guaranteed by statutory tax, some ministers became less concerned with keeping the flock in church and attracting new converts as their interest in mundane pastoral matters flagged. This chagrined the laity, who became drawn by the allure of itinerant ministers, such as George Whitefield and James Davenport, whose sermons represented if not a direct attack on the Standing Order, then at least an appealing alternative. Only unified action by the Standing Order checked the dangerous invasion of enthusiasm in the years of the Great Awakening.[30]

---

28. Conrad Wright, "Institutional Reconstruction in the Unitarian Controversy," in *American Unitarianism, 1805–1865*, ed. Conrad Wright (Boston, 1989), 23.

29. The history of Puritan Massachusetts suggests that the ministers and magistrates were rather prudent in the exercise of their considerable power, so it is not surprising that the Standing Order eventually gave out in the 1820s and 1830s. By then, religious belief was far from homogeneous.

30. On the Great Awakening in Massachusetts, see Perry Miller, "Jonathan Edwards' Sociology of the Great Awakening," *New England Quarterly* 21 (1948): 50–77; Edwin S. Gausted,

The tumultuous events of the 1730s and 1740s proved far less severe in Massachusetts than in other New England States, such as Connecticut, where religious controversy virtually rent the Standing Order in two. Massachusetts's Congregational church, while threatened and attacked, managed to weather the storm relatively intact. Unlike its southern neighbor, Massachusetts Bay emerged from the ordeal with a more unified Congregational church at the cost of the birth of separating Baptist congregations.[31] On the whole, the Old Light ministers succeeded in portraying their New Light's rivals as outsiders, preaching as they did with exaggerated emotion and excitement. Once the thrill wore off and the hysteria burned itself out, the ministers convinced most of their flocks that their opponents were little more than intruders likely doing Satan's bidding rather than the Lord's. Old Lights concurred with Timothy Cutler that, as often as not, the New Light preacher was "a monster, impudent & noisy."[32] Itinerants were outsiders and they were dangerous.

On the other hand, the New Lights struck a responsive chord among at least some of the laity with their "new methods" of exaggerated excitements and frequent warnings of damnation for the unregenerate. In numerous congregations, the increasing sacerdotalism of the "learned" ministers had created a widening gap between clergy and flock. Whatever the apparent unity demonstrated during the crisis, it was clear that there was disagreement about what the Awakening had meant, what should be done in its aftermath, and how, if at all, the clergy should reach out more toward those members of the community dissatisfied with the Congregational church. In short, should new methods be adopted in some modified form? Or was enthusiasm the work of the devil, to be eliminated entirely?

The events of the so-called Great Awakening did not resolve these questions. In its aftermath, the Standing Order learned that it could, and must, tolerate internal doctrinal differences. By uniting to ward off the outside itinerant preachers and those few among them who exhibited "an excess

---

The Great Awakening in New England (New York, 1957); J. M. Bumstead, "Religion, Finance, and Democracy in Massachusetts: The Town of Norton as a Case Study," *Journal of American History* 57 (1971): 817–31; and Patricia J. Tracy, *Jonathan Edwards, Pastor: Religion and Society in Eighteenth-Century Northampton* (New York, 1979).

31. See C. C. Goen, *Revivalism and Separatism in New England, 1740–1800: Strict Congregationalists and Separate Baptists in the Great Awakening* (New Haven, Conn., 1962).

32. Timothy Cutler, letter of September 24, 1743, as cited in Eugene E. White, "Decline of the Great Awakening in New England, 1741–46," *New England Quarterly* 24 (1951): 37.

of enthusiasm," all the clergy had benefited. The ministry, while coming to see its internal divisions, vigorously defended its institutional prerogatives. The Standing Order was too important to risk a crisis like that suffered by Connecticut's ministers. That experience was to be avoided at all costs.[33]

In the Nutmeg State, as Richard Bushman has shown, the bifurcation into Old Lights and New Lights had ramifications far beyond the Congregational church.[34] The people of Connecticut came to see the utterances of their ministers no longer as the credited speech of divines specially trained in interpreting the word of God; rather, they were the words of defenders of selfish interests. If there was not one univocal truth, then perhaps there was none. The ministers lost a great deal of the status they had formerly enjoyed as the laity ceased to defer to their ministers as they once had.[35]

While the turbulence and divisiveness of the Great Awakening passed, it left in its wake a heightened recognition of internal divisions and doctrinal differences, which were not going to disappear. Nonetheless, Massachusetts's Congregational clergy, unlike that of Connecticut, managed to remain united. In fact, the intrusion of itinerants and their divisive behavior compelled the established ministers to lobby the General Court to enact a new statute to specify the qualifications of ministers. The court incorporated its desires into the Massachusetts Religious Act of 1760.[36] The General Court now granted tax support solely to ministers who had a formal college education or the "testimony of the clergy in his county that his learning was sufficient."[37] In the end, common institutional interests outstripped potentially divergent doctrinal ones during the period of the

---

33. Conrad Wright traces the origins of Unitarianism to the Arminian stance of the Old Lights from the Great Awakening. See Conrad Wright, *The Beginnings of Unitarianism in America* (Boston, 1955).

34. Richard Bushman, *From Puritan to Yankee: Character and Social Order in Connecticut, 1690–1765* (New York, 1967).

35. See Alvin Gouldner's insightful discussion of credited speech in his trilogy *The Dark Side of the Dialectic*, especially *The Dialectic of Ideology and Technology: The Origins, Grammar and Future of Ideology* (New York, 1976).

36. See Joseph Sylvester Clark, *A Historical Sketch of the Congregational Churches in Massachusetts* (Boston, 1858), 141–50.

37. See Gerard Gawalt, *The Promise of Power: The Emergence of the Legal Profession in Massachusetts, 1760–1840* (Westport, Conn., 1979), 19.

Great Awakening. Institutional breakdown did not occur in most towns until the nineteenth century.

The imperial crisis and the declaration of American independence strengthened the Standing Order. The Congregational clergy's near-universal Whig sentiment and devoted service in behalf of the patriot cause reclaimed for their members the status and prestige they had lost in the Great Awakening. The twenty years between the defeat of the French and the retreat of the British would prove to be a time of hardship for all New Englanders, not least the clergy. "It must be admitted," one nineteenth-century minister claimed, "that New England was never at a lower point religiously" than during the Revolutionary period.[38] While Congregationalists made similar laments throughout the eighteenth century, there can be little doubt that the ministers of the Standing Order, like their flocks, were preoccupied with politics and war. Indeed, some ministers tried to transform the revolution into a "Sacred War."[39] Their devotion to the patriot cause would leave them in a favorable position in the revolution's aftermath, a station from which they made important contributions to the postrevolutionary political and social order.

The ministers of the Standing Order of Massachusetts had as much to lose as anyone by increased imperial meddling in Massachusetts society, or so many of them contended. Several ecclesiastical developments at mid-century prompted the clergy to sound the alarm of imperial encroachment. The principal point of conflict concerned the Church of England, whose activities in the colony had always caused more than a little anxiety for Congregationalists. In the aftermath of the Seven Years' War, Congregational ministers expected the early establishment of an Anglican episcopate in the colonies. As early as 1763, Jonathan Mayhew, the outspoken minister of Boston's West Church, had publicly expressed concern about the ex-

---

38. Tarbox continues: "For fifty years and more from the middle of the last century the minds of men in this country were peculiarly absorbed by questions of politics and war." Tarbox, "Congregational Churches," 3:403.

39. Ronald Formisano uses the term "Sacred War" in his study of early state politics in Massachusetts. In *The Transformation of Political Culture: Massachusetts Parties, 1790s–1840s* (New York, 1983), 57, Formisano says that politicians of both political parties—Federalist and Democrat—claimed the mantle of the "sacred" American Revolution. "Service in the Revolutionary War or in public life in the 1770s and 1780s identified a man inextricably with the center of politics, whatever his views on particular issues."

panding activities of the Anglican Society for the Propagation of the Gospel and the danger of Anglican bishops on colonial soil.[40] In fact, such heightened apprehension seemed very much in concert with the general suspicion of British motives throughout the 1760s and 1770s.[41] The diplomatic resolution of the Seven Years' War, in which the French Catholics retained Quebec, caused further alarm. The people of Massachusetts had made significant sacrifices in the war effort, a primary objective of which had been the eradication of this main bastion of Catholicism in such close proximity. As a result, no group felt more betrayed by the 1763 Treaty of Paris than the Congregational clergy.[42]

The ministers of the Standing Order had been intimately concerned with politics from provincial days, so it is no surprise that political issues would be mixed with those of doctrine and church polity. Christian beliefs have always contained convictions about correct laws in society. For most people, the pulpit was a source of both ecclesiastical and political discourse, a fact not lost on John Mayhew, who declared that the "common people of New England, by means of our schools and the instructions of our 'able, learned, orthodox ministers,' are, and have been all along, philosophers and divines in comparison to the people of England, of the communion of the church there established."[43] Whatever New Englanders' preoccupation with politics prior to the imperial crisis, in the months immediately following the Stamp Act of 1765 they would garner much of the information and interpretations they might need in the meetinghouse. Until the Whigs created the Massachusetts Committees of Correspondence, the ministers were a vital, if not the exclusive, source of information on imperial matters. This was the case particularly in the interior, where, as one minister noted, "the small village pulpits rang throughout the years with

---

40. See John Mayhew, *Observations of the Charter and Conduct of the Society for the Propagation of the Gospel* (Boston, 1763).

41. Gordon Wood puts the issue of paranoia in perspective in "Rhetoric and Reality in the American Revolution," *William and Mary Quarterly*, 3d ser., 23 (1966): 3–32.

42. For the contribution of Massachusetts to the Seven Years' War and the resulting sense of betrayal concerning the peace treaty, see Fred Anderson's articles "Why Did Colonial New Englanders Make Bad Soldiers?: Contractual Principles and Military Conduct during the Seven Years' War," *William and Mary Quarterly*, 3d ser., 38 (1981): 395–417, and "A People's Army: Provincial Military Service in Massachusetts during the Seven Years' War," *William and Mary Quarterly*, 3d ser., 40 (1983): 501–27.

43. Mayhew, *Observations*, 39.

the sentiments of election sermons, that they served as textbooks in politics."[44] Harry Stout echoes this sentiment by noting that in "America's predominantly 'aural' culture, speech was even more important than print in mobilizing a revolutionary mentality."[45] Ministers were instrumental in inciting rebellion.[46]

The interconnected nature of church and state in Massachusetts enabled the Congregational clergy to transform a political struggle over colonial rights into a quasi-religious war. Ministers had little trouble marrying religious and secular issues, which were never really distinct in the first place. Numerous colonial historians from Alice Baldwin to Harry Stout have demonstrated this point persuasively. "From the repeal of the Stamp Act on," writes Stout, "New England's ministers played a leading role in fomenting sentiments of resistance and, after 1774, open rebellion."[47] Secondly, the close connection of the Congregational Standing Order and the state apparatus, together with the culturally dominant position of the clergy, made it inevitable that, along with the emerging coterie of colonial lawyers, the Congregational clergy would assume leadership positions in the movement for independence.[48] As long as the Bible remained the basic source of political ideas among the people, ministers, as the sole members of society able and authorized to interpret the deep structural meanings

---

44. Andrew P. Peabody, "The Unitarians in Boston," in *The Memorial History of Boston*, ed. Justin Winsor (Boston, 1881), 3:470.

45. Stout, *New England Soul*, 283.

46. The most recent work to establish the importance of the Standing Order in the Revolutionary movement is Dale S. Kuehne, *Massachusetts Congregationalist Political Thought, 1760–1790: The Design of Heaven* (Columbia, Mo., 1996).

47. Stout, *New England Soul*, 283; Alice Baldwin, *The New England Clergy and the American Revolution* (Durham, N. C., 1928), 7, 121. Baldwin makes what seems to be a more dubious claim that the Congregational clergy was "already developing and teaching, on the basis of traditional theories, the conceptions of a fixed constitution, and the organization of a free government which were later to lead to the demand for a constitutional convention and a written constitution." Alan Heimert took issue with Baldwin's interpretation a half century later, saying that, New Light Congregationalist ministers played the key role in fomenting revolution, and an overwhelmingly ideological one at that. See Heimert, *Religion and the American Mind: From the Awakening through the Revolution* (New York, 1966).

48. John Adams, of course, is just the best known example of the growing practice of Harvard students opting for the bar over the ministry in the eighteenth century, as John Murrin has pointed out.

embedded in that text, would elucidate key political issues. In many cases, the parish minister explained what the struggle was all about.[49]

Ministers throughout the Bay Colony were preaching independence long before 1776. During the Stamp Act Crisis, Boston's leading lights—Charles Chauncy, Jonathan Mayhew, and Samuel Cooper Thacher chief among them—actively organized colonial opposition. One historian has noted how during the crisis the Congregational clergy "served to spread and intensify a spirit of resistance among the people and to convince them that such resistance was but the carrying out of ideals and practices of their ancestors. Every villager who attended a church on the Sabbath day could talk learnedly of the reasons for refusing to pay the [stamp] tax."[50] It was clear early in the conflict on which side the Standing Order stood. They were Whigs.[51]

The various servants of the empire took note of the not-so-otherworldly activities of the Congregational clergy. They did not like it at all, but there was precious little even the governors and imperial placemen of Massachusetts could do to quell it. After Parliament repealed the Stamp Tax, Congregational activist Charles Chauncy applied to the governor for permission to conduct a day of fasting and prayer, ostensibly to celebrate the peaceful settlement of the crisis. While a measure of tranquillity had returned to the colony, Gov. Thomas Gage summarily refused Chauncy's application. With as much realism as cynicism, he concluded that "the request was only to give an opportunity for sedition to flow from the pulpit."[52] Thomas Hutchinson, the last native governor of the colony, harbored no illusions about the role of religion in the crisis. He wrote to a friend in 1770:

> It is certain that the present leaders of the people of Boston wish for
> a general convulsion, not only by harangues but by the prayers and
> preaching of many of the clergy under their influence, inflame the

---

49. The population of Boston and a few other seaboard towns were likely more influenced by lay leaders and secular sources of information, including sea captains and lawyers, as well as from reading newspapers. It was in the outlying villages that the minister was so vital for information and the weaving of that information into some ideological framework.

50. Baldwin, *New England Clergy,* 104.

51. Again, Heimert takes exception to Baldwin, arguing that New Lights were instrumental in fomenting resistance and revolution. See Heimert, *Religion and the American Mind.*

52. General Gage's acerbic comments are quoted in Baldwin, *New England Clergy,* 123.

minds of the people, and instill principles repugnant to the fundamental principles of government. . . . Our pulpits are filled with
such dark covered expressions and the people are led to think they
may as lawfully resist the King's troops as any foreign enemy.[53]

Hutchinson was not the only one to divine the sentiments of the ministry.
Peter Oliver, Hutchinson's relative, wrote with particular venom about the
role of the Congregational clergy in the revolution, whom he designated
as the "black Regiment." "As to their Pulpits," he wrote in his *Origins and
Progress of the American Revolution*, "many of them were converted into
Gutters of Sedition, the Torrents bore down all before them. The clergy
had quite unlearned the Gospel, & substituted Politicks in its Stead." And
after the Boston Massacre, "the Pulpits rang their Chimes upon blood
Guiltiness, in Order to incite the People."[54] There was no love lost here.

The clergy did not halt its activities at the outbreak of hostilities. When
revolution and war became inevitable, the overwhelmingly Whig clergy
"not only blessed it," but joined the fray, contributing to the war effort in
several vital areas.[55] Some served as officers, some as privates, while most
found more direct ways to apply their religious calling to the Whig cause.
Ministers recruited soldiers, served as information conduits, and contributed their—rather meager, as it turned out—personal savings to the drive
for independence. In addition, they "responded with patriotic fervor to the
plea of the provincial Congress for chaplains for the army, announcing
their willingness to serve in rotation, subject to the consent of their several
congregations."[56] The Reverend John Cleaveland of Ipswich saluted his
brethren's overwhelming support for the patriot cause by hanging upon
them the sobriquet "Clericus Americanus."[57]

By the end of the American Revolution, Clericus Americanus found itself in a remarkable and enviable position—remarkable particularly if one
considers that the clergy managed to assume leadership in a distinctly political movement. After all, even couched in theological terminology and

---

53. Letter of June 8, 1770, to John Pownall, as quoted in the *(Boston) Massachusetts Spy* on
    August 9, 1775.
54. See Peter Oliver, *Origins and Progress of the American Revolution: Tory View*, ed. Douglas
    Adair and John A. Shutz (New York, 1961), 128–31, 148.
55. See Atkins and Fagley, *American Congregationalism*, 121.
56. Worthley, "Massachusetts Convention," 59.
57. Quoted in Baldwin, *New England Clergy*, 115.

biblical allusion, politics and power defined the imperial struggle, while militia and minutemen waged the war. As they emerged from the war, the ministers proved to be more united and respected than at any time in more than a century. Nathan Hatch deems the "overwhelming political unity of the Congregational clergy the most towering feature" of the religious history of the period.[58] With power and prestige intact because of their overwhelming support of the war at every turn, ministers of the Standing Order were situated to maintain their preeminent position when it came time to write the first Bay State constitution.

In many ways, the Massachusetts Constitution of 1780 was one of the most important documents in early American history. Written in large measure by John Adams, it served more than any other as the model for the federal Constitution. Together with several ministers of the Standing Order, Adams incorporated into the constitution many progressive notions of American governmental forms, including a bicameral legislature, an executive veto, an independent judiciary, and a bill of rights.

One section stands apart from the rest of the Massachusetts Constitution, as well as from the republican thinking characteristic of Adams. In contrast to the national government, and virtually alone among the states, Massachusetts chose to embrace state support for the Christian religion in its constitution.[59] Article 3 of the bill of rights invested "the Legislature with power to authorize and require the several towns, parishes, precincts, and other bodies politic, or religious societies, to make suitable provision, at their expense, for the institution of the public worship of God, and for the support and maintenance of publick *Protestant* Teachers of piety, religion and morality."[60] The wording left no doubt that the Bay State was Protestant and that its freeholders would finance the Congregational

---

58. Nathan O. Hatch, *The Sacred Cause of Liberty: Republican Thought and the Millennium in Revolutionary New England* (New Haven, Conn., 1977), 7.

59. Contrast, for example, Article 5 of the New Hampshire Constitution: "The future legislature of this State shall make no laws to infringe the rights of conscience, or any other natural, unalienable rights of Men, or contrary to the laws of God, or against the Protestant religion." New Hampshire Declaration of Rights, *Collections of New Hampshire Historical Society*, 4:155.

60. Quotations from the constitution cited from *Journal of the Convention for Framing a Constitution of Government for the State of Massachusetts Bay, from the Commencement of Their First Session, September 1, 1779, to the Close of Their Last Session, June 16, 1780* (Boston, 1832).

church. The framers, institutionalizing the status quo, opted not to alter in any significant way the intimate relationship of church and state Massachusetts had enjoyed throughout its colonial history.[61] Clearly, the Standing Order was alive and well in 1780.

No article was seemingly more discordant with the sentiments of the times than Article 3 of the Massachusetts Bill of Rights. Few contemporary observers failed to point out the anachronistic standing of the Massachusetts Congregational church, particularly when compared with that in other states, where, for the most part, there was a distinct movement toward the separation of church and state. A delegate to the North Carolina constitutional convention, for example, quipped that "even the Pope of Rome might become President of the United States."[62] President or no, if the Pope moved to Massachusetts he would have to support the Congregational church.

Historians, too, have found the 1780 de facto establishment of the Congregational church anomalous. Several generations of scholars have criticized Article 3 as a decidedly peculiar and retrograde addition to the constitution. At the end of the nineteenth century, Justin Winsor, in his four-volume history of Boston, cited the "disastrous results of the long-continued union of church and state" maintained by the state constitution,[63] while Samuel Eliot Morison concluded that "Article III was reactionary."[64] Although the framers made no direct reference to Congregationalism, they unequivocally embedded the Standing Order within the constitution.

If a religious establishment clashed with most popular sentiments in other states, it certainly had strong support in Massachusetts where exertions toward separating the Congregational church from state support had faltered. In 1777, Joseph Hawley, a prominent Northampton lawyer and ardent Whig, had attempted without success to bring before the General Court a bill toward disestablishment. Hawley could not muster enough support even to bring it to the floor for a vote.[65] Similarly, voters rejected

---

61. See Cushing, "Notes on Disestablishment."
62. Quoted in Paul E. Lauer, *Church and State in New England* (Baltimore, 1892), 96.
63. Tarbox, "Congregational Churches," 3:403.
64. Samuel Eliot Morison, "The Struggle over the Ratification of the Constitution of 1780," *Publications of the Massachusetts Historical Society* 50 (1917): 371.
65. E. F. Brown, *Joseph Hawley* (New York, 1931), 180–85.

a 1778 draft of a proposed new constitution because, according to several contemporary commentators, it neglected to address religious issues adequately. The sole clause on the subject stated that the "free exercise and enjoyment of religious profession and worship shall be allowed to every denomination of Protestants within the State."[66] One legal historian concluded that several Massachusetts towns rejected the 1778 draft because

> it contained no statement of rights and did not discuss religious issues. Several factors guaranteed that a bill of rights would make some comment about religion. Precedent for using tax monies to pay ministers and religious teachers extended back to the earliest days of Massachusetts Bay Colony, when the Boston clergy alone were supported by voluntary contributions and all others were paid from the public coffers.[67]

With so much at stake, the clergy of the towns played a large role in defeating the 1778 constitution. Many ministers, like Henry Cummings of Billerica, "who laboured, both in the pulpit and out of it, to diffuse the patriotic spirit,"[68] were in a strategic position to influence the proceedings since they were both their town's minister and its representative to the 1778 and 1780 constitutional conventions.[69] Roxbury's minister, William Gordon, used his important station as chaplain to the General Court to publish an influential series of letters in the Boston *Independent Chronicle.* In these editorials, Gordon spoke out so strongly against the constitution that the General Court summarily fired him for offering so vigorous a critique of its labors.[70] Contending that the "importance of religion to civil society and government is great indeed," so great as to demand its incorporation into the constitution, most ministers of the Standing Order actively sought the rejection of the constitution of 1778.[71]

---

66. This draft: "A Constitution and Form of Government for the State of Massachusetts" is in Henry Cushing, *Government in Massachusetts* (New York, 1896), 214.

67. Charles Lippy, "The 1780 Massachusetts Constitution: Religious Establishment or Civil Religion?" *Journal of Church and State* 20 (1978): 536.

68. William Sprague, *Annals of the American Pulpit* (New York, 1865), 8:57.

69. Henry Hazen, *History of Billerica* (Boston, 1883), 238–40.

70. Cushing, *Government in Massachusetts*, 220.

71. Phillips Payson, *A Sermon Delivered before the Honorable Council of State of Massachusetts* (Boston, 1778), 529.

The Congregational clergy, realizing the importance of the constitution for its future, made sure it was well represented at the 1779–80 constitutional convention. Sent by their respective towns, thirteen ministers in all attended the convention. Prominent among them were Peter Thacher of Malden, Samuel West of Dartmouth, and Henry Cummings of Billerica, all Congregationalists; and Baptist Noah Alden of Bellingham, who chaired the committee that finally recommended Article 3 to the convention as a whole.[72]

The constitution itself was drafted during the month of September 1779 by a committee chosen by the convention. Its principal authors were John and Samuel Adams. John Adams left the state, however, before the convention took up the bill of rights. Accordingly, it seems likely that William Wells was right when he claimed that "Sam Adams was the principal agent in preparing the Declaration of Rights."[73] Regardless of who wrote it, when the committee submitted the bill of rights to the entire convention in January of 1780, it included Article 3. Providing for the "maintenance of publick Protestant teachers," Article 3 secured the prominent position of the Standing Order.

Article 3 engendered considerable excitement. Isaac Backus, a Baptist with great interest in matters of church and state, commented that the "Third Article therein was to give civil rulers power in religious matters, which occasioned much debate."[74] It stirred so much debate that even Noah Alden declined to vote in favor of Article 3. Only after much wrangling and after gaining all the concessions he could—Article 2's gesture at religious toleration in particular—Alden agreed to abstain from the vote while offering no objections to the third article.[75] The final draft incurred

---

72. See *Journal of the Convention*, 40.

73. William V. Wells, *Life and Public Service of Samuel Adams* (New York, 1888), 3:71

74. Isaac Backus, *A History of New England with Particular Reference to the Baptists* (New York, 1871), 2:225–26.

75. Not everyone present remembers the article engendering much debate. According to Caleb Strong in a letter dated 1819: "the committee met several times . . . at length agreed to report the third article as it now stands in the Declaration of Rights,—all members [including Alden the chairman] engaging to support it. . . . When the report was made to the convention there was little or no debate, and it was adopted by an almost unanimous vote." Letter to Samuel Adams as quoted in Wells, *Life and Public Service*, 3:88.

resistance on the convention floor, including "a motion to expunge the entire article."[76] The debate was so heated that a procedural rule, which provided that no delegate could speak more than twice on any particular issue, was waived temporarily. Convention President James Sullivan stated that Article 3 "underwent long debates, and took time in proportion to its importance."[77] Opponents argued that Article 3, by effectively establishing the Congregational church, would engender persecution of minority sects. Echoing these sentiments, one commentator claimed that "in order to obtain the vote, it was asserted that there never was any persecution in this land; but that what had been so called were only just punishments upon disorderly persons, and disturbers of the peace."[78]

Despite all the heated debate, the incorporation of Article 3 into the bill of rights was never really in doubt; its supporters had many important factors on their side. First, advocates of Article 3 correctly claimed that they were not offering any great innovation, merely extending a practice that dated back to the earliest settlements and that had been incorporated in Massachusetts law for a century. "New England's fathers," wrote Reverend William Sprague, "thought it incumbent on them to incorporate the church with the state in some form."[79] Omitting state support of the Standing Order as opponents of Article 3 demanded would have constituted a sea change for Massachusetts, which for the longest time had essentially taxed parishioners for the support of the Congregational clergy. To the objections of those who claimed that the convention had abridged religious liberty, supporters pointed to the inclusion of Article 2 in the bill of rights, which explicitly gave all citizens the right to worship God as they saw fit. Samuel Adams, in drafting a circular letter above the name of convention president, anticipated many of the concerns about religious liberty expressed by leery citizens. The letter outlined the middle position the authors of the bill of rights believed they had assumed. Adams wrote:

> In the third article of the Declaration of Rights, we have, with as much precision as we are capable of, provided for the free exercise of *the rights of conscience.* We are very sensible that our constituents

76. Cushing, *Government in Massachusetts,* 237.
77. Sullivan's statement is quoted in Thomas Amory, *Life and Times of James Sullivan* (Boston, 1859), 342.
78. Backus, *History of New England,* 226.
79. Sprague, *Annals,* 2:xx.

hold these rights infinitely more valuable than all others; and we flatter ourselves that, while we have considered morality and the public worship of GOD as important to the happiness of society, we have sufficiently guarded the rights of conscience from every possible infringement.[80]

For Adams and the drafters of the constitution, the financial support of one religion, even in the state constitution, would not impinge upon the rights of those of dissenting religious views. Their aim was and had always been, they argued, "to secure religious liberty without increasing infidelity."[81]

Advocates of the continued and unique Massachusetts establishment had several demographic and social elements on their side. Whereas the Anglican church had been dominant in such Southern provinces as Virginia, and on a par with the Presbyterians in North Carolina, its close affiliation with the Tory cause had prejudiced the inhabitants against any type of church establishment. Massachusetts had no such history. The Standing Order was a native institution whose ministers had fought vigorously for independence. Consequently, with the exception of the Baptists, few considered the Congregational establishment a political threat. Furthermore, as William McLoughlin has pointed out, Massachusetts had never been home to any popular deists, such as Thomas Jefferson and Benjamin Franklin, who might have led the fight against incorporating the Congregational clergy in the constitution.[82] Bay State religious liberals were, for the most part, firmly in the Congregationalist camp.[83]

---

80. Quoted in Wells, *Life and Public Service*, 3:92–93.

81. Amory, *Sullivan*, 344.

82. The best recent study of Jefferson's religious sentiments is Kerry Walters's *The American Deists: Voices of Reason and Dissent in the Early Republic* (Lawrence, Kans., 1992); quotation is from William G. McLoughlin, "The Role of Religion in the Revolution: Liberty of Conscience and Cultural Cohesion in the New Nation," in *Essays on the American Revolution*, ed. Stephen G. Kurtz and James H. Hutson (Chapel Hill, 1973), 227–28.

83. It is instructive to note the suggestions of the various states concerning a religious amendment to the federal Constitution. New Hampshire's, for example, said, "Congress shall make no laws touching religion, or to infringe on the rights of conscience"; while Virginia suggested, "That religion, or the duty which we owe to our Creator, and the manner of discharging it, can be directed only by reason and conviction, not by force or violence; and, therefore, all men have an equal, natural and unalienable right to the free exercise of religion, according to the dictates of their conscience." See Lauer, *Church and State*, 96.

Demographics played an important part in the debate as well. Over 80 percent of the population of Massachusetts considered itself Congregationalist; Congregationalism predominated in virtually every parish in the state.[84] After the revolution, it was a vigorous and confident confession. If the Standing Order was going to compromise at all, it would do so from a position of almost unassailable strength. "There was never a time," wrote Increase Tarbox, "when the Churches of the Standing Order in New England were forced by outside majorities to change their early policy."[85] Congregationalists outnumbered dissenters four to one.

All other reasoning notwithstanding, it is clear that considerable pressure to retain state support for "public Protestant teachers" was exerted by the teachers themselves. Bearing in mind its critical role in fomenting and leading the revolution, the Congregational clergy was one of the most powerful elements in the state in 1780. It made no sense for the constitution's drafters to strip the long-standing public financial support of the clergy, especially considering that the practice dated back to at least 1693, if not 1631. In addition to the undeniable prestige and persuasive power of the several ministers who served as delegates to the convention, even the lay members understood that they could not well antagonize the Congregational ministers and churches of their own communities and expect them to endorse the constitution. The clergy's important role in the defeat of the 1778 constitution had vividly demonstrated the consequences of leaving religion out. "Ignoring the interests of religious institutions," one historian explains, "would have been tantamount to defeating the constitution also."[86]

In March of 1780, the convention finally concurred upon the wording of the constitution and the bill of rights and "ordered it published and sent to the several towns in the state. The votes of the people on this subject were directed to be returned in the June following."[87] Thus, the people had from March 2 to June 7 to decide the issue in town meetings.

It did not take long for the citizens to ratify the constitution. Some histo-

---

84. See Anne C. Rose, "Social Sources of Denominationalism Reconsidered: Post-Revolutionary Boston as a Case Study," *American Quarterly* 38 (1986): 243–64.
85. Tarbox, "Congregational Churches," 3:405.
86. Lippy, "Civil Religion," 536.
87. Alden Bradford, *History of Massachusetts from the Year 1790 to 1820* (Boston, 1822–29), 2:171.

rians have raised questions about the meaning of the freeholders' votes. One scholar has pointed out the intriguing fact that "there was no complete publication of the proposed constitution in the newspapers" during the two and a half months when the people of the towns were debating the merits of the proposed constitution.[88] Many citizens, especially those in the hinterlands, found perusing a copy of the proposed constitution impossible. Nonetheless, there was a fair amount of discussion, some of it very heated, about parts of the proposed constitution. Not surprisingly, Article 3 "produced more discussion and opposition than any other part of the constitution."[89]

The Baptists denounced Article 3 most vociferously. Having failed to convince the convention delegates to keep matters of church and state separate, they took their case to the people. Opponents of the Standing Order since the Great Awakening, the Baptists had hoped that Massachusetts would finally leave the church out of politics or, at the very least, out of the foundational political document of the state. Isaac Backus, the most outspoken critic of the 1692 general-assessment statute, for years had cautioned that "ministers ought to be supported by [God's] laws and influence, and not by tax and compulsion by the civil power."[90] Backus had gone to greater lengths than anyone else to seek redress; in 1774, he traveled to Philadelphia to plead the Baptist case against the Standing Order in front of the Continental Congress. He urged the members, "as our highest civil resort, . . . for the restoration and establishment of our just rights, civil and religious."[91] John Adams himself responded to the charge by acknowledging Backus's claims for the most part. "There is, indeed, an ecclesiastical establishment in our province; but a very slender one, hardly to be called an establishment." Nonetheless, Adams, the religious skeptic, dismissed Backus and counseled his colleagues to do the same. When Backus had finished lobbying the delegates, Adams, ever the wit, quipped that Backus "might as well expect a change in the solar system, as to expect they would give up their religious establishment."[92] Backus left the Continental

88. Arthur Lord noted this fact in an article entitled "Some Objections to the [Massachusetts] Constitution, 1780," in *Publications of the Massachusetts Historical Society* 50 (1917): 57.
89. Morison, "Struggle," 368.
90. Backus, *History of New England,* 232.
91. Ibid., 200.
92. Ibid., 202n.

Congress with only Adams's promise to "invite the Baptists to lay their grievances before the first regular legislature."[93]

Other prominent persons expressed their misgivings about Article 3 of the bill of rights. Joseph Hawley, the Northampton lawyer with impeccable patriot standing, had tried for several years to get the General Court to disestablish the Congregational church. He led his town's opposition to Article 3, writing that "it is far from indisputable, and positively denied by many, viz, That it is the duty of all men in society, publicly and at stated seasons to worship, &c. . . . It is inconsistent with the unalienable rights of conscience, which rights are certainly unalienable, if mankind have, (as the first article [of the bill of rights] avers they have) any such rights."[94] In addition to Northampton, several other towns expressed concern over the general assessment for their minister's salary. "At least twenty-nine towns," according to Morison, "distinctly stated their opposition to Article 3."[95]

There were four types of resistance from one end of the spectrum to the other. Some responses complained that the declaration did not go far enough in ensuring the "worship of GOD." Specifically, it was said, the General Court should amend the constitution to include Congregationalism by name. It should make explicit the Standing Order's position of preeminence, since four out of five citizens were Congregationalists.

A second criticism, that Article 3 was too vague, proved to be more common. The response of the town of Grafton was typical; it cautioned that the article "is very ambiguously expressed," and that this would lead to problems of interpretation later on. Raynham's delegation expressed similar concerns:

> It is our opinion that the Said Third Article in the Bill of Rights ought to be more explicit so that it may be easily understood by all men. If there will not be a danger of Different Societies Quariling and Contending in the Law about their Rights which will tend to the destruction of Piety, Religion and Morality and Entirely Subvert the Intention of said Third Article.[96]

---

93. Morison, "Struggle," 376.

94. Joseph Hawley, "Protest to the Constitutional Convention of 1780," in *Smith College Studies in History*, ed. Mary Catherine Clune (Northampton, Mass., 1917–18), 3–4, 40–41.

95. Morison, "Struggle," 378.

96. Ibid., 371–72.

The authors of both the Grafton and Raynham documents proved prescient. Much of the wording of Article 3 was ambiguous and unclear. Years of litigation and acrimonious debate ensued until the state eliminated all vestiges of the Standing Order in 1833.

By far the most significant objections to Article 3 proved to be those which directly challenged the basic notion of an established church paid for from the public coffers. These objections took two forms: those concerning issues of church and state, and those addressing the issue of taxation versus voluntary support for the ministry. The Baptists expressed the most vehement displeasure, criticizing Article 3 on both fronts. Some Congregationalists also contributed dissenting views, especially lawyers who paid lip service to the importance of religion, but strongly warned against using civil authority to instill or encourage private religious belief. Some ministers, particularly those in Boston, were among the first of the Standing Order to suggest that Article 3 was simply out of step with the times. "The time is hastening," noted Thomas Bernard, "when all unnatural mixtures of civil and religious power will be taken away."[97]

According to Isaac Backus, time was not hastening fast enough. Backus was convinced that Article 3 was a retrograde action on the part of the Congregationalists. Previously, dissenting sects such as his Middleborough Baptists were exempted from taxation, whereas under Article 3, everyone, dissenting or not, would be taxed. Only after dissenters documented that they had their own "publick Protestant teachers" could they get their duly paid taxes turned over to their own minister. In addition, the number of Baptist churches was growing; Backus foresaw that it would be a struggle for every new minority church, whether Baptist, Methodist, Universalist, or whatever, to secure recognition as an incorporated church. Without official status—including a charter and an ordained minister—no church was eligible to receive its share of the general assessment. Even after recognition, new churches would be beholden to the tax man, likely a Congregationalist, to get their worshippers' levies turned over to them. In short, Backus had good reason to make an immediate stand.

Paying taxes, even to their own minister, Baptists found anathema. Their objections to Article 3 made clear their belief that religious societies must be on a voluntary basis. The voluntarist principle, not unknown within the Congregational creed, was at the core of Baptist objections to the general

---

97. Bernard is quoted in Worthley, "Massachusetts Convention," 58.

assessment, particularly as it concerned ministerial pay. In many ways, the Baptists anticipated a growing trend within all Protestant denominations. The most ardent nineteenth-century advocate of voluntarism would prove to be Lyman Beecher, an orthodox Congregationalist, whose defense of Connecticut's establishment before 1818 had soured him on state-supported religion. In 1780, however, ministerial pay was at the heart of the dispute between Baptists and Congregationalists. According to Backus, it was axiomatic "that the government of the church should be wholly by the laws of Christ, enforced in his name, and not at all by the secular arm. That gospel ministers ought to be supported by his laws and influence, and not by tax and compulsion enforced by the civil power. . . . True religion is a *voluntary* obedience unto God."[98] Article 3, then, fundamentally contradicted Baptist belief.

The debate over the constitution spilled over into the newspapers. Since the beginning of the imperial crisis some twenty years earlier, pamphlets and newspapers had become, in addition to pulpits, an important forum for most public disputes. Article 3, and the proper relation of church and state, engendered a series of articles, both for and against, in the *Continental Journal,* the *Boston Gazette,* and the *Independent Ledger.*[99] The primary disputants wrote under the pseudonyms Irenaeus and Philanthropos; Irenaeus was Boston minister Samuel West, "who always took a deep interest in political concerns,"[100] while Philanthropos has never been identified.[101]

In the course of their exchange, Philanthropos offered several principled objections to Article 3. Since religious expression was a private, not a public, concern, he contended that the state should not interfere in it; ministers

---

98. Backus, *History of New England,* 223 (emphasis his).

99. There had been an ongoing newspaper exchange between Isaac Backus and a defender of the Standing Order, who wrote above the pseudonym Heironymous. Their debate, which was published in the two years prior to the constitutional convention, presaged virtually all the arguments over Article 3, both in the convention and after. For a summary, see Charles Lippy, "Civil Religion," 543–44.

100. See Samuel West's biographical sketch in Sprague, *Annals,* 8:55.

101. William McLoughlin has suggested that Philanthropos might have been David Sanford of Medway. That Philanthropos was a member of the convention, he states himself, and there seems little reason to doubt it. Alice Baldwin states that Sanford was a member of the committee that drafted Article 3. See McLoughlin, *New England Dissent,* 1:608–9, and Baldwin, *New England Clergy,* 145n.

were not agents of the state and should not enjoy any special privileges; accordingly, voluntary contributions constituted the only equitable means of financing religion in Massachusetts or anywhere else. On a practical level, the creation of a religious establishment was an impossible task, declared Philanthropos, which invariably would cause a decline of religious goodwill, the very purpose for including Article 3 in the bill of rights. In short, Philanthropos argued, the state should let the people choose to support religion as they saw fit.[102]

Samuel West's Irenaeus called for the ratification of Article 3. His answer to Philanthropos consisted of two rejoinders. In the first place, West agreed that religious liberty constituted an undeniable right of all Bay State residents. The bill of rights, he said, did not abridge the rights of conscience at all; it affirmed them. Baptists and other dissenters were free to practice their faith as their consciences dictated. As for Article 3, West defended the mandated public support of religion. Since everyone acknowledged the importance of religious instruction for the good of society, the drafters of the constitution had only fulfilled the state's responsibility.[103] If, as all agreed, Christianity was essential to the commonwealth, then the state had to ensure its continued good health. Public support of "Protestant teachers" did just that.[104]

Samuel West was hardly the only minister to call for state support. The Congregational clergy came out in strength in defense of the constitution. Like West, the ministers carefully avoided the fact that they were in essence defending their own pecuniary interests. Instead, they emphasized the import of religion for civil society. "The fear and reverence of God, and the terrors of eternity," declared Phillips Payson, "are the most powerful restraints upon the minds of men; and hence it is of special importance in a free government."[105] Simeon Howard, one of the most outspoken advocates of Article 3, stated the issue unequivocally when he wrote that government "should have the power to provide for the institution and support of

---

102. The best summaries of Philanthropos's position are in his last two articles, both from the *Boston Gazette*. See issues August 14 and 21, 1780.

103. An intriguing parallel might be drawn with later public school efforts.

104. See Irenaeus's arguments in consecutive issues of the *Independent Ledger* from April 17 through May 22, 1780.

105. Payson, *A Sermon Delivered*, 529.

the public worship of God, and public teachers of religion and virtue . . . without which there can be no confidence, no peace or happiness in society."[106]

Using the press and their pulpits to great effect, Samuel West, Simeon Howard, and their cohorts were, in the end, able to convince most communities that the bill of rights in general, and Article 3 in particular, did not infringe upon anyone's religious liberty. According to the convention notes, over two-thirds of the towns conveyed their acceptance of Article 3 as it was written, or offered only minor revisions, although Samuel Eliot Morison, in his tabulation of the plebiscite in more than two-thirds of the 290 towns voting, concluded that only 58.8 percent voted in the affirmative on Article 3. Morison also noted that the convention counted votes by means of some legislative legerdemain, counting as "yeas" all votes affirming Article 3 "as amended" by the town committees considering the constitution. As noted above, some proposed revisions were so extensive as to call into question whether those votes should not have been interpreted as "nays." By means of this fiat, the convention, upon reconvening in June 1780, concluded that the constitution had received the required two-thirds vote needed for ratification. The convention thus declared the Massachusetts Constitution duly adopted and sent it to the General Court for implementation.[107] Massachusetts had its constitution, religious establishment and all.

Just what the third article meant for religion in the Bay State was unclear. For the Baptists and others who opposed it, Article 3 reestablished and strengthened the Standing Order of Congregational clergy. In fact, as Isaac Backus and others argued, it bound church and state closer together than it had been since the Restoration. Creating a religious establishment, Article 3 under any interpretation was an assault on their "rights of conscience."

To its advocates, the bill of rights guaranteed religious liberty while Article 3 reinforced the state's responsibility to support "publick Protestant teachers." The state, they argued, had some responsibility for religion; accordingly, the clergy concurred with Samuel West that if there was "no law

---

106. Simeon Howard, *A Sermon Preached before the Honorable House of Representatives of the State of Massachusetts* (Boston, 1780), 374–75.

107. Morison, "Struggle," 411. There were 8,885 out of 16,235 who voted in favor of Article 3 in the 220 towns Morison surveyed.

to support religion, farewell meeting-houses, farewell ministers, and farewell all religions."[108] While most delegates did not go as far as West, they did acknowledge the state's responsibility in this matter. The members of the Boston ratifying committee, explaining their decision to vote in favor of the constitution, Article 3 included, asked rhetorically: "Though we are not supporting the Kingdom of Christ, may we not be permitted to assist civil society by an adoption, and by the teaching of the best act of Morals that were ever offered to the world?"[109] The Boston delegates answered their own question: "Suspend all provision for the inculcation of morality, religion and piety, and confusion and evil work may be justly dreaded; for it is found that with all the Restraints of Government enforced by Civil Law, the World is far from being as quiet an abode as might be wished."[110] The Boston Committee, it seems clear, understood Article 3 to be less a measure about religious conscience than about education and morality.

The adoption of Article 3 was simply one means by which the state carried out its obligation to ensure domestic tranquillity. Most advocates believed Article 3 would support religion without punishing dissenters. "Your delegates," concluded James Bowdoin, president of the constitutional convention, "did not conceive themselves to be vested with the power to set up one denomination of Christians above another, for religion must at all times be a matter between GOD and individuals."[111] Clearly, a majority of freeholders agreed.

Congregationalists were one with the dissenters on the principle of religious liberty, or so they declared. The second article explicitly provided for freedom of religious expression. Why, then, did they advocate and insist upon the inclusion of Article 3 in the constitution? It seems plausible that Massachusetts might have chosen the course followed by the architects of the federal Constitution, who all but left religion out. Perhaps the Congregationalists and their supporters were dissembling as they sensed all along that they would never have a better chance to reestablish once and for all the intimate church-state relations of their forebears. John Adams certainly did not think so. Looking back in 1807, he remarked that the convention

---

108. *Independent Ledger*, April 17, 1780.
109. Boston Committee Report as quoted in Morison, "Struggle," 380.
110. Ibid.
111. Wells, *Life and Public Service*, 3:96.

might have created a religious establishment "had they so desired." According to Adams, the "convention delegates had held the power to establish Congregationalism legally, but they had not done so."[112]

The question remains of what the delegates had intended by inserting Article 3 into the constitution. Charles Lippy, in a recent analysis of the debate over religion in the 1780 constitution, concluded "that the authorization of a religious establishment was not the intention of these legal provisions, nor was it the result once the various constitutions were in effect. Rather, they saw public support for religious instruction as a way to promote political stability and social cohesion by guaranteeing that individuals would receive instruction in moral principles."[113] In short, as the title of Libby's article suggests, Article 3 did not create a religious establishment but secured Congregationalism's place as a "civil religion."

It seems likely that Article 3 was really a compromise on the issue of religious establishment. It represented a sort of lowest-common-denominator type of agreement between the Congregational clergy and the laity. The article did not enforce any doctrinal creeds yet effectively established the Congregational majorities in each parish, giving them a number of critical prerogatives concerning matters of religion. Most importantly, precisely what constituted an "able learned and orthodox minister" or a "Protestant teacher of piety, religion and morality" was left to the interpretation and discretion of the majority in the towns.

Article 3 was substantially about money. While many of the debates surrounding ratification focused on religious liberty, religious taxes constituted the core of the argument. Article 3 said, after all, that "the Legislature shall, from time to time, authorize and require, the several towns . . . to make suitable provision, at their own expense, for the institution of the publick worship of God and for the support and maintenance of publick Protestant Teachers." Isaac Backus claimed that the Baptists only desired "the liberty they enjoy in Boston," where the residents had long been exempted from religious assessments.[114] Article 3, dissenters argued, was really about getting as large a tax base as possible for the support of the Congregational clergy.

---

112. Quoted in Lippy, "Civil Religion," 544.
113. Ibid., 534–35.
114. Quoted in Alvah Hovey, *Memoir of the Life and Times of Rev. Isaac Backus, A.M.* (Boston, 1859), 221.

The chief difference between Article 3 and the general assessment of 1692 concerned money. Article 3's wording sought to change one of the problems of the earlier tax policy. Previously, an individual had only to join a dissenting sect to get himself exempted from the assessment, as the law provided for the exemption of various dissenting groups. Article 3 changed this phraseology, closing what many considered a loophole that had allowed the irreligious to avoid supporting the establishment. Congregationalists had long been wary of wealthy converts to dissenting religions. One observer said as much in a letter to the *Boston Gazette* during the debate over ratification. "Last summer, a certain rich man in the county of Plymouth, altered his principles with regard to Baptism, was rebaptized, and admitted into Mr Backus' church in Middleborough. Some neighbors were so uncharitable and censorious as to imagine that this person changed his religion in order to be freed from ministerial taxes."[115] The wording of Article 3 made the nature of such convenient conversions moot because henceforth everyone had to pay the tax. Whether or not the monies eventually went to a dissenting church was another matter.

The Congregationalists and dissenters carried on the bulk of the debate over Article 3, but the framers of the article may well have had in mind another segment of Bay State society. The number of non-churchgoers had been on the rise in Massachusetts, the war no doubt augmenting their ranks. It is altogether likely that the specific wording of Article 3 was intended to ensure this group's contribution to the establishment. Article 3 only allowed the privilege of requesting the general assessment be paid to a legally recognized dissenting Protestant teacher. People who did not go to church or who belonged to a small unincorporated church were in the same situation as were the irreligious when it came to the general assessments. Without a recognized church society to receive their taxes, they were forced simply to support the Congregational minister of their town; everyone was considered a member of her or his Congregational parish, since it was the first incorporated society in each town.

Article 3, then, expanded the tax base of the ministers of the Standing Order. "The preoccupation of numerous precincts with the problem of ministerial tax evaders," wrote one historian, "suggests that in addition to an increasingly vocal sector of institutionally contained religious dissenters there were also present in many communities a sizable element that was

---

115. Reported in the *Boston Gazette*, February 5, 1781.

unconcerned with religion in any form."[116] It is altogether likely that, while various groups supported Article 3 for different reasons, the majority of the framers sought to ensure that the growing number of non-churchgoers support the Congregational church. Robert Treat Paine said as much when commenting to a group about dissenters in his home state: "There was nothing of conscience in the matter, it was only a contending over paying a little money."[117]

In sum, Article 3 proved a compromise. Its framers sought to write a document that satisfied the conservatives, who urged the state to embrace explicitly the Congregational church as the established church of the Bay State, as well as the growing number of religious dissenters and others, who argued for the complete separation of church and state. In large measure the conservatives won. Article 3 did not establish the Congregational church, but it did establish its clergy. The Congregational clergy, transformed into civic teachers, managed to secure a guaranteed salary with the assistance of the tax man.

The dissenters, their heated arguments notwithstanding, also won. It became clear within a few years that the constitution did not abridge religious liberty in any meaningful way. Under the new constitution, dissenting sects flourished, none more so than the Baptists. The framers had simultaneously guaranteed religious freedom and privileged the Standing Order. While dissenters could, and did, go their own way, the Congregational clergy had secured its salary by means of a public tax, as decreed by Article 3. The unity of the Congregational ministers in the face of concerted opposition proved crucial to the ratification of the 1780 constitution, as many observers shrewdly noted. "It is fortunate for us that the clergy are generally with us," noted Levi Lincoln in a letter to George Washington a few years later. "They have in this state a very great influence."[118] When Massachusetts finally disestablished the Standing Order over half a century later, the Congregational clergy was a shell of its former self, having fissured into competing camps.

---

116. See Alliman, "Incorporation of Massachusetts," 196.
117. Quoted in Morison, "Struggle," 376.
118. Atkins and Fagley, *American Congregationalism*, 136.

CHAPTER 2

The Birth of the Brahmins

*Boston or Brattle Street Christianity is a compound force
or the best diagonal line that can be drawn between Jesus
Christ and Abbot Lawrence.*

—RALPH WALDO EMERSON

A T THE TURN of the nineteenth century, Boston was home to nine Congregational churches. The Puritans founded First Congregational Church in 1630, while their descendants established the ninth, West Church, over a century later.[1] In these Boston churches—Brattle Street, Second Church, New North, Hollis Street, and Federal Street, in particular—liberal ministers and wealthy pew owners joined together to constitute the Brahmins. William Emerson, Joseph Stevens Buckminster, John Thornton Kirkland, John Eliot, Jeremy Belknap, Samuel West, Charles Lowell, William Ellery Channing, and others self-consciously transcended the traditional "office" of the Congregational ministers of the Standing Order. As the transitional generation between Charles Chauncy and Jonathan Mayhew, who preached an accommodating arminianism, and the leading Unitarians of the Jacksonian era, Emerson, Buckminster, Kirkland, et al., both intellectually and socially re-created themselves as high priests of culture. Encouraged and funded by their well-healed parishioners,

---

1. After First Church's founding in 1630, Congregationalists built Second Church in 1650, Old South in 1669, Brattle Street in 1699, New North in 1714, New South in 1719, Federal Street in 1727, and Hollis Street in 1732, before West Street in 1737. Two others, Samuel Mather and School Street, were constructed in the 1740s but disbanded in 1785.

they proved instrumental in fostering a Boston-based secular highbrow culture.

Long before the turn of the nineteenth century, Boston's churches possessed essential characteristics distinct from those of the rest of the Standing Order. For better or worse, Boston's houses of worship reflected the capital's importance as the political and commercial center of Massachusetts. From the founding of the colony through the War of Independence, the merchant adventurers, living primarily in Boston, and the ministerial leadership of the Massachusetts Bay Company had distinct, and often opposing, visions of the goals of the Puritan enterprise. Inevitably, the merchants, having contributed large sums toward the undertaking, believed that the settlements should be geared toward profits. There is ample evidence that from the founding of the Massachusetts Bay Company in England, they resented the ministerial domination of the adventure.[2] As early as the Antinomian Crisis of 1636, there proved an unmistakable "divergence between the merchants and most of the rest of the Puritan population."[3] Deeply religious for the most part, the merchant community nonetheless desired to make the city more profitable and less Puritan.[4]

By the end of the seventeenth century, Boston boasted a sizable merchant community that was rapidly growing prosperous as a result of the lucrative fishing and shipping industries. One consequence of this increasing wealth was the construction in 1698 of the Boston's fourth Congregational church. Brattle Street Church, as it came to be known, was the first Congregational society formed in Boston since the 1660s. Its organization marked a significant turning point in the city's religious history as well as that of Massachusetts Bay.

Brattle Street Church proved innovative in many respects. Merchants donated the funds to build the church and supported it generously in subsequent years. Accordingly, they greatly influenced the doctrinal and policy

---

2. See Darren M. Staloff, *The Making of an American Thinking Class: Intellectuals and Intelligentsia in Puritan Massachusetts* (New York, 1997).

3. Bernard Bailyn, *The New England Merchants in the Seventeenth Century* (Cambridge, Mass., 1979), 41.

4. "Boston was fragmented from the very beginning," wrote Darrett Rutman in *Winthrop's Boston: A Portrait of a Puritan Town, 1630–1649* (Durham, N. C., 1965), 21. Winthrop's vision of a city upon a hill "was doomed to failure." Other towns in Massachusetts Bay came far closer to Winthrop's ideal Christian commonwealth.

developments within the church. What the mercantile elite created proved to be Boston's most exclusive church, encompassing the wealthiest members of the Congregational community. The exclusivity of the Brattle Street churchgoers manifested itself in the way the society conducted its business. Members purchased their pews essentially according to social status. Pew rents paid the bills, including, most importantly, the ministers' salaries, which were the most ample in the colony. In contrast to the other churches of the Standing Order, Brattle Street conducted its business through several committees, dominated by the wealthiest pew proprietors, in conjunction with the church communicants. Brattle Street proved to be the sole Congregational church in which the church communicants did not possess the prerogative of calling the minister. Brattle Street's unique parishioner status resulted in its reputation as the "aristocratic society" among Boston's Congregational churches.

The relative power of the wealthiest pew proprietors over the church communicants had important ramifications for this newest Congregational society. In matters of church doctrine, Brattle Street became more liberal, eventually latitudinarian, as it increasingly reflected the sentiments of its urbane and successful proprietors. The communicants, or full church members, upon whom fell the job of ensuring doctrinal uniformity, simply had too little power within the church structure to press their case. Through the course of the eighteenth century, largely as a result of the relative strength of proprietor over communicant, Brattle Street's ministers retreated from the doctrines of Calvin. While neither Samuel Cooper nor Peter Thacher can be called incipient Unitarians—they would have been deeply distressed by the materialism of Joseph Priestly's four-volume *History of the Early Opinions Concerning Jesus Christ*—both ministers' writings reflected some form of the rationalism and latitudinarianism so characteristic of Unitarians.

Brattle Street proved to be the first, but not the last, Congregational church in Boston to embrace the views associated in Europe with the teaching of Jacobus Arminius, the sixteenth-century Dutch theologian.[5] In

---

5. In addition to Brattle Street, First Church, New North, New South, Federal Street, Hollis Street, and West Street gradually adopted some form of Arminianism. Two other churches, Samuel Mather and School Street, were absorbed into the eight societies mentioned above in 1785.

the latter half of the eighteenth century, many of Boston's churches drifted away from strict Calvinist doctrines.[6] As in the case of Brattle Street, the ascendancy of pew proprietors over church communicants precipitated the transformation. Convinced they were masters of their own fate, Boston's elite sought pastors like Jonathan Mayhew, Charles Chauncy, and John Lathrop, who served a rational and benevolent deity.[7] Minister and parishioner were highly devout to be sure; yet, as they repudiated the orthodoxy of their Puritan predecessors, they mutually agreed that the pulpit could do without fire and brimstone. Few Boston ministers admonished the pew owners with the parable of the rich man and the camel. Likewise, wealthy Bostonians did not go to church to hear admonitions in front of their neighbors and ne'er-do-wells. Rejecting the doctrines of double predestination and human depravity, they considered themselves neither sinners nor in the hands of an angry God.

Jonathan Edwards's "Sinners" sermon, as well as many others like it, rocked the Massachusetts countryside between 1734 and 1742. Yet, the mass conversions and general excitement of the so-called Great Awakening, while profoundly important for the later development of religion in New England, affected Boston only modestly. On the whole, the bifurcation of New Lights and Old Lights served to increase greatly the separation of Boston's liberal churches from the rest of Massachusetts. Itinerant preachers and their enthusiastic ranting acted, it seemed to Boston ministers, like intoxicants upon many of the people of the Bay Colony, particularly as it became evident that religious enthusiasm could wane as rapidly as it waxed. As a result, by the 1750s many ministers concluded that the successive revivals had done much more harm than good. When George Whitefield made his second tour of New England in 1745, Harvard College's president officially ridiculed him as "a censorious, uncharitable person, and a deluder of the people."[8] For young Boston ministers like Charles Chauncy, Simeon Howard, John Lathrop, and James Freeman, the "enthu-

---

6. Arminius and his followers, as embraced by Unitarianism, emphasized the development of Christian character, rather than the personal experience and display of conversion, and thus came to doubt the doctrine of universal predestination. See Williston Walker, *A History of the Christian Church* (1919; rev. ed., New York, 1959), 399–401.

7. For an interesting discussion of proto-Unitarian views, see Robert Wilson's biography of Ebenezer Gay: Robert J. Wilson III, *The Benevolent Deity: Ebenezer Gay and the Rise of Rational Religion in New England, 1696–1787* (Philadelphia, 1984).

8. See Josiah Quincy, *History of Harvard University* (Boston, 1860), 2:48.

siasm" of the itinerants, and of the New Lights generally, had demonstrated itself to be a grave deception unleashed on naive people by ignorant, unscrupulous, and dangerous men.[9] During the years of awakening, Boston's leading ministers fought, individually and collectively, against any further encroachments of the unschooled itinerant preachers and the religious enthusiasm they engendered. They turned increasingly toward the predictable doctrines of what they called rational religion, a set of beliefs that reconciled Enlightenment thought with Puritan theology. "Change in belief came gradually and almost imperceptibly," wrote Octavius Brooks Frothingham.[10] "There was simply a more generous interpretation of ancient formulas."[11] As their parishioners grew prosperous and sophisticated, Boston's ministers adopted a more learned, practical, and "rational" set of religious doctrines that ultimately formed the basis of Unitarianism, or what Ralph Waldo Emerson sardonically styled "Boston religion."[12]

"Boston religion" should not be understood as a doctrinal revolt against Calvinism or any religious creed. In fact, it was not a revolt at all, but rather more of an evolutionary change.[13] It proved to be more of a "humanitarian" than a theological attitude. "Boston was liberal before it became Unitarian," wrote Joseph Haroutunian, "and its Unitarianism was primarily ethical and social."[14] Few debates or disputes over church doctrine erupted among the clergy or anyone else, as the early transition to "rational reli-

---

9. Chauncy's most vituperative critique of the itinerants' "enthusiasm," especially that of Davenport, can be found in his *Seasonable Thoughts on the State of Religion in New England* (Boston, 1743), 198–215.

10. Octavius Brooks Frothingham, *Boston Unitarianism* (New York, 1890), 41.

11. Ibid.

12. Neither Emerson nor the author means to suggest by "Boston religion" that all churches in Boston were Unitarian or would shortly become so. In 1800, in addition to the eight incipient Unitarian churches, Boston was home to the orthodox Congregationalist Old South; Episcopalian King's Chapel; two Baptist houses of worship; and a Catholic, Methodist, and Universalist church. See *The Boston Directory, Containing the Names of the Inhabitants, Occupations, Place of Business and Dwelling Houses* (Boston, 1798), 7.

13. For a fine discussion of the evolution of "unbelief" over more than a century, see James Turner, *Without God, without Creed: The Origins of Unbelief in America* (Baltimore, 1985).

14. Joseph Haroutunian, *Piety Versus Moralism: The Passing of New England Theology* (New York, 1932), 179–80. Liberalism did not mean the same thing to all people. Rather, it signified a constellation of non-Calvinist beliefs including a rejection of universal and unconditional predestination.

gion" proved seamless for the most part. The advent of Unitarian, or "anti-Athanasian," belief in Boston has never been dated precisely. By William Ellery Channing's 1819 Baltimore sermon, Boston's leading churches had already embraced for some time the sensibilities associated with Unitarianism. In an 1815 letter to the orthodox cleric, Jedidiah Morse, former President John Adams demurs when Morse argues that "Unitarianism is represented as only thirty years old in N England. I can testify as a witness to its old age—65 years ago my own minister," Adams writes, could be called Unitarian.[15] The relative ease of this transition resulted, in part, from the American Revolution, which inaugurated a limited moratorium on theological controversy. In an era when liberty was on everyone's lips, movement away from enforcing religious orthodoxy was inevitable. More significantly, Boston ministers and laity rarely engaged in doctrinal disputation in large measure because it no longer interested them; neither the liberal clergy nor their affluent parishioners cared for such seemingly unimportant hairsplitting upon which nothing seemed to hang.[16] Liberal, or what more suitably can be called Brahmin, ministers and their lay allies understood themselves more by means of their social sensibilities than their adherence to any dogma. Elizabeth Palmer Peabody characterized the Brahmins' preaching as "always ethical rather than theological."[17] They embraced New England's version of latitudinarianism, devoting themselves to the preservation of the established order and the maintenance of a deferential society. Doctrine proved secondary to the subtle issues of class and culture.

In choosing the label "liberal," the ministers meant to suggest something

---

15. Adams to Morse, May 15, 1815, copy in Morse Papers, Massachusetts Historical Society. Morse calls his opponents Unitarians as early as 1805. See Morse to Joseph Lyman, June 15, 1805, Morse Family Papers, Yale University Archives.

16. A fine example of putting social issues ahead of theological ones is the case of John Murray, the evangelist. Murray's preaching of the doctrine of universal salvation during his 1770 visit to the Bay City should have found a ready audience among the liberal clergy, especially Charles Chauncy, who was about to publish his *Salvation for All Men*. Instead, Chauncy and his colleagues virtually hounded Murray out of Boston, citing him as an example of the vulgar and uneducated ministers who had caused so much disruption during the Great Awakening. Here, theological belief was secondary to social status.

17. Elizabeth P. Peabody to William Sprague, June 3, 1854, in William Sprague, *Annals of the American Pulpit* (New York, 1865), 8:279.

quite distinct from present usage and connotations; they were gesturing at their openness, catholicity, and latitudinarian generosity to diverse doctrinal positions. Far from being devoted to any dogmatic positions, Boston's ministers, William Emerson declared in an 1803 sermon, "religiously avoided the metaphysical subtleties, with which some adherents to Calvin bewilder themselves and their hearers."[18] The term *Brahmin*, however, seems preferable to *liberal* for several reasons. In the Hindu religion, Brahmin refers to the highest status of thinkers, thus specifically connoting intellectual achievement.[19] Not only does it convey the clergy's class commitments and cultural values, something that even to them proved more important than any doctrinal revisionism, but it suggests their status as America's first coterie of professional intellectuals.[20] Representative of the more affluent and socially prominent Bostonians, the Brahmin ministers sought to preserve the social order as they defended the existing distribution of wealth and status. Virtually without exception, they attended Harvard, not Yale, their distant Connecticut cousin. Culturally, they were cosmopolitan in outlook and secure in wealth and social standing. Preaching accommodation to an increasingly comprehensible world composed of modern science and literary expression, they justified the pursuit of wealth and status, celebrated reason and good order, and embraced symbols of class standing.[21] Calling themselves "enlightened Christians," they argued

---

18. William Emerson, *A Sermon on the Decease of the Rev. Peter Thacher, D.D.* (Boston, 1803), 20.

19. The ministers saw themselves in some measure related to their Hindu counterparts. The *Monthly Anthology* published the *Sakuntala*, which Van Wyck Brooks claims to have been "the first Hindu work to appear in the country." See Van Wyck Brooks, *The Flowering of New England, 1815–1865* (New York, 1936), 20.

20. Both David Tyack and Lawrence Lader employ the term *Brahmin* in the more traditional sense for the Boston's antebellum elite. Richard Brown uses the term almost precisely, as I do, in a recent review article. See Tyack's *George Ticknor and the Boston Brahmins* (Cambridge, Mass., 1967); Lader, *The Bold Brahmins: New England's War against Slavery* (New York, 1961); and Richard Brown, "Who Should Rule at Home? The Establishment of the Brahmin Upper Class," *Reviews in American History* 9 (March 1981): 55–61.

21. Donald Scott describes the transformation of ministerial responsibilities in a different context in his *From Office to Profession: The New England Ministry, 1750–1850* (Philadelphia, 1978). He focuses broadly on the entire Congregational clergy, while I am here differentiating between two different factions within the denomination. The transformation from office to profession was by no means uniform over the entire Congregational clergy.

that "the God of scripture is the same being as the God of nature."[22] In a review article about the relationship of religion and science, one Brahmin went so far as to proclaim that "the phenomena and operations of the natural world, as explained and illustrated by philosophy, might furnish most important means . . . communicating to all, new and sublime views of the attributes, character and intentions of God."[23]

While the Congregational ministers vehemently disagreed about the precise origins of Unitarianism in the United States, all concurred that it was a Boston phenomenon.[24] Becoming the creedless stance of the Brahmins, who came together in the first decades of the nineteenth century as a powerful alliance of grand bourgeoisie and liberal ministers, they constituted, as Henry Adams observed, "a social hierarchy of . . . respectability, education, property and religion."[25] The enterprising grand bourgeoisie, grown prosperous from a boom in overseas trade, and the educated elite of the Standing Order, many of whom had become acquainted with one another while attending Harvard College several years earlier, joined together to form a remarkable union. Out of this alliance developed an important symbiotic relationship—not unlike that which has become almost commonplace today—between a culturally committed bourgeoisie and an enlightened clique of intellectuals. This union signaled a degree of financial and intellectual freedom previously unheard of for Congregational ministers, or any other American intellectuals for that matter; at the same time, it legitimated the wealthy's claim to an exclusive cultural and social status. Patronage of the arts, initially through subsidy of Brahmin ministers, helped distinguish the Brahmin merchant from the pretentious philistine "trader."[26] The birth of the Brahmins eventually set Boston apart from its neighbors, making it a sanctuary to some and a Sodom to others.

---

22. *Christian Examiner* 3 (1826):15.

23. Ibid., 17.

24. If the key tenet of the Unitarian sensibility is the restoration of everyone to salvation, then Charles Chauncy, as early as the 1750s, can be called a proto-Unitarian. His first defense of the doctrine was not published until 1784.

25. Henry Adams, *The History of the United States of America during the Administrations of Jefferson and Madison* (New York, 1921; reprint, Chicago, 1967), 76.

26. For the importance of cultural virtuosity in the self-identification of Brahmin status, see Frederic Cople Jaher, "Nineteenth-Century Elites in Boston and New York," *Journal of Social History* 6 (1973): 32–77. Patronage of the arts was part of Boston's "civic role characteristic," notes Jaher on page 66.

The intellectual freedom enjoyed by the Brahmin ministers of Boston proved extremely important for subsequent developments within the Standing Order. This freedom, so vital to the ministers, stemmed from two conditions unique to Boston. In the first place, Boston's bourgeoisie had a strong sense of civic duty—a legacy, perhaps, of their Puritan past. As politics diminished as an outlet for civic sensibilities, the Brahmins turned increasingly to the arts as an alternative, or at least as a complement to political activity.[27] "If the affluent would patronize the arts," declared Robert Field in 1806, "they would be looked up to with veneration by . . . every subordinate class of society."[28] Second, since Boston churches were funded by their parishioners, the status of the church communicants had declined compared to the rest of the state. Therefore, communicants were not in a position to demand the same kind of doctrinal conformity and dogmatism from the minister as their counterparts in outlying parishes. As a result of the comparative intellectual freedom granted their ministers, Boston churches became an arena for enlightenment, high cultural virtuosity, instead of old-time religion. Boston let its ministers, deeply religious to be sure, act as cultural gatekeepers as opposed to stern shepherds ever vigilant lest their flock should stray.

In other parts of Massachusetts, liberal-leaning ministers confronted problems that their colleagues in Boston did not. Everywhere but Boston, the church communicants instead of the parishioners held the bulk of power. They enjoyed significant control over the calling of a minister as well as over other church matters. Not surprisingly, the church communicants, having professed their faith before the entire congregation, tended to be more dogmatic and far more concerned about doctrine than other parishioners. In virtually every dispute between church and parish during the first decades of the nineteenth century, the church communicants tended to be conservative theologically and orthodox doctrinally. As the parishioners and communicants diverged, conflict between them proved

---

27. Not only was elective politics becoming more populist, which prompted one Federalist to exclaim that "the herd is now walking on its hind legs," but even appointive office proved increasingly out of reach of civic-minded Federalists. When it came to governmental appointments, Jefferson and Madison failed to treat aspirants as "all Republicans, all Federalists." See Carl Prince, "The Passing of the Aristocracy: Jefferson's Removal of the Federalists, 1801–1805," *The Journal of American History* (1966): 563–75, and Shaw Livermore, *The Twilight of Federalism* (Princeton, 1962), ch. 3.

28. *Monthly Anthology* 3 (1806): 300.

inevitable. Accordingly, a minister espousing liberal views virtually guaranteed himself some sort of conflict with the church communicants.

For a number of reasons, full church members in Boston were inclined to be less steadfast in their devotion to religious orthodoxy; more significantly, whether Brahmin or orthodox, they possessed diminishing authority in church governance as well as in the calling of the minister. For example, a dispute broke out in 1806 when pew proprietors of Old South Church, the only orthodox church remaining in Boston, attempted to assume complete control of church property. The proprietors wanted to exclude non-pew owning members from meetings in which church property was discussed. Old South's minister, Joseph Eckley, opposed the proprietors, even though this put him at odds with "Dawes, Salisbury, and Phillips, the most influential men in the church and congregation at that time," who were more sympathetic to Eckley's increasing liberalism than most full church members. Instead, Eckley supported the full church members (who still had the official voice in appointing the minister) in their bid to retain their traditional role as keepers of all church land and property. In a compromise settlement forged by Eckley, Old South broke tradition by allowing pew proprietors to join in the call for a new assistant pastor, a prerogative members previously had kept for themselves.[29] On the whole, Boston ministers, even such luminaries as Charles Chauncy, found that their relations with the church communicants remained generally cordial. In any event, church matters were increasingly transacted between the minister and the parishioners, not the communicants; accordingly, ministers, over time, allied themselves with their parishioners, the leading pew owners particularly, at the expense of the church communicants.

The significant social differences between Boston and the outlying areas in Massachusetts were exacerbated by the constitution of 1780 when it came to church polity matters. Since Article 3 exempted Bostonians from paying their ministers with tax money, allowing the town to continue "its accustomed way and practice,"[30] "the Salary of the Minister [was] raised by a Voluntary Contribution."[31] "The ministers of Boston," wrote Edward Randolph in 1799, "are paid by a Collection weekly made in the several

29. Hamilton Hill, *History of the Old South Church* (Boston, 1889), 2:309–42.

30. See *Acts and Resolves, Public and Private, of the Province of Massachusetts Bay* (Boston, 1869–1922), 1:103.

31. Cotton Mather, *Ratio Disciplinae Fratrum Nov-Angolorum* (Boston, 1726), 20.

Congregations by the Elders, who give the ministers what they think fit, but in other towns they have a settled maintenance by a rate laid down upon every inhabitant."[32] This voluntary system had several significant ramifications for Boston's houses of worship. In the capital, ministerial salaries depended on the satisfaction of the congregations: the larger the congregation, the higher the salary. Likewise, ministers of wealthier congregations garnered higher salaries. Federal Street Church, upon calling Jeremy Belknap in 1787, effectively offered him a year-end bonus if he augmented the society's membership, stipulating that "in the case our society shall increase, and the pews be all occupied, the salary shall then be increased to a comfortable support."[33] Church policy devolved to those with the largest material stake in the society, those who held the most valuable pews.[34] As pew owners gained authority, church communicants as a distinct group lost theirs, especially the right to call the minister. In Boston churches, then, the authority of those in full communion, which had never been equal to that of rural churches, declined precipitously as the century drew to a close. Clearly, Boston's Congregational churches changed with their society as a whole far more dramatically than those outside the capital. Where the Congregational churches had once served as a bridge between Boston and beyond, they now showed signs of fracturing along the same social lines as society at large.

None of this discussion is meant to suggest that Boston's wealthy parishioners were irreligious, or even that they were less so than the church members in full communion. While there surely is a connection between the development of Unitarianism and Universalism and "the origins of unbelief," as James Turner has suggested, it seems clear that pious Bostonians, minister and laity alike, took their churches very seriously.[35] The orthodox *Spirit of the Pilgrims* may have gone a bit overboard when it cited the "testimony of a Unitarian minister," which claimed that the Boston elite "join that kind of church which imposes the fewest restrictions, and makes the

---

32. Randolph excerpted in Bliss Perry, ed., *Historical Collections* (Boston, 1911), 3:22.
33. *Church Records of Federal Street Society,* as cited in Sprague, *Annals,* 8:77.
34. The voluntary system "caused the pews in their several houses to be valued according to the convenience and situation thereof, and a new estimate to be put upon said pews from time to time, as shall be found necessary." Arthur B. Ellis, *History of the First Church in Boston* (Boston, 1881), 186.
35. Turner, *Without God,* chs. 3, 4.

fewest demands; they care little for any of the religious interests of the community, and are sure to avoid exertion and contribution."[36] Similarly, Boston ministers would shortly react so vehemently to the orthodox's charges of infidelity not because they sought to hide the truth, but because they thought the charges so utterly baseless.

Boston ministers were more vulnerable under the voluntary system than their rural colleagues. If they failed to attract a sizable audience, they jeopardized their own livelihood. In contrast to his counterparts in outlying regions, the parishioner in Boston "had the option, denied to those residents of a country parish, of withdrawing his support from a minister with whom he was displeased."[37] This seems to have been a genuine problem in only a few exceptional cases. Joseph Eckley sided with the "bare majority" of his church that decided to revert to the seventeenth-century practice of refusing to baptize children of attendees not in "full communion."[38] Eckley alienated so large a proportion of the Old South society that "from the largest Society in Boston," wrote Rev. William Bentley, "the Old South had become the smallest."[39] In much the same way, Edward Dorr Griffin— minister at Park Street Church, the new orthodox society in the center of Boston—so antagonized a sufficient proportion of his parishioners that, by his second year as pastor, he preached regularly to a half-empty church. In no time, Park Street Church would have become insolvent. Griffin resigned by mutual agreement within two years.[40]

Throughout the Bay State the role of the church communicants, while diminishing in the course of the eighteenth century, remained privileged within the Congregationalist order. Several factors contributed to the communicants' elevated place in the congregation. Communicants' public profession of faith allowed them the generally exclusive right to partake in all the sacraments, including participation at the Lord's Supper. In addition, communicants traditionally enjoyed specific ecclesiastical rights: they formed congregations, called the ministers, and, importantly for developments into the nineteenth century, owned the church property. In Boston,

36. "Testimony of a Unitarian Editor," *Spirit of the Pilgrims* 1 (June 1828): 296.

37. Seymour Katz, "The Unitarian Ministers of Boston" (Ph.D. diss., Harvard University, 1961), 10.

38. See letter from John Eliot to Jeremy Belknap in *Collections of the Massachusetts Historical Society*, 6th ser., 4 (1891): 144.

39. William Bentley, *The Diary of William Bentley* (Salem, 1905–14), 4:18.

40. The best book on Park Street Church is H. Crosby Englizian, *Brimstone Corner: A History of Park Street Church* (Chicago, 1968). Chapters 1–3 deal with the nineteenth century.

all these privileges had come under assault, eventually devolving to others in the church society. Before the turn of the century, Boston churches formally denied communicants their exclusive say in choosing the minister. A 1799 state statute confirmed this practice by declaring the election of a minister the exclusive right of pew proprietors and allowing "the church as such no rights whatsoever in the selection of a minister."[41] One prominent minister faithfully reported that the "ruling elders, who had figured so prominently in the early generations, had taken their departure."[42]

As the status of church communicants in Boston congregations diminished in importance, fewer parishioners sought to testify as to their conversion in front of the assembled congregation. Perhaps they had become less religious; more likely they realized the decreasing prestige associated with full communicant status and decided to forgo the ordeal of public examination. Not surprisingly, as ministers placed less value on this traditional ritual of testimonial, fewer of the laity attempted it. In any case, whatever individuals' particular reasons for holding back, that the first decades of the nineteenth century witnessed a precipitous decline in the number of church communicants was unmistakable. "All the churches in Boston," according to Salem minister William Bentley, "have not so many male church members as one Church half a century ago did contain."[43] It is worth noting that Bentley mentions gender; the trend in the nineteenth century toward overwhelmingly female church societies, as pointed out by Bentley, was unmistakable. From attending preparatory lectures and morning services to becoming members of the church, women came to predominate. Ann Douglas characterized this development as one part of a larger trend she styled the "feminization of American culture," the consequences of which, she asserted, damaged the prestige of a ministerial career. As a result, ministers "lost status and respect."[44] Even the increasingly important role of women in religion, which continued throughout the nineteenth

41. See Edward Buck, *Massachusetts Ecclesiastical Law* (Boston, 1866), 252–55. Citation is from William Wallace Fenn, "The Revolt against the Standing Order," in *A Religious History of New England—The King's Chapel Lectures* (Cambridge, Mass., 1917), 107.

42. Increase N. Tarbox, "The Congregational Churches of Boston since 1780," in *The Memorial History of Boston,* ed. Justin Winsor (Boston, 1881), 3:404.

43. Bentley, *Diary,* 3:282.

44. Ann Douglas, *The Feminization of American Culture* (New York, 1977). See especially the chapter "Clerical Disestablishment." Douglas's argument derives, in large measure, from the "status anxiety" thesis of Richard Hofstadter and Stanley Elkins. For Douglas, "the case of the ministers is clear-cut."

century, could not reverse the decline in the imputed value of church membership and the resulting contraction in the number of communicants. Within the Congregational churches, full communion was so rapidly diminishing in status and significance that, by the 1830s, it "functioned largely at the level of ritual."[45]

One result of the declining status of the church communicants within the congregation was that, as the power of the communicants declined, theological disputes diminished proportionally. There are several reasons for this. Without doubt, communicants were the best versed in matters of doctrine; they oversaw, in conjunction with the ministers, all complex doctrinal issues. In hiring the minister, it fell to the communicants to examine prospective candidates on the soundness of their training and beliefs. When parishioners stripped church communicants of their authority to call ministers, they decided for the most part to abandon examining candidates on matters of theology altogether. Bostonians desired ministers who, as William Emerson declared, "religiously avoided metaphysical subtleties."[46] Almost axiomatically, Boston ministers eschewed wasting their time on the old doctrinal disagreements that had repeatedly caused rifts in the Standing Order. As a result, after independence theological disputes within Boston congregations all but disappeared until the Unitarian controversy erupted in 1805.

The case of John Thornton Kirkland, candidate at Boston's New South Church, is instructive. Named for the celebrated English philanthropist, Kirkland was a recent graduate with high honors of Harvard College who went on to study theology under Stephen West of Stockbridge. It was not long before West's Hopkinsian sentiments "found little favor in the eyes of his pupil"; Kirkland fled Stockbridge for the more congenial confines of the Harvard campus, where with William Emerson he tutored young students in metaphysics and logic.[47] In 1794, Boston's New South congregational church asked the young man to preach on successive Sundays. A short time later, after the Boston Association of Ministers approved Kirkland's credentials, New South Church unanimously offered him its vacant pastorate. Significantly, during the candidate's examination no ordaining

45. Anne C. Rose, "Social Sources of Denominationalism Reconsidered: Post-Revolutionary Boston as a Case Study," *American Quarterly* 38 (1986): 250.

46. Emerson, *Sermon,* 20.

47. Sprague, *Annals,* 8:263.

council nor any other group queried him as to his theological convictions. Beyond assurances that Kirkland harbored no heretical views, it appeared the New South society did not particularly worry about his specific beliefs. Like many ministers after him, Kirkland kept his doctrinal opinions to himself during his examination; nor is there any record of doctrinal controversy in the course of his tenure at New South. The Boston Association of Ministers did not concern itself with these matters either. Upon the basis of "his public education in the University at Cambridge" and after a cursory perusal of a "specimen of his composition," the association concluded that Kirkland was "qualified for a preacher of the Gospel."[48] Clearly, neither the New South Church nor the Boston Association was looking for theological novelties or nuances from Mr. Kirkland.

During the succeeding decade, the Boston Association modified its policy in regard to examining prospective ministers. Rather than choosing to delve into the specific theological beliefs of candidates, the association went in the opposite direction. Far more concerned about competency than creed, the association devised a rather simple scheme for approbation in which candidates, after studying "under the direction of some able, judicious, and respectable divine," were given "a portion of scripture" upon which they were to base a sermon.[49] Latitudinarian and learned, Boston ministers openly declared that they sought candidates as much for their "literary abilities" and moral character as anything else.[50] Clearly, for the ministers of the Boston Association, talent in textual exegesis had supplanted doctrinal uniformity.

The increasingly latitudinarian views of Boston's ministers had significant consequences for issues of church polity. In lieu of the church communicants, pew proprietors emerged as the dominant group in Boston churches, garnering to themselves the real power.[51] "In the most prestigious churches," writes one historian, "the owners of the pews held control."[52]

---

48. Boston Association of Ministers, *Records: 1755–1803*, March 12, 1792.
49. Ibid., January 1803.
50. Ibid.
51. I am not suggesting that the church communicants and the pew proprietors were mutually exclusive. Communicants owned pews in every church. The point is that the groups differed in how they were constituted, the pew owners by wealth and the communicants by religious fervor for the most part—and that made all the difference.
52. Robert Stanley Rich, "Politics and Pedigrees: The Wealthy Men of Boston: 1798–1852," (Ph.D. diss., University of California at Los Angeles, 1975), 201.

They negotiated the settlement of the minister and determined his annual wage. In addition, pew owners handled all money-related matters, from maintaining the house of worship to assessing annual fees, the chief source of income for the congregation. The wealthiest pew owners, if they so desired, served on the important church committees for years at a time. In Boston churches, as Anne Rose notes, "the most influential man was also the richest."[53] By the beginning of the nineteenth century, it can fairly be said that Boston ministers did the preaching, and pew owners' money did the talking.[54]

As early as 1803, when New North Church began construction of a new, more spacious meetinghouse, evidence of proprietor domination could readily be detected. The congregation decided to incorporate itself as the New North Religious Society, officially conjoining the deacons and pew owners, the latter referred to as "such persons as are or may become engaged in building the house of worship now erecting."[55] This newly constituted society ensured that pew proprietors would never again suffer all the "difficulties" that had traditionally arisen "from the members of the church voting separately from the congregation."[56] New North's incorporation worked well enough that before the decade was out, Federal Street, West Church, and Hollis Street had followed its lead. In each case, pew proprietors flexed their muscle. In exchange for putting up the money to build new buildings, to pay ministers' salaries, and otherwise maintain the society, proprietors demanded exclusive control of fiscal matters.

Raising money was always an important issue for Boston churches. As they sought to attract promising ministers, congregations looked for ways to bring in more money. They found the most promising means to accom-

---

53. Anne C. Rose, "Denominationalism," 251.

54. A partial list of wealthy vestrymen and church officers by their institutional affiliation includes the following: First Church: David Tildon (treasurer and deacon) and John and Benjamin Austin; King's Chapel: Perez Morton (vestryman), Ebenezer Oliver (vestryman), Abiel Smith (vestryman), George Minot (vestryman), the Lowells, Lees, Shaws, and, later, Appleton, Bowditch, and Forbes; Federal Street: Jonathan Phillips, John Bryant (one of the wealthiest of all Bostonians before the Civil War), Thomas Perkins, and John Salisbury; Brattle Street: Harrison Gray Otis, James Austin, James Sullivan, James Bowdoin, Jonathan Chapman, John C. Gray, William and Abbot Lawrence, Amos Lawrence (deacon for twenty years), Moses Gill, Moses Grant Sr., and Moses Grant Jr.; Hollis Street: Elisha Ticknor (deacon).

55. Ephraim Eliot, *Historical Notes of the New North Religious Society in the Town of Boston* (Boston, 1822), 43.

56. Ibid., 39.

plish their purpose proved to be removing the galleries, where the less affluent worshipped for free, and installing pews in their place.[57] Boston's congregations began to do just that. In Old South Church, for example, parishioners paid anywhere from twenty dollars for gallery seats to over one hundred for the best pews. Charging rent throughout the church proved particularly effective in large measure because no new Congregational societies were gathered in the Boston area between 1748 and the completion of the orthodox Park Street Church in 1809. As Boston's population doubled, its Congregationalist churches failed to keep pace; by the turn of the century, they simply lacked room to accommodate the increase of potential worshippers. With space at a premium, it was not long before entire churches comprised pew proprietors whose annual fees filled their society's coffers.[58]

The pew proprietor arrangement under which only those who could afford to purchase a seat were welcome precipitated a fundamental, albeit evolutionary, transformation in Boston's Congregational churches.[59] Predictably, pew ownership entailed a degree of social homogeneity unimaginable a century earlier.[60] The encroachments of Boston's rich elbowed the poor out of the meetinghouse and encouraged them to join the growing Baptist and Methodist denominations.[61] "There is very little room in many of these churches," declared Joseph Tuckerman, "to which the poor have any more right (and of which they may more freely avail themselves) than they have in our homes."[62] Pew levies became, in essence, the membership

---

57. Two prominent examples are the First Church, Boston's oldest, and King's Chapel. Of course, King's Chapel, while technically not Congregationalist but Episcopalian, demonstrated the latitudinarian principles of the Brahmins. See Henry W. Foote, *Annals of King's Chapel* (Boston, 1881–96), 2:340–41, 375, and Ellis, *First Church*, 39–40. Historians from Foote to Paul Conkin claim that King's Chapel was "virtually Unitarian" even before the revolution.

58. Hill, *Old South*, 213–26.

59. Evolutionary in the sense that indigent members who could no longer afford to buy pews were not expelled.

60. Boston churches were increasingly called Unitarian by contemporaries as well as by later historians. I use the term Congregational here because the transformation to Unitarianism was incomplete at this time.

61. Anne Rose notes that the Baptists and Methodists "gave ordinary people opportunities for religious self-expression and practical autonomy largely blocked by the formality and deference of Unitarian congregations." Rose, "Denominationalism," 250.

62. Joseph Tuckerman to George Bond, April 11, 1835, in George Bond Papers, Boston Public Library.

fees of an exclusive club, while pews became status symbols. By the second decade of the nineteenth century, Boston Brahmins dominated their Congregational churches.[63]

Brahmin ministers and parishioners no more abandoned the disadvantaged than they banned them from their churches altogether. In fact, the beginning of the nineteenth century witnessed a sea change in Bostonians' charitable and philanthropic endeavors.[64] Rev. Joseph Tuckerman, classmate of William Ellery Channing and Joseph Story at Harvard and for twenty-five years a minister at Chelsea, moved to Boston in 1824 to become "Minister at Large." Frequently in poor health, Tuckerman spent the rest of his life defining a unique office specifically created for ministering to the poor and destitute. Raising both money and awareness, "endeavoring to recover the lost, helping the feeble minded, and recognizing the unknown brethren, who were not perhaps sealed with the name of Christ," Tuckerman attempted to bridge the widening gap between the Brahmins and underprivileged.[65] The first of its kind and funded by Brahmin largesse, Tuckerman's enterprise spurred the creation of the Benevolent Fraternity of Churches as well as similar ministries in eastern Massachusetts. In an 1835 letter to one of his English counterparts, Tuckerman boasted, "We have now seven Ministries at Large, [of which] three are Unitarians."[66] The Brahmins assiduously sought to help those less privileged than themselves. However, their charity did not extend to church services. As church membership took on an increasingly social significance, Sundays were not the day when the classes would mingle.

Affluent parishioners changed many features of the old Congregational system in creating "Boston religion." In the last two decades of the eighteenth century, no fewer than 12 percent of affluent Bostonians changed denominations, mostly joining the elite, incipient Unitarian churches.[67] Boston religion, as the domain of the wealthy, proved to be as much about

---

63. In Federal Street Church, for example, an 1814 list of the 116 pew owners reads as a veritable "who's who" of Brahmin elite. Parishioners included Nathan Appleton, Henry Wainwright, John McLean, Josiah Quincy, Haslett Sturgis, Jonathan Phillips, William Smith Shaw, Thomas Dawes, William Jackson, and a host of others.
64. Conrad Edick Wright, *The Transformation of Charity in Revolutionary New England* (Boston, 1992).
65. Elizabeth Palmer Peabody to William Sprague in Sprague, *Annals,* 8:355.
66. Cited in Sprague, *Annals,* 8:347.
67. Rich, "Politics and Pedigrees," 207.

this world as the next, as well-to-do proprietors looked upon the churches as a commentary on their secular success.[68] The stern Calvinist God gave way to a benevolent deity that blessed the Brahmins with a fine life. To make their point, they began to spend lavishly on their houses of worship. Bostonians undertook a spate of new construction at the cost of many thousands of dollars derived from private donations. Proprietors of no less than four societies erected new buildings in the first decade of the nineteenth century. Hollis Street, New North, West Church, as well as the First Church of Boston, moved into spacious new dwellings, each one larger and more expensive than the former.[69] To the tastes of Congregationalists of an earlier generation, these new structures would have been utterly ostentatious; to affluent Bostonians, their "very liberal scale of church expenses" was fitting testament to a simple fact; they had arrived.[70]

Besides being expensive, the new churches were large. Greater space promised more money in pew levies, provided that the larger churches could sell all the pews. Accordingly, congregations sought preachers who would pack the hall, whose virtuosity and literary skills promised a large and congenial audience. Doubtless, Brattle Street lured Peter Thacher to its vacant pulpit because of his oratorical virtuosity. The great George Whitefield, "in reference particularly to the fervor of his prayers, called him 'the Young Elijah.'" Securing young, talented candidates like Thacher proved to be no easy task, since available ministers were in short supply after the Revolution. Their numbers had diminished to such an extent that many churches had to convince their aging pastors to remain in the pulpit even after their effectiveness had all but ceased. Other churches, according to Jeremy Belknap, simply had to go without a settled minister for long periods.[71]

---

68. An analysis of the 1798 *Boston Directory* by Robert Rich reveals that for the 149 of the 255 persons listed as wealthy property holders classified by religious affiliation, 70 percent attended incipient Unitarian churches. That is, of the 149 wealthiest churchgoers, 103 were Unitarians, compared to a scant 21, or less than 15 percent, who were orthodox. See *Boston Directory*, 5–7; Rich, "Politics and Pedigrees, 207."

69. For a general description of the new structures and their cost, see Andrew Peabody, "The Unitarians in Boston," in *The Memorial History of Boston*, ed. Justin Winsor (Boston, 1881), 3:468–79.

70. Joseph A. Allen, *Our Liberal Movement in Theology* (Boston, 1882), 25.

71. See Jeremy Belknap, Belknap Papers, *Collections of the Massachusetts Historical Society*, 6th ser., 4 (1891): 608–11.

Of course, while not fabulously wealthy by any means, Boston churches had far greater resources upon which to draw than their rural counterparts. "Rural pastors were starving," one historian aptly states; so why not offer them promising positions in Boston?[72] This task proved not so easily accomplished. From the founding of Massachusetts Bay Colony, Congregationalists frowned upon offering a call to a settled pastor. Churches understood that when they offered their pastorate to a candidate, they were essentially granting him lifetime tenure. In turn, ministers obligated themselves to remain in their chosen pulpit for the duration of their careers. Although ministers inevitably quit their posts for myriad reasons, they did not do so just to move up the Congregational pecking order. If they left their congregations in the lurch, as it were, ministers often had trouble procuring calls from other Congregational societies. While no one put it precisely so, quitting a pulpit to seek another spoiled a minister's reputation. Similarly, congregations of the Standing Order deferred to one another. They refrained from seeking the services of a settled minister.

Congregational ministers themselves undertook to end the "deep-seated prejudice against translation."[73] In the seventeenth and eighteenth centuries, a secure position was a boon to young ministers; but after the Revolution, "tenure" had become more of a burden than an opportunity. Salaries were meager, and parishes often found themselves far in arrears in their obligations to their minister. As a result, when Boston churches offered lucrative and prestigious positions, even settled ministers quickly jumped at the bait. Not less than four of Boston's most beloved ministers had fled the countryside for the city. Wealthy Boston parishioners, ever eager to find suitable ministers to fill their new expansive churches, quickly took advantage of the increasingly fluid situation.

The 1785 "translation," as the resettlement of a minister was styled, of Peter Thacher to the Brattle Street Church from "an obscure parish in Malden" appeared initially to be an exception to long-established church practice. Instead, Thacher's translation, "the first instance of the kind which occurred in our region," set an important precedent.[74] Emboldened by

---

72. Evelyn Marie Walsh, "The Effects of the Revolution on Boston," (Ph.D. diss., Brown University, 1964), 204.

73. Ibid.

74. "Peter Thacher Memoir," in *Collections of the Massachusetts Historical Society*, 6th ser.,

Brattle Street, Federal Street Church in Boston offered a call to Jeremy Belknap, former minister of Dover, New Hampshire, the very next year. Belknap had suffered a series of disagreements with his congregation in large measure because he had condemned some of his parishioners for their participation in local uprisings associated with Shays' Rebellion. Unhappy and "subject to no little pecuniary embarrassment," Belknap quit his post in Dover.[75] Federal Street transgressed accepted practice when it called Belknap to its pulpit exactly because, having resigned from Dover without the approval of his congregation, he was available. That Belknap had unceremoniously broken his bond with the Dover church seemed to bother Federal Street not in the least. Its offer to Belknap was generous. "We promise to pay him for his support," the contract stated, "from the time he commences his charge, the sum of two pounds, eight shillings, lawful money, per week, or quarterly, if he chooses it, during the whole time of his ministry among us."[76] Belknap was installed as pastor in April of 1787.

For Belknap, the call to Boston meant a great financial relief. Yet, his prompt acceptance of Federal Street's offer turned on more than monetary matters. Having published the first installment of a three-volume *History of New Hampshire* that he had commenced on a 1784 trip to the White Mountains, Belknap was especially eager to pursue the professional opportunities presented by the city. Whereas some members of the Dover congregation had expressed reservations about Belknap's literary excursions, Belknap's Boston parishioners actually promoted his historical writings. Federal Street was enthralled by their minister's efforts on behalf of Boston's emerging secular high culture. With his congregation's blessing, Belknap became the embodiment of the Brahmin minister, establishing himself in conjunction with several important literary and philanthropic endeavors. Instrumental in the establishment of the Massachusetts Historical Society, plans for which he had first conceived in 1790, Belknap became a member of the American Academy of Arts and Sciences, the Humane Society, as well as an honorary member of Philadelphia's American Philosophical Society. He contributed to the development of his alma mater, becom-

8 (1893): 282; Sprague, *Annals*, 8:435; and "Jubilee of Rev. Dr. Snell," *Collections of the Massachusetts Historical Society*, 19 (1905): 430.

75. Sprague, *Annals*, 8:76.

76. Ibid., 77.

ing an overseer of Harvard, as well as the recipient of an honorary Doctor
of Divinity degree in 1792. Both minister and parish took special pride in
the publication of the second and third volumes of his still noteworthy
History of New Hampshire.

For the other ministers who, like Belknap, moved to Boston around the
turn of the century, their flight to the capital spelled freedom. With better,
more secure salaries, latitudinarian and learned colleagues, vastly greater
literary opportunities, and Harvard just across the Charles River, the life
of the Boston minister proved far more appealing than that of a rural pastor. Boston's willingness to offer positions to promising ministers, whether
settled or not, helped to loosen the tight grip of rural church communicants, so often the bane of liberal ministers.

The Boston Association of Ministers, rather than Federal Street Church,
took the most significant step concerning translations. Traditionally com-
prising ministers of all stripes, the Boston Association served many formal
and informal functions. While its primary role was approbating ministers
to preach, it also served as the clearinghouse for changes in the policies of
Boston's churches. Increasingly dominated by Boston's Brahmin ministers,
the association acquitted Belknap of all wrongdoing in moving from Dover
to Federal Street. Its members effectively assented to churches offering
their pastorates to settled ministers. As a result, the clergy commenced a
remarkable migration from outlying areas toward Boston. Within two
years, Hollis Street called Samuel West from Needham, while First Church
made an ample offer, gratefully accepted, to Harvard, Massachusetts's William Emerson, father of Ralph Waldo Emerson. By 1800, Boston had fractured the commandment "thou shalt not covet thy neighbor's minister."

Not all parishioners thought these developments universally beneficial,
but most accepted the changes as unavoidable. Benjamin Austin, a senior
member of the First Church of Boston, fretted over luring Emerson away
from another post. Publicly lamenting his congregation's decision in verse,
Austin declared:

> Farewell, Old Brick—Old Brick, farewell,
> You bought your minister and sold your bell.[77]

---

77. Ellis, *First Church,* 235. Alternatively, Austin also wrote: "Alas! Old Brick, you're left in
    the lurch, / You bought your Pastor, and sold the church." See *Independent Chronicle,*
    July 5, 1808.

Boston's novel policy in regard to ministerial translations did not sit well in the outlying towns. To say the least, rural congregations were displeased. It was clear to them that Boston was prepared to assault their pulpits, as it "drains a large watershed of New England's intellect."[78] Boston's high-handed forays raised the ire of rural societies, but they had little recourse when Boston raided their pulpits. The case of the Congregational church of Harvard, Massachusetts, is a good example. Livid over the translation of its minister, William Emerson, to the First Church of Boston in 1800, the Harvard society demanded some sort of compensation from their high-handed urban counterparts. Restitution proved rather difficult.

In the absence of a Presbyterian system, Harvard lacked a suitable means to gain a hearing to air its grievances. Massachusetts Congregationalists, long protective of their decentralized church polity, had for years resisted any attempt to go the route, for example, of Connecticut; the Bay State boasted nothing like the Saybrook Platform. At the beginning of the nineteenth century, several orthodox divines, led by Jedidiah Morse of Charlestown, campaigned vigorously for the adoption of a Presbyterian-like body as a means of combating the "evils in the present state of ecclesiastical affairs."[79] To protect rural, less powerful societies and to ensure doctrinal unity, Morse warned of the need for a "regular and acknowledged method in which Congregational churches can exercise a Christian watch over each other."[80] As for the Harvard society, proprietors of the First Church negotiated a most favorable settlement in which Harvard received a lump-sum payment, ostensibly to defray the costs of settling a new pastor, in exchange for relieving Emerson of any further obligations to them.[81] Brattle Street, just a few years earlier, had lured away Peter Thacher from Malden by agreeing to pay the balance due on his salary, a major source of Thacher's disenchantment with his Malden congregation. Ultimately, rural societies had little recourse but to resign themselves to the inevitable encroachments of the larger and wealthier Boston congregations, which had breached the

---

78. Oliver Wendell Holmes's *Autocrat of the Breakfast Table* (Boston, 1891), 1:127. Of course, Holmes had in mind more than just ministers; he was thinking of all intellectuals, particularly those with literary talent.

79. Jedidiah Morse et al., "Report to the General Association," *Panoplist* 13 (August 1815): 240.

80. Ibid., 244.

81. *Records of the First Church*, September 25, 1799; reprinted in the *Colonial Society of Massachusetts Collections* 40 (1961): 589–603.

"almost universal understanding that ministers were ordained for life, and that it was sinful to separate them, except in cases of imperious necessity,—especially for ministers to leave their people for more eligible situations." The payment came to one thousand dollars, "which sum you will consider our ultimate and will not be exceeded," curtly wrote David Tildon, First Church's treasurer.[82]

Not surprisingly, congregations outside of Boston remained very bitter about the high-handed actions of their urban colleagues well into the nineteenth century. Their resentment exacerbated the emerging fissure between Boston and the remainder of the Congregational churches of Massachusetts at a time when other significant issues would divide the Brahmins and orthodox. From differences over public funding of ministerial salaries to refusal to continue the long-standing Congregational policy of pulpit exchanges, the Standing Order began to fracture along precisely the fault lines that witnessed the rumblings over ministerial translations.

At the turn of the century, Boston's leading churches were well on their way to fulfilling their ambition of attracting a young and talented clergy. With resources unmatched by rural congregations, wealthy Boston societies had a great deal to offer prospective divines. Desperate for the "life of a scholar," William Emerson vividly expressed his sense of exile in a letter to William Farnham in 1792.[83] "It may be well for you to come and see how we *up in the country folks live*," he wrote. "The taste of our homely fare will give new and pleasing relish to the dainties of *Port*."[84] Higher wages proved to be more of an enticement than dining opportunities, although one commentator wondered which was more important to John Thornton Kirkland. "So often did he dine in public, and so much of his time was occupied in company, that many wondered how he could find time for writing his fine sermons."[85] It is not difficult to imagine the relief many a minister felt upon translating to the metropolis from the country, where likely he had been obliged to supplement his meager income by farming or tutoring the

82. Ibid., 601–2.
83. Samuel Cooper Thacher, "Memoir of the Life and Character of the Late Rev. William Emerson," *Collections of the Massachusetts Historical Society*, 2d ser., 1 (1812): 254–58.
84. William Emerson to William Farnham, April 24, 1792, Emerson Collection, Massachusetts Historical Society.
85. "Notes on President Kirkland," *Proceedings of the Massachusetts Historical Society*, 2d ser., 147 (June 1894): 144–51. Kirkland was notorious for composing sermons from a jumble of papers while in the pulpit.

children of his few well-to-do parishioners. Ministers filled their diaries with laments over their pecuniary straits and the necessity of supplementing their income by other means. A secure salary without repeatedly having to beseech church members proved equally important. So long as the pews were packed, their stipends were safe. For Boston ministers, puerile bickering over salary and the necessity of having to go without became only unpleasant memories.[86]

The Boston elite offered more than money to its young ministers. The diminished status of church communicants in their congregations as a whole proved to be an important attraction for prospective ministers. As John Kirkland had discovered, an acquiescent church promised an end to theological squabbles, long a bitter nuisance for rural pastors who often found themselves less orthodox than the communicants of their churches. Joseph Stevens Buckminster experienced a great relief upon translating to Brattle Street Church for just this reason. Buckminster's "intellectual developments," wrote William Sprague, "had been so remarkable and so well-known, that the Congregation in Brattle Square, Boston, then recently rendered vacant by the death of Dr. Thacher, fixed upon him as a suitable person to fill that important vacancy."[87] Proud of their new pastor's literary abilities and "enraptured by his eloquence,"[88] Brattle Street's parishioners would not induce him incessantly to discuss "the humiliating state of man as a fallen and apostate creature, his helplessness and danger, the glorious character of Christ as a DIVINE person, the special influence of the Spirit, the necessity of regeneration, and the awful prospects of the impenitent and the unbelieving."[89] The majority of proprietors, Buckminster was convinced, believed their prospects to be pretty good, even if they had not made "a profession of their repentance towards God and faith in our Lord Jesus Christ."[90] As Francis Bowen asked of his contemporaries:

---

86. See Belknap in *Collections of the Massachusetts Historical Society*, 6th ser., 4 (1891): 608–11, for a review of ministerial salaries and other money matters at the end of the eighteenth century.

87. Sprague, *Annals*, 8:386.

88. Ibid., 387.

89. Buckminster to Jedidiah Morse in a 1799 letter, as quoted in Eliza Buckminster Lee, *Memoirs of Rev. Joseph Buckminster, D. D., and of His Son, Rev. Joseph Stevens Buckminster*, 2d ed. (Boston, 1851), 327.

90. Ibid.

How many of those who read this page have been plagued by fam-
ines, inundations, earthquakes, the assassination of friends, robbery,
ravenous beasts, tyranny, the necessity of slaying a fellow creature
for sustenance, or the like? And if, which is very improbable, there
be an individual who had experienced one of these calamities, how
small a portion of his whole existence had been immediately sad-
dened by the event?[91]

In place of heavy-handed admonitions, minister and parishioner explicitly agreed to substitute a refined, measured, literary style in their sermons
that reflected a decidedly post-Calvinist accommodation to their salubri-
ous station. For the new Brahmin ministers, preaching to Boston congregations proved an entirely different undertaking than elsewhere in the
Bay State.

The city of Boston presented different opportunities and challenges for
a young minister. Boston was booming in the decades after independence,
and, doubtless, this made ministering there a rather daunting proposition
for young divines. In rural parishes, the minister was the only show in
town; in Boston, the sermon competed, as it were, against the entertain-
ments and distractions of the entire metropolis. Henry Wansey, an Englishman who visited New England in 1794, remarked that Bostonians were
not as "vigilant" about worship as the "country" folk, noting with some
sarcasm that Boston's citizens had "in a great measure lost that rigidity of
manners, and vigilant way of keeping the Sunday, as to put people in stocks
who were seen walking the streets during service."[92] In order to compete
with the myriad secular distractions, sermons had to be entertaining. They
also had to be competent, thorough, and of a high caliber. "To be the pastor," worried John Pierce upon his move to Brookline, "of men of fortune
and of education . . . filled me with painful apprehensions. I had studied
for so short a time in my profession, and was so doubtful of my ability
to interest people of distinguished talents and attainments."[93] Boston-area
divines realized that they were preaching to "an intelligent and discrimi-

---

91. Francis Bowen, *Principles of Metaphysics and Ethical Science* (Boston, 1826), 373.
92. Henry Wansey is excerpted from "An Excursion to the United States of North America
    in the Summer of 1794," in *America through British Eyes*, ed. Allen Nevins (New York,
    1948), 39.
93. Pierce Memoir, January 1797, John Pierce Papers, Massachusetts Historical Society.

nating congregation," as Kirkland called his New South parishioners.[94] Discriminating proved to be an accurate description, because Boston pew proprietors, unlike their rural counterparts, were likely educated, a number having attended Harvard College. They demanded literary, contemporary sermons delivered in a clear style. In short, Boston pulpits promised to good preachers first-rate salaries for top-notch Sunday performances.

Boston was not wanting in attractions during the remainder of the week. Accepting a call at one of the elite Boston churches became an entry into society, as ministers discovered with barely disguised relish. No sooner had Peter Thacher been called to Brattle Street than he received social invitations from Boston's most prominent families. Thacher's "society was constantly sought by Bowdoin, [Governor] Hancock, and all the dinner-giving gentry of that day."[95] Of course not all the consequences of joining the circle of Boston's elite were beneficial. After several years at Brattle Street, Thacher came to realize that "when he was brought in contact with the world politically and socially at so many points, the fervour of his religious feelings … considerably abated."[96] What was bad for the soul proved equally taxing on the body. One traveler in Boston masquerading as an English visitor went so far as to suggest that some ministers "injured their health and shortened their days by eating and drinking too much."[97]

When New South Church extended its vacant pastorate to John Thornton Kirkland, his former mentor, David Tappan, Hollis Professor of Divinity at Harvard, congratulated his protégé on his "destined lot" of being called to a Boston pulpit.[98] From the outset, Kirkland found himself welcome in the best sitting rooms of Boston. He "lived on the most intimate terms," writes his biographer, "with all the leading men of his time in this part of the country—with [Fisher] Ames and [John] Cabot, and [Theophilus] Parson, and [Christopher] Gore, and [Charles] Lowell, and [William] Prescott and [Josiah] Quincy. His society was courted by them, for he

94. Alexander Young, *Discourses on the Life and Character of John Thornton Kirkland* (Boston, 1840), 36.

95. Sprague, *Annals*, 1:721.

96. Ibid., 720.

97. Elias Boudinot, *Journey to Boston in 1809*, ed. Milton H. Thomas (Princeton, 1955), 37.

98. Quoted in Alexander Young, "Memoir of John Thornton Kirkland," in *American Unitarian Biography*, ed. William Ware (Boston, 1850), 292. For more on David Tappan, see below.

threw a charm over every circle by his urbanity."[99] As David Tappan had aptly noted, by becoming Boston ministers, Thacher and Kirkland had gained admittance into the New England's emerging Brahmin class. Josiah Quincy, longtime president of Harvard, went so far as to proclaim that "on the topmost round [*sic*] of the social ladder stood the clergy."[100] The fact that Kirkland was "courted" because of his urbanity and "unusual social charm" revealed much about what Bostonians sought in their new generation of young divines.[101] Kirkland appealed to them because, according to his colleague Abiel Abbot, he "was by nature and habit a perfect gentleman"; whether he displayed an especially earnest religiosity or whether he inspired religious devotion in others seemed ancillary.[102] Likewise, it signified little if his sermons were less deep and awe-inspiring than his Puritan predecessors, just so long as they "abounded in striking thoughts and pithy expressions."[103] At the turn of the century, then, Boston courted a cultured as well as a religious ministry.

The proprietors of Boston's elite churches sought a specific constellation of intellectual qualities in its new ministers. They had the money, so they knew they could recruit the talent. Brattle Street proprietors, declared Harrison Gray Otis, "were regarded as somewhat fastidious in their estimate of the qualifications requisite for the pulpit," preferring "an established celebrity."[104] The necessary characteristics—clarity of thought, breadth of learning, and an upbeat preaching style—revealed most clearly the Brahmins' desire to have their churches reflect their gentility, more than the desire to seek spiritual regeneration. Prospective ministers especially needed excellent oratorical skills; the Sunday sermon had to be lucid and literary and delivered in an entertaining manner in order to attract a large congregation. A boring preacher, no matter how personally devout or doctrinally sound, would lead to empty pews and diminished returns. Proprietors well understood that Boston parishioners had the option of joining

---

99. Ibid.

100. Josiah Quincy IV, *Figures of the Past, from the Leaves of Old Journals*, ed. M. A. DeWolfe Howe (Boston, 1926), 303.

101. Henry Adams, *The Education of Henry Adams* (Boston, 1918), 27.

102. Abiel Abbot to William Sprague, September 22, 1853, in Sprague, *Annals*, 8:269.

103. Ibid.

104. Quoted in Sprague, *Annals*, 1:719; see also, Samuel Eliot Morison, *Harrison Gray Otis, 1765–1848: The Urbane Federalist* (Boston, 1969), ch. 4.

any one of several other religious societies in the environs of Boston. In short, calling an unsuitable divine would likely spell financial disaster for a congregation.[105]

Boston churches knew what they did not want as well. Out was the old-fashioned domineering minister who issued decrees from on high; out was the jeremiad, together with "Hopkinsian subtleties" and "cold subtleties of metaphysic."[106] Preaching had to have a literary quality, with "scarcely a doctrinal tinge."[107] Preaching damnation and hellfire to the "unfaithful and unregenerate" unfit a minister for office. Boston ministers praised the wealthy, reassuring them that although "we are not of this world, it is not necessary that we should absolutely refuse its riches, honours and pleasures."[108] "Our Savior's instructions," declared Joseph Stevens Buckminster in remarkably un-Puritan terms, "do not require men . . . to throw their wealth into the sea or to inflict upon themselves unnatural austerities."[109] Provided hardworking Congregationalists used their wealth appropriately, Buckminster and his colleagues saw no reason to admonish them for their toils and tenacity. They facilely distinguished between wealth and luxury. Commenting on the Brahmins' recalibration of the worthiness of wealth, an orthodox preacher offered this observation: "A preacher pays a visit to a wealthy, fashionable family, if he should introduce a discourse upon the important subject of salvation, what would probably be the effect? The company would be struck dumb at his rudeness."[110] By mutual agreement, then, discourses of damnation made poor table fare.

Young Boston ministers disavowed many of their former pastoral obligations, opting instead for a new professionalism that encouraged and re-warded secular literary and social gifts. Parishioners of Boston's churches

---

105. The case of Edward Dorr Griffin is instructive. His style proved so acerbic that many Bostonians quit attending his sermons. Within a little more than a year, Griffin found himself lecturing to a half-empty hall. The Park Street society had to choose between either keeping its minister and going broke or showing Griffin the door. It chose the latter.

106. Kirkland, in a letter to Stephen Palmer, as quoted in Young, *Kirkland*, 32; and, Kirkland again in his "Belknap Funeral Sermon," as reproduced in Sprague, *Annals*, 8:82.

107. Abbot to Sprague, September 22, 1853.

108. John Clarke as quoted in Wright, *Beginnings of Unitarianism*, 259.

109. Joseph Stevens Buckminster, *Works* (Boston, 1839), 2:228.

110. *Panoplist* 3 (May 1808): 555.

no longer required, nor did they desire, many of the duties traditionally associated with the pastoral office.[111] While Bostonians remained devoted churchgoers, they increasingly contented themselves with relegating their religious activities to Sunday. Accordingly, ministers found themselves emancipated from the old parish tasks of conducting meetings for mutual instruction of the laity or inspiring religious devotion. "It is not so many years since the death of a clergyman of eminent piety, and not given to boasting, who to the very last deemed it a title to commendation that he had never in his life been at a 'night meeting,'" noted Rev. Andrew Peabody. "[T]o the two Sunday services there was very little of week-day supplement."[112]

Boston's solicitations proved extremely successful. A gaggle of talented, young ministers accepted calls from Boston churches between 1785, when Peter Thacher translated to Brattle Street, and 1803, when William Ellery Channing settled at Federal Street. With their newly constructed houses of worship and aspiring ministers, Bostonians took the first crucial steps toward remaking their churches. In addition to Thacher, Channing, Kirkland, and Buckminster, Boston boasted the likes of William Emerson, called to the First Church in 1799; Henry Ware Sr., shortly to become the Hollis Professor of Divinity at Harvard; Jeremy Belknap, colleague of Channing at Federal Street; Samuel West, minister at Hollis Street; and James Freeman, reader at the formerly Episcopalian King's Chapel. These divines both reflected the ambitions of the Boston elite, to whom in many ways they were beholden, and their own vision of a novel, literate, elitist, and increasingly well-to-do professional clergy. "People here," wrote William Ellery Channing, "are attached to religion, not so much by a sense of the value of religion as by their love to their minister."[113]

Their backgrounds had striking similarities. In addition to accepting calls from Boston churches, they had each been reared in the Boston area, with the exception of Channing, who hailed from Newport, Rhode Island. All of them, Channing included, attended Harvard College. Belknap and

---

111. Donald Scott characterizes this as a transition "from office to profession." The main problem of Scott's study *From Office to Profession* is that by generalizing over the entire ministry, orthodox and Brahmin alike, Scott fails to distinguish between the greatly dissimilar experiences of the two increasingly opposing factions.

112. Peabody, "Unitarians in Boston," 3:469.

113. William Ellery Channing, as quoted in William Henry Channing, *The Life of William Ellery Channing* (New York, 1880), 124–25.

West entered together in 1758, while Emerson and Kirkland, "congenial minds engaged in the same pursuit," were both members of the Harvard class of 1789.[114] Buckminster, the youngest, matriculated in 1796. While the professors and curriculum had changed significantly between Belknap and Buckminster, Harvard proved an important institutional tie binding the Brahmins together. The new clergy of Boston, together with the succeeding generation, bore a decidedly crimson stamp, as Harvard increasingly "became an important stage for socialization, and graduation a rite of passage and a credential for recruitment in upper-class Boston."[115]

Harvard proved significant in a number of ways; its import was not lost on these graduates, who had installed Ware as Hollis Professor of Divinity and Kirkland as president in the first decade of the nineteenth century.[116] Besides making mutual friends, the young ministers had undertaken a similar regimen of studies, principally under the tutelage of divinity professor David Tappan. Nominally a Calvinist, Tappan avoided dense doctrinal debates, "sensible of the difficulties connected with the doctrines of his system."[117] Channing recalled that "in his Lectures he had delivered in college on Theological questions, he scarcely intimated his own opinions, but gave impartial views of the best arguments on opposite sides, and led his pupils to weigh and balance the evidence for themselves."[118] Critical examination, argued Tappan, provided a sounder basis for anchoring religious belief among those, like himself, steeped in classical learning and Enlightenment physics and metaphysics. Over his many years at Harvard, Tappan successfully transmitted his open-mindedness and lack of doctrinal rigidity to his students. "The book of Nature and the book of Scripture," wrote one Tappan student, "[are] works of the same Author."[119]

Whatever the nuances of their varied personal religious beliefs, "the catholic air we breathe[d] at our Cambridge" produced ministers greatly reticent about engaging in theological disputation.[120] This reluctance man-

---

114. Kirkland, quoted in Young, *Kirkland*, 33.

115. Frederic Jaher, *The Urban Establishment* (Urbana, 1982), 17.

116. The Ware installation proved a huge, protracted battle. See J. W. Alexander, *Life of Archibald Alexander* (New York, 1894), ch. 3.

117. Dr. Archibald Alexander, as cited in Alexander, *Life of Archibald Alexander*, 254.

118. Channing is cited by his brother in William Henry Channing, *Life*, 86.

119. Jeremy Belknap in a letter to Ebenezer Hazard in *Collections of the Massachusetts Historical Society*, 5th ser., 2 (1877): 325.

120. Ibid.

ifested itself both in public and in private. Publicly, "there was an almost passionate desire," wrote Rev. Joseph Allen, "to escape from controversy"; while to themselves, the ministers had grown distrustful of creeds generally.[121] Privately, Brahmin ministers expressed their frustration with metaphysical speculation. "Hopkinsian subtleties have puzzled and bewildered me," admitted John Thornton Kirkland. "They certainly attempt to explain what is, in the nature of things, inexplicable, and to carry the mind higher than it will bear to rise without swimming."[122] From their studies with Tappan at Harvard, many ministers had taught themselves to wield Occam's razor, becoming increasingly skeptical about religious dogma. Belknap stated as much when he declared that "what there appears sufficient evidence for I admit as truth; where the evidence is not sufficient to induce belief, I allow myself to doubt."[123] The Trojan horse of skepticism had entered the citadel of religion.[124]

As a group, the Boston clergy decided that it was neither its duty nor desire to enforce specific creeds. The Boston Association of Ministers, to whom earlier enforcement had devolved, went so far as to declare that "the expectation of attaining uniformity of sentiment upon subjects either of faith or of practice, every one must consider as chimerical."[125] Accordingly, the association consistently opposed later attempts to compel divines to swear to any creed or confession. Not surprisingly, orthodox ministers, who urged some sort of mandatory subscription to a creed, criticized Boston's laxity most vehemently. "It matters not what a man believes, or does not believe," the orthodox Samuel Melancthon Worcester caustically observed of the Brahmin ministers. Their "charity, catholicism, or liberality of sentiment, at present so popular," he continued, constituted

---

121. Joseph Allen, "Historical Sketch of the Unitarian Movement since the Reformation," in Joseph Allen and Richard Eddy, *History of Unitarians and Universalists in the United States*, American Church History Series, (New York, 1894), 10:190.

122. Letter from Kirkland to Stephen Palmer, as quoted in Young, *Kirkland*, 31–32. In this letter, Kirkland refers specifically to Dr. Stephen West of Stockbridge, a disciple of Hopkins with whom Kirkland studied in 1790.

123. Letter to parish committee, April 4, 1787, reprinted in Sprague, *Annals*, 8:77–78.

124. For a fine examination of the intellectual development of Harvard's moral philosophers, see Daniel Walker Howe's *The Unitarian Conscience: Harvard Moral Philosophy, 1805–1861* (Cambridge, Mass., 1970). On the movement from rational religion to atheism, see Turner, *Without God*, 154–58.

125. Boston Association of Congregational Ministers, *Records: 1803–1836*, 10.

a "pernicious sentiment" destined to undermine the Congregational religion.[126]

Boston divines assiduously kept doctrinal matters out of their sermons. According to Hugh Blair's *Lectures on Rhetoric and Belles Lettres,* for years the standard text at Harvard, the "end of all preaching is to persuade men to become good. . . . It is not to discuss some abstruse point [or] . . . illustrate some metaphysical truth. . . . Sermons are always the more striking, and commonly the more useful, the more precise and particular the subject of them is."[127] Sensible to Blair's admonitions, ministers prepared sermons with the avowed aim of stressing moral values over doctrinal subtleties. "To insist much on controverted points," wrote Belknap, "is not good for the use of edifying."[128] Elias Boudinot, during a stay in Boston in 1809, found Brahmin sermons to be quite different from what he expected. "I had gone," he wrote, "with a full persuasion that most of the ministers were Socinians, and did not believe in the divinity of the Savior. I heard nothing like this from the pulpit. . . . I never heard a doctrine advanced in the Pulpit, that I could not have subscribed to. Indeed the Sermons I heard were universally practical."[129] Boudinot aptly perceived that Boston ministers rejected "the divinity of the Savior," but the profession had developed in such a way within the metropolis, as to make the point virtually moot. Deeply devout and loved by their congregations, Boston divines preached how to live morally, not how to believe dogmatically.

By the turn of the nineteenth century, as is evident from their sermons and correspondence, Boston Congregationalists harbored a distinct antipathy to religious dogma. Tolerance proved to be the key byword, as Boston ministers defined themselves and their brethren increasingly in terms other than those of creed or doctrine. "Thus in the year 1800 it comes to pass,"

126. Worcester's comments are cited in *Facts and Documents, Exhibiting a Summary View of the Ecclesiastical Affairs, Lately Transacted in Fitchburg; Together With Some Strictures on the Result of a Late Party Council, in Said Town, and General Observations: The Whole Designed to Vindicate the Rights of the Churches, and to Illustrate the Subject, and Enforce the Importance, of Church Discipline* (Boston, 1802), 87.

127. Hugh Blair, *Lectures on Rhetoric and Belles Lettres* (London, 1785), 2:304. For its use at Harvard, see for example, the comments of Belknap in a letter reproduced in *Collections of the Massachusetts Historical Society,* 5th ser., 2 (1877): 346.

128. Jeremy Belknap, *A Sermon, Preached at the Installation of Jedidiah Morse* (Boston, 1789), 21.

129. Boudinot, *Boston in 1809,* 50.

Rev. Joseph Allen commented, "that while scarce one Congregational preacher can fairly be called a trinitarian, there is as yet no 'line of demarcation.' Eckley is rated 'orthodox,' Eliot and Howard as 'Arian,' Emerson as 'Unitarian,' Kirkland as simply 'liberal.'"[130] Two decades into the nineteenth century, Boston ministers almost to a man came to accept the title of Unitarians, the sobriquet stuck to them by their erstwhile orthodox colleagues. Significantly, however, Unitarianism was not the religious movement so many churchmen and historians have made it out to be; it had "no creed, no platform, no policy."[131] For the Brahmin intellectuals and their merchant-patrons, Unitarianism proved to be as much a social as a religious enterprise.

A healthy and growing alliance of hard-bitten merchants and haughty clerical intellectuals was never guaranteed. Merchants who devoted their lives to the pursuit of wealth questioned, at times, the rationale for spending so lavishly on the arts. Was it their function to provide sustenance for great minds? And where was the payoff? Ministers, for their part, occasionally voiced concerns about what they were forfeiting in exchange for support by these emerging capitalists, while at the same time prodding their patrons for more money. The nascent Brahmin alliance needed cementing.

Family ties served as a critical bond between mercantile interests and the intellectual elite. Like Oliver Wendell Holmes's Brahmins of a half century later, these Bostonians formed something of a caste, an intertwined group of wealth and knowledge. Boston's great fortunes and great minds intermarried in remarkable numbers, as ministers found nuptials to be the best way to secure "easy circumstances."[132] Contemporary satirist Francis Grund noted that Boston's leading intellects "marry rich women, who can afford paying for being entertained."[133] Merchant princes, for their part, proved all too happy to see their daughters betrothed to Brahmin ministers and professors, while the young women—taking their fathers at their word—married the most eligible intellectuals in Boston. John Thornton Kirkland wedded the daughter of George Cabot, one of his most devout and rich supporters; William Ellery Channing upon marrying Ruth Gibbs,

130. Allen, "Historical Sketch," 186–87.

131. Allen, *Liberal Movement*, 31.

132. Quoted in Francis J. Grund, *Aristocracy in America: From the Sketchbook of a German Nobleman* (1839; reprint, New York, 1959), 156.

133. Ibid.

daughter of the wealthy Portsmouth merchant and his cousin, not only gained a bride but her Beacon Hill mansion as well.[134] Marriage conjoined many first families of wealth with the top intellects of Harvard College. Two Cambridge professors, Andrews Norton and George Ticknor, wedded the daughters of Samuel Eliot, Ticknor receiving a dowry of $84,394, more than he would earn in salary in the course of many years.[135] The familial connection of Harvard and Brahmin Boston proved most conspicuous with the marriage of Edward Everett, the silver-tongued orator at Cambridge, and the daughter of Peter Chardon Brooks, the wealthiest man in Boston. When Brooks donated ten thousand dollars toward the repair of the Harvard president's official residence, his daughter and son-in-law were its inhabitants![136] Grund offered the most salient observation concerning the conjoining of rich daughters and wily intellectuals when he claimed that "Proper Boston" considered it altogether appropriate for "our rich girls to *buy themselves a professor.*"[137] In several ways, then, the mercantile elite were the fathers of America's first group of Brahmin intellectuals. From this alliance, the Brahmins were born.

The clerical liberalism of the early nineteenth century depended in great measure upon Boston. Essential to the success of the Brahmin clergy was that Boston alone boasted churches in which the parishioners, not the church communicants, held the bulk of the power. Additionally, only in Boston arose a class of bourgeoisie with the wealth and desire to patronize a coterie of enlightened and literary intellectuals. It was only a natural progression, then, for the Brahmins to move beyond the confines of the Congregational church into new arenas of high culture, where they directly cultivated the arts and sciences. With their patron's backing, the Brahmin clergy began the process of making "Proper Boston the nineteenth century center for historians, poets, educators and philosophers."[138]

---

134. See Walsh, "Effects of the Revolution," 224.
135. See Tyack, *George Ticknor*, 90.
136. Paul R. Frothingham, *Edward Everett, Orator and Statesman* (Boston, 1925), 34.
137. Grund, *Aristocracy in America*, 156.
138. Frederic Jaher, "Nineteenth Century Elites," 63.

CHAPTER 3

Toward a Secular High Culture

*From what other body of men in proportion to their
numbers, has this country drawn so largely its men of
letters, its poets, its historians . . . as from the Unitarian
denomination and even the Unitarian pulpit?*

—HENRY BELLOWS

WHEN BOSTON MERCHANT Samuel Dexter died in 1810, he bequeathed the sum of five thousand dollars to Harvard College for the encouragement of the study of religion. His bequest, earmarked for the "critical study of the Holy Scriptures," led to Harvard establishing the Dexter Lectureship shortly thereafter. When Joseph Stevens Buckminster, Brahmin minister of Boston's Brattle Street Church, accepted the first Dexter Lectureship the following year, he became the first American professor of literary biblical studies. The most vocal advocate of German higher criticism in America, Buckminster almost single-handedly commenced what Jerry Wayne Brown called "the rise of Biblical criticism."[1]

It is as fitting that Samuel Dexter should have endowed the Harvard chair as it is appropriate that Harvard tapped Buckminster to be the first lecturer. Both men's lives reveal the interconnectedness and interdepen-

---

1. The Dexter lectureship was the first instance in America of the higher criticism typical of German scholars, who took a decidedly historical and critical approach to the study of the books of the Bible. It is worth noting that the first Dexter lecturer, Joseph Buckminster, was only New England's first advocate of German higher criticism. See Jerry Wayne Brown, *The Rise of Biblical Criticism in America, 1800–1870: The New England Scholars* (Middletown, Conn., 1969).

dency of Boston's ministry and mercantile elite. Following shortly on the heels of Dexter's bequest, the Brahmin alliance published the *Monthly Anthology and Boston Review* (hereafter *Monthly Anthology*), its own journal of secular high culture; founded the exclusive Boston Athenaeum; and en-gineered the first key moves in the secular transformation of Harvard. As this chapter will demonstrate, businessmen generously supported arts and letters, while ministers championed the bourgeoisie's generosity.[2]

Samuel Dexter, the son and grandson of Congregational ministers, had been raised by his father to succeed him in the clerical profession. His father's prompting notwithstanding, Samuel chose, like many of his con-temporaries, the more promising career of merchant and businessman. He seems to have opted for the right calling, as he met with considerable suc-cess. Dexter had amassed a large enough fortune by his thirtieth birthday to retire in considerable comfort. Jettisoning the business world, he then became, as his longtime intimate Josiah Quincy styled it, "a theological dilettante."[3] Dexter's religious sentiments corresponded to a pattern typical of his class and community. Seeking "a devotional pattern consonant with [his] status," Dexter rejected the Calvinist nostrums of innate human de-pravity and double predestination in favor of a system in which the Chris-tian merchant held the rank of cultural and moral steward.[4] For Boston's "men eminent for ability, worth and beneficence, and most of the principal merchants," wrote the Reverend Andrew Peabody, the reasonable and be-nevolent deity of the Unitarians proved most appealing.[5]

By endowing a series of lectureships on the Bible, Dexter was able to use the wealth he had accumulated to satisfy his unfulfilled religious ambi-tions. Dexter's choice of Harvard for his bequest is not surprising, but not

---

2. Daniel Walker Howe comes to much the same conclusion about his clique of Jacksonian-era Harvard professors. "The implicit bargain that the Harvard moral philosophers were trying to drive with the merchants came down to this: the moralists would provide a rationale for capitalism and protection of property, if the merchants would grant them the positions of cultural and moral leadership." Howe, *The Unitarian Conscience: Harvard Moral Philosophy, 1805–1861* (Cambridge, Mass., 1970), 140–41.

3. See Josiah Quincy, *The History of Harvard University* (Boston, 1860), 2:296–97; quoted in Brown, *Biblical Criticism*, 10.

4. Ronald Story, *Harvard and the Boston Upper Class: The Forging of an Aristocracy, 1800–1870* (Middletown, Conn., 1980), 8.

5. Andrew Peabody, "The Unitarians in Boston," in *The Memorial History of Boston*, ed. Justin Winsor (Boston, 1881), 3:479.

solely because the university at Cambridge was the Bay State's preeminent institution of higher education. Seen in the context of the growing controversy surrounding religious liberalism, Dexter's motives were clearly partisan, particularly considering that the orthodox Andover Theological Seminary had been established little more than a year earlier. His selection of Harvard constituted one of a series of maneuvers, philanthropic and institutional, to ensure that Harvard would bear the Brahmin stamp of the Boston elite. Dexter's contribution proved to be only one of many philanthropic activities undertaken by affluent Bostonians to ensure the success of their enterprise.

The selection of Joseph Stevens Buckminster as the first Dexter Lecturer demonstrated the close ties of Boston merchants and ministers. As stipulated in Dexter's bequest, a committee to administer the funds was assembled by the members of the Harvard Corporation. It consisted of two merchants, including Samuel Dexter Jr., and three Brahmin ministers, most notably William Ellery Channing of Federal Street Church. In selecting Buckminster, the committee tapped one of Boston's leading Brahmin clergymen. A Harvard man, a preeminent preacher, and a man of letters, Buckminster had secured his literary rank as a member of the Anthology Society that published the *Monthly Anthology,* as well as with the publication of a number of his occasional sermons in the preceding years. A fine scholar, Buckminster was one of the best examples of the new breed of clerical intellectuals, who "blessed" their affluent parishioners with "elegant manners" and "the refined pleasures of reason."[6] The growth and prosperity of Boston's churches testified to their worldly success. In appreciation and thanks to the generous bequest of the wealth of Samuel Dexter, Buckminster became the first Dexter Lecturer at Harvard.

The Dexter Lectureship at Harvard was only one of many donations and initiatives made in behalf of Brahmin religion and polite letters in Boston. At the urging of the young, energetic Congregational ministers, Boston's elite commenced a wave of philanthropy, the first of its kind in America, which underwrote projects as varied as social libraries, the Harvard Medical School, literary journals, the Massachusetts Historical Society, the Lowell Institute, and the Boston Athenaeum. It can fairly be claimed that large

---

6. Thaddeus M. Harris, "An Oration on Learned Associations," Phi Beta Kappa Address at Harvard, Pierce Collections, Massachusetts Historical Society, 1790, 48.

scale patronage of the arts and sciences in America began in early-nineteenth-century Boston.[7]

There are several explanations for the rise of philanthropy. Among them is the fact that Boston businessmen were making money. Independence and the new Federalist regime ushered in a period of great economic expansion, especially in overseas trade, which lasted for several decades, the Jeffersonian embargo and the War of 1812 notwithstanding. In these decades, the great firms of State Street and the family fortunes of Brahmin Boston came into being. Boston's first families—the Lowells, the Saltonstalls, the Lodges, the Quincys—amassed great wealth on the basis of a favorable economic climate and lucrative overseas trade.[8] Peter Chardon Brooks became Boston's first millionaire.[9] For perhaps the first time in American history, money was available for philanthropic activities.[10]

One of the most interesting facts about the advent of philanthropic giving was its timing. The wealthy men of Boston created a slew of elite cultural institutions at the very moment when their political fortunes, in the form of the Federalist party, had reached their nadir. This burst of philanthropic activity coincided with the rise of Jefferson and the Republican party. From the turn of the century, the Federalist party, the party of Boston's mercantile elite, found itself as the minority party in Congress and hopelessly locked out of the executive branch. Not coincidentally, as the members of the elite shrank from politics, hastening to point out its "popular" turn, they sought to create exclusive cultural outlets for their stirring civic spirit. Encouragement and endowment of high culture supplemented, and increasingly replaced, politics as a source of social legitima-

---

7. For an interesting contrast with New York City and Charleston, see Frederic Jaher, *The Urban Establishment* (Urbana, 1982).

8. Cleveland Amory gives a fine literary account of the "first families" in his *Proper Bostonians* (New York, 1947), while a more scholarly account can be found in Samuel Eliot Morison's *A Maritime History of Massachusetts, 1783–1860* (Boston, 1921).

9. See Robert Rich, "A Wilderness of Whigs: The Wealthy Men of Boston," *Journal of Social History* 4 (spring 1971): 263–76.

10. In a recent book on charities in New England, Conrad Edick Wright notes the irony of Brahmin donations to charities; he finds it peculiar that they gave more money after 1800, when charity was far less necessary, than immediately after the revolution. The simple explanation is that charity is directly tied not to demand but to supply. Brahmins got rich, so they made charitable contributions. See Conrad Wright, *The Transformation of Charity in Revolutionary New England* (Boston, 1992).

tion and status. As in the case of the Dexter Lectureship, the production of Brahmin culture resulted from the growing alliance of merchants and ministers, both of whom found themselves and their interests increasingly at odds with the growing popular culture of Massachusetts society. Brahmin culture fulfilled the mercantile elite's sense of civic pride, enabling it to constitute itself as blue bloods while it freed the ministers from the narrow confines of traditional doctrines and promised them a fine living.

There was no want of sour grapes among Boston's first citizens, as they blamed everyone and everything but themselves for their political plight. Jefferson, the three-fifths clause of the constitution of 1787, and, of course, the people, for not deferring to their "betters," shouldered the vast bulk of the blame. "There was never a country, which calls itself enlightened, in which talents, property and virtue have so little influence," lamented Rev. John Gardiner; "the people are unwilling to trust it to the only hands capable of preserving it pure and unsullied."[11] The democratization of politics curtailed the aspirations of the elite for office, as their laments, omnipresent in the writings of Federalist politicians, State Street merchants, and the Brahmin clergy, so amply demonstrated.

Boston Brahmins derided the democratization of American politics in no uncertain terms.[12] Fisher Ames called democracy, "the sure forerunner and irresistable engine of tyranny," while George Cabot declared it to be, "in its natural operation . . . the *government of the worst.*"[13] To a man, the Federalist elite believed that a republic had little, if anything, in common with democracy; the founding fathers "intended our government should be a republick," wrote Fisher Ames, "which differs more widely from a democracy than a democracy from a despotism."[14] Federalist fear of democracy stemmed from a visceral distrust of the people. If democracy was to succeed, Stephen Higginson wrote to his friend Timothy Pickering, "the people must be *taught* to confide in and reverence their rulers."[15] Similarly,

11. John Sylvester John Gardiner, *Fast Day Sermon Preached at Trinity Church, in Boston, April 7, 1808* (Boston, 1808), 20–21.

12. Fisher Ames in *Works of Fisher Ames,* ed. Seth Ames (1854; reprint, Indianapolis, 1983), 1:229.

13. George Cabot in *Life and Letters of George Cabot,* ed. Henry Cabot Lodge (Boston, 1877), 322.

14. Fisher Ames, "The Mire of a Democracy," *Monthly Anthology* 2 (November 1805): 563.

15. Stephen Higginson to Timothy Pickering, May 27, 1797, Pickering Papers, Massachusetts Historical Society.

Alden Bradford made respect for rulers the subject of his 1804 Fourth of July sermon; it was necessary, he stated, "to inculcate on their expanding minds the necessity of subordination and obedience to their superiors."[16]

The democratization of politics meant that candidates for office had to appeal to the populace. Of course, in some measure, Federalists and Republicans alike paid obeisance to some form of popular political participation. New England leaders had long sought voter approval of their actions. Federalists, however, drew the line at specifically currying favor with the people, who should automatically defer to their betters. Reticent about ingratiating themselves with their constituents, Federalists repeatedly made remarks like those of Ames in an essay appropriately titled "The Mire of a Democracy." "Of all flattery," wrote Ames, "the grossest (gross indeed to blasphemy) is that the voice of the people is the voice of God; that the opinion of the people, like that of the Pope, is infallible. . . . The temple of publick liberty has no better foundation than the shifting sands of the desert."[17] John Howe, an Englishman visiting Massachusetts, observed in a letter to an associate why Boston's "men of property and standing" had quit politics.[18] "So annoyed by the servile means necessary to gain power, and by the violence and licentiousness connected with it," he noted, "they are generally shrinking from the scene."[19] It may be difficult to determine whether most Federalists quit politics because they would not undertake the new style of campaigning and solicitation of the electorate or whether they and their programs simply proved unpopular. In either case, the results were the same. "I renounce the wrangling world of politics," declared Fisher Ames, "and devote myself in the future to pigs and poultry."[20] Democracy was in and the Boston elite was out.

As the "middling sorts" of farmers, shopkeepers, artisans, and mechanics took an increasingly active role in politics, the Brahmins turned not to pork, as was the case with Ames, but to private philanthropic endeavors, which proved to be overwhelmingly elitist in nature. Just as their churches

---

16. Alden Bradford, *An Oration, Pronounced at Wiscasset, on the 4th of July, 1804* (Boston, 1805), 13.

17. Ames, "Mire of a Democracy," 564–65.

18. John Howe, "Reports of John Howe," as quoted in David Hackett Fischer, *The Revolution of American Conservatism: Federalist Party in Jeffersonian Democracy* (New York, 1965), 197.

19. Ibid.

20. Ames, "Mire of a Democracy," 565.

had become the domain of those who could afford to worship in the "high rent district," so the newly endowed cultural institutions became the dominion of the well heeled. If the people would not have them in politics, they would not have the people in their privately endowed, elitist institutions. As Richard Brown comments, "Brahmins ruled high culture in Massachusetts."[21]

The merchant princes of State Street threw themselves into philanthropic projects with great zeal, generously making donations to many projects. "The denomination—that is, the men composing it—have never been stingy; none less so," wrote Rev. Joseph Allen looking back a generation later. "It would be," he continued, "within the bounds to say that their gifts for religious, charitable, and other public objects (especially educational) . . . could be reckoned by a good many millions of dollars in these last fifty years."[22] In an article published in 1860, Samuel A. Eliot estimated that since the turn of the century, "Bostonians expended at least ten million dollars in charitable funds."[23] Their pet projects proved as numerous as varied. Like Samuel Dexter, many wealthy Bostonians made Harvard their chief beneficiary, donating some $1.2 million to the university. The Boston Athenaeum and the Lowell Institute received gifts totaling some $600,000, while the Massachusetts Historical Society, the American Academy of Arts and Sciences, and the Boston Society of Natural History each received gifts totaling not less than $30,000.[24] Lesser contributions to many smaller organizations were made as well. In his 1992 study of charities in New England, Conrad Edick Wright lists some forty-six Boston charitable organizations founded in the first two decades of the nineteenth century alone.[25] "It is not too much to say," wrote Octavius Brooks Frothingham of his Brahmin predecessors, "that they started every one of our best secular charities. The town of Boston had a poor-house, and nothing more until

---

21. Richard D. Brown, "Who Should Rule at Home? The Establishment of the Brahmin Upper Class," *Reviews in American History* 9 (1981): 60–61.

22. Joseph A. Allen, *Our Liberal Movement in Theology* (Boston, 1882), 25.

23. Samuel A. Eliot, "The Charities of Boston," *North American Review* 91 (July 1860): 154–57, and his earlier estimates in *North American Review* 61 (1845): 135–39. Evelyn Walsh comes to the same conclusions in "The Effects of the Revolution on Boston" (Ph.D. diss., Brown University, 1964), 224.

24. Eliot, "Charities," 154–57, and Story, *Harvard and the Boston Upper Class*, 8.

25. Wright, *Transformation of Charity*, app. 3.

the Unitarians."[26] A transformation of charity and philanthropy was underway.

Brahmin ministers were instrumental in stimulating the development of philanthropic activity. The first families of Boston received a great deal of encouragement for their patronage activities from the Brahmin clergy, who found a generous portion of this largesse coming their way. The ministers especially encouraged mercantile underwriting of literary activities, such as Dexter's endowment of his Harvard lectureship on biblical criticism; the patronage of literary journals, such as the *Monthly Anthology* and the *North American Review;* and the underwriting of the Boston Athenaeum. In each case, the Brahmin clergy promoted these projects by appealing simultaneously to several points of Brahmin sensitivity, smarting, as it were, from their political demise. Referring to elitist notions of social responsibility that were no longer fulfilled by politics and governance, the ministers argued that philanthropic support of literary activities promised one important way of satisfying civic duty. John Thornton Kirkland of New South church went so far as to write: "A nation, that increases in wealth, without any corresponding increase in knowledge and refinement, in letters and arts, neglects the proper and respectable uses of prosperity. A love of intellectual improvement, and of the various objects of literature and taste, in a state or society enjoying freedom and affluence, is to be coveted and maintained."[27]

Boston's clerical intellectuals, together with other contributors to the pages of the *Monthly Anthology,* had little difficulty pointing out, and they did so frequently, the dearth of high culture in the new nation. William Emerson, minister of First Church and editor of the *Monthly Anthology,* drew attention to the barrenness of native literature with an apt metaphor. "American literature," he wrote, "is rather a kind of half cleared and half cultivated country, where you may travel til you are out of breath, without startling any rare game."[28] Fisher Ames struck the same chord in an article requested by Emerson for the *Monthly Anthology.* "Excepting the writers of two able works on our politics," he declared, "we have no authors. . . . If, then, we judge of the genius of our nation by the success with which American authors have displayed it, our country has certainly hitherto no

---

26. Octavius Brooks Frothingham, *Boston Unitarianism* (New York, 1890), 127.
27. John Kirkland in *Monthly Anthology* 2 (November 1805): 333.
28. "Address of the Editors," *Monthly Anthology* 6 (1809): 4.

pretensions to literary fame. The world will naturally enough pronounce that what we have not performed we are incapable of performing."[29] In a Phi Beta Kappa oration at Harvard in 1809, fittingly titled "The Dangers and Duties of Men of Letters," Joseph Stevens Buckminster, pastor of Brattle Street Church, wondered aloud whether and where men of genius were to be found in a democratic society. "Is it probable," he queried, "that you will have the honour of belonging to a nation of men of letters? The review of our past literary progress does not authorize very lofty expectations."[30] Among the distinguished guests in the audience that day was Samuel Dexter. Taking Buckminster's admonitions to heart, he bequeathed funds for the Dexter Lectureship in biblical studies.

An interesting and important transformation was taking place in the utterances of the Brahmin clergy. Kirkland, for example, was making the same type of appeal his Congregational forefathers had delivered about the importance of considering the greater good of the community. The striking difference between his appeal and that of his predecessors is that the arts had displaced religion. The measure of a nation, urged Kirkland, was not the quality of its theology but of its literature.[31] Octavius Brooks Frothingham claimed precisely this as he looked back a generation later. The Brahmin clergy of Boston proved to be "the first who deliberately substituted a rational idealism for the creed; who adopted art, humanity, literature as expressions of the divine mind; who set up social morality as a means of grace."[32]

The problem proved to be, then, the dearth of men of letters in Boston, or anywhere else for that matter. The clergy blamed an increasingly democratic society for the paucity of culture in New England and in the nation as a whole.[33] "God preserve us," William Emerson wrote to his sister, Mary

---

29. Fisher Ames, "American Literature," in Ames, *Works of Fisher Ames,* 24.

30. Joseph Stevens Buckminster, "The Dangers and Duties of Men of Letters," Phi Beta Kappa Address as quoted in *Monthly Anthology* 7 (1809): 145.

31. Lewis P. Simpson has made a similar interpretation. To wit: "In the Early nineteenth century the image in the New England mind of the old theocratic polity begins to become the image of a literary polity." Simpson, *The Man of Letters in New England and the South* (Baton Rouge, 1973), 23.

32. Frothingham, *Boston Unitarianism,* 24.

33. From the 1740s an interesting semantic irony developed in which religious liberals were well-nigh conservative in everything else. "Liberalism was a profoundly elitist and conservative ideology, while evangelical religion embodied a radical and even democratic

Moody Emerson, "in this howling and tempestuous world! One might almost as well be overwhelmed by the floods of democracy."[34] Emerson and his colleagues believed that in a democracy the arts needed special care and nurture, as they made clear in the pages of the *Monthly Anthology*. Fisher Ames was one of the first to fault the growth of a democratic, popular culture for the plight of high culture. In an article entitled "American Literature" published in one of the first issues of the *Monthly Anthology*, Ames made his case:

> At present the nature of our government inclines all men to seek popularity as the object next in point of value to wealth; but the acquisition of learning and the display of genius are not the ways to obtain it. Intellectual superiority is so far from conciliating confidence, that it is the very spirit of democracy, as in France, to proscribe the aristocracy of talents. To be the favorite of an ignorant multitude, a man must descend to their level. . . . Surely we are not to look for genius among demagogues: the man who can descend so low has seldom very far to descend.[35]

Even more than the Federalist politicians, the Brahmin clergy of Boston refused to "descend" to the popular level. For the politician, this refusal to adapt virtually doomed his public career. For the minister, who already appealed to a select crowd in Boston's exclusive churches, the rejection of democratic culture spelled a decline in overall influence and a rethinking of his belief in the minister's direct obligation to all of society.

Brahmin aversion to democracy notwithstanding, there was little Boston ministers or their allies could do to stem the rising tide of the Jeffersonian democracy. The Congregational clergy, like its Federalist politician-allies, reacted in various ways to the seemingly inevitable encroachment of democratic politics. For the Boston clergy, the popular political ferment was not a particularly pressing problem, as the pew proprietor system had already insulated them at least to some extent from the general population. Almost to a man, Brahmin ministers had begun to eschew the kind of

---

challenge to the standing order." Alan Heimert, *Religion and the American Mind: From the Awakening through the Revolution* (New York, 1966), 5–6.

34. William Emerson to Mary Moody Emerson in a letter of 1807. Mary Moody was the aunt who raised Ralph Waldo Emerson and figured so prominently in his religious and literary development.

35. Ames, "American Literature," 36.

active participation in politics entailed in the election-day sermons and fast days of the colonial era. By the turn of the nineteenth century, many Boston ministers had started to disavow any direct connection between religion and politics, choosing to avoid soiling themselves with political activism. The wife of Josiah Quincy came away from an 1808 sermon by John Thornton Kirkland miffed because he had failed to attack Jefferson's embargo. She complained that his sermon was "less political than on any former occasion when it was expected to be the reverse."[36] Following their churches, Boston's Congregational ministers simultaneously became more literary and less political in the first decades of the nineteenth century. This choice had its consequences; jettisoning their traditional political role, and with it the Puritan notion of God's covenant with the entire community, in favor of literary, high-cultural activities implied a distinct class bias.

The decline of deferential politics had limited the clergy's importance in the community at large and had effectively circumscribed its role in politics. Yet, in many respects, Boston's ministers were never better off than in the opening decades of the nineteenth century. These years witnessed the development of an increasingly cozy relationship between Boston's ministers and the merchants and financiers of State Street. Joseph Stevens Buckminster, one of the beneficiaries of this relationship both as minister of Brattle Street Church and Harvard lecturer, made no bones about the attention paid to the ministers "by the most enlightened."[37] Recognizing this unique situation, he observed: "Those very men [wealthy merchants], who in New York and Philadelphia, would be unbelievers because they could not be Calvinists, are among us in Boston, rational Christians,—the most constant supporters of public worship, the most intimate friends of the clergy."[38] The combination of enlightened rationalism and social elitism proved to be the fundamental basis of the Brahmin union of merchant princes and learned ministers.

---

36. Quincy is quoted in Hamilton Hill, *History of the Old South Church* (Boston, 1889), 2:333–34.
37. James Savage, "Patronage of Letters and National Prosperity," *Monthly Anthology* 4 (1807): 244.
38. Buckminster in *Memoirs of Rev. Joseph Buckminster, D. D., and of His Son, Joseph Stevens Buckminster*, ed. Eliza Buckminster Lee, 2d ed. (Boston, 1851), 335–36. Jon Butler makes a similar observation stating that "Unitarians kept a crucial elite moored to a Christian dock." *Awash in a Sea of Faith: Christianizing the American People* (Cambridge, Massachusetts, 1990), 221.

As the high culture split off from popular culture, the enlightened businessmen of Boston began to patronize in earnest the literary ambitions of
the Brahmin clergy.[39] In addition to paying their ministers comfortable
salaries for literary Sunday sermons, these wealthy Bostonians opened their
purses to support new literary institutions. In the opening decade of the
nineteenth century, the first families underwrote a literary journal, the
Monthly Anthology, under the editorship of William Emerson, minister of
the First Church of Boston; generously endowed America's first private social library, the Boston Athenaeum; and, most importantly, took over and
transformed Harvard College. These undertakings proved to be the important first steps in the creation of a secular high culture in New England.
As William Charvat observed, "in no other period had the economically
dominant class exhibited such an interest in the arts."[40]

At the same time, wealthy pew owners, in conjunction with the Brahmin
clergy, significantly altered the responsibilities and burdens placed upon
their ministers and teachers. No longer expected or required to perform
onerous pastoral chores, ministers devoted themselves to shepherding the
development of an indigenous high culture.[41] Increasingly, they shed such
traditional clerical duties as conducting night meetings and holding devotional discussions.[42]

Founded in 1803, the *Monthly Anthology* was one of the earliest American literary journals as well as one of the most influential, inspiring both
positively and negatively the generation of scholars and writers of the

---

39. James Savage, "Patronage of Letters," 244.

40. William Charvat, *The Origins of American Critical Thought, 1810–1835* (Philadelphia, 1936), 173.

41. Ralph Waldo Emerson offers the best testament as to how the Brahmin minister-
intellectual felt impossibly uncomfortable when attending to traditional pastoral duties.
Feeling hopelessly out of place at a parishioner's sickbed, Emerson concludes that he is
not cut out for the cloth. In fact, it is my sense that he quit the ministry because he
wrongly expected his church to treat him like his father and Buckminster and the like
had been treated after establishing their literary reputations. Henry Nash Smith suggests
different reasons in "Emerson's Problem of Vocation: A Note on the 'American Scholar,'"
New England Quarterly 12 (1939): 52–67.

42. Donald Scott describes the transformation of ministerial responsibilities in a different
context in *From Office to Profession: The New England Ministry, 1750–1850.* (Philadelphia,
1978). He focuses broadly on the entire Congregational clergy, while I am here differentiating between two different factions within the denomination.

"American Renaissance."[43] According to George Willis Cooke, "the *Monthly Anthology* was the first distinctly literary journal published in this country. It had an important influence in developing the intellectual tastes of New England, and of giving initiative to its literary capacities."[44] The *Monthly Anthology* was conceived and published by the Anthology Society, predominantly a group of Brahmin Boston clergymen and their intellectual associates. The composition of the society, its sources of funding, its ambitions, and the content of the journal reveal the close ties of the clergy to the mercantile elite.

William Emerson, minister of the prestigious First Church of Boston, took over the foundering *Monthly Anthology* in May 1804. With a number of like-minded ministers, he undertook what he was convinced would be the successful operation of an entirely new type of literary endeavor. Due to his prominent position at the First Church, Emerson felt he could engender enough interest and financial backing to "give to our charge expensive advantages."[45] Emerson aptly perceived that his wealthy parishioners would be willing to patronize an undertaking designed to pique their cultural sensibilities and legitimate their social position. For the next decade, the success of the journal depended on Emerson and his colleagues' status and connections.[46]

Emerson's first order of business involved organizing a coterie of "literary gentlemen" to assume the primary responsibilities of editing, writing, and securing a large enough readership to keep the nascent publication going.[47] By the beginning of the *Monthly Anthology*'s second year, Emerson had assembled the Anthology Society, with the Reverend John S. J. Gardiner, the versatile rector of Trinity Church of Boston, as president. That Gardiner, an Episcopalian, proved so prominent in the society serves to

---

43. See Lewis P. Simpson's introduction to his *The Federalist Literary Mind: Selections from the* Monthly Anthology and Boston Review, *1803–1811* (Baton Rouge, 1962). Simpson revised the Transcendentalist claim that nothing of literary value was produced by the first generation of Boston's liberal clergy.

44. George Willis Cooke, *Unitarianism in America* (Boston, 1902), 96.

45. William Emerson, "Preface," *Monthly Anthology* 1 (1804): iv.

46. Emerson succeeded admirably as the journal issued ten volumes, a substantial run, according to Frank Luther Mott; see his *History of American Magazines: 1741–1850* (New York, 1930), 255.

47. The anthologists called themselves "a society of gentlemen" as well as "a society of literary gentlemen." See Andrews Norton in the *Monthly Anthology* 9 (1810): 350.

underscore the members' assertion that religious affiliation and conviction had no part in their undertaking. Of the original handful of members of the society, six were ministers. In addition to Emerson and Gardiner, the "clerical band" consisted of Joseph Stevens Buckminster, minister at Brattle Street and future Harvard professor; Joseph Tuckerman, who left his Chelsea parish to become Boston's first Unitarian Minister-at-Large; Thomas Gray, minister of the Third Church in Roxbury since 1793; and Samuel Cooper Thacher, Harvard librarian and longtime minister of the New South congregation.[48] Ministerial predominance did not abate with the first members. Other men of the cloth soon joined the society; they included Joseph McKean, the second Boyleston Professor of rhetoric and oratory at Harvard; Sidney Willard, Harvard's Hancock Professor of Hebrew; John Pierce, longtime minister of the First Church of Brookline; and John Thornton Kirkland, predecessor of Thacher at New South Church and future Harvard president. These men were without doubt the leading ministers of the Boston area. This "bright circle of personal force and culture," the first of its kind in America,[49] bore the liberal stamp of Boston's churches.[50]

Other members of the Anthology Society included several prominent lawyers, Daniel Webster among them; three doctors, one of whom, John Collins Warren, founded the Harvard Medical School; and such scions of the Boston business community as James Savage, president of the Provident Institution for Savings; William Tudor, principal founder of the Boston Athenaeum and longtime secretary to John Adams; William Smith Shaw, who served as the Anthology Society treasurer; as well as book publisher and schoolmaster William Wells. "A rallying-ground for those of known liberal sympathies," the society constituted a remarkable combination of wealth and talent, ministers supplying the talent and men of business supplying the funds. It became, as Lewis Simpson writes, "the focus of an incipient community of Boston-Cambridge literary intellectuals."[51]

The genteel Anthology Society was the very embodiment of the new

---

48. See Richard Parker Harrington, "The *Monthly Anthology:* Literary Excellence as Interpreted by a 'Society of Gentlemen'" (Ph.D. diss., University of Texas, 1964), 35.

49. Allen, *Liberal Movement*, 37.

50. Some comparison might be made with Benjamin Franklin's famous "Junto" or with the American Philosophical Association in Philadelphia.

51. Lewis P. Simpson, *Man of Letters*, 28.

Brahmin minister. It "met once a week in the evening" to conduct its business, according to William Tudor's reminiscences.[52] At these evening meetings, members combined the necessary tasks of selecting and editing submissions for the *Monthly Anthology* with the more agreeable endeavor of mutual entertainment. Tudor wrote that "after deciding on the manuscripts that were offered, [the members] partook of a plain supper, and enjoyed the full pleasure of a literary chat."[53] Several accounts in the *Anthology Society Journal* describe suppers of "widgeons and teal," "brants," "very good claret," and the like, which were always followed by a healthful smoke on some "segars."[54] While orthodox ministers of the Standing Order condemned this type of secular camaraderie as unbefitting a man of the cloth, the anthologists embraced this "club sociability" as an expression of enlightened thinking and behavior. When Jedidiah Morse, orthodox minister at Charlestown, printed a blistering denunciation of the Masonic lodges, several Brahmin ministers forcefully took to their defense, calling Morse's attack "ignorant."[55] To the Brahmins, a gathering of Masons, like their own literary society, proved a fitting expression of Enlightenment rationality and taste.[56]

From the first issue to the last, the anthologists made clear that their goal was not religious but literary, even though the cloth was prominent in the club's activities.[57] "Undertaken by a society of gentlemen for the diffusion of literary taste," the *Monthly Anthology* promised to be "a repository for correct notices of all American publications; for just criticism; for

---

52. William Tudor Jr., *Miscellanies* (Boston, 1821), 3.

53. M. A. DeWolfe Howe, ed., *Journal of the Proceedings of the Society Which Conducts the Monthly Anthology and Boston Review* (Boston, 1910), 148, 159.

54. Ibid.

55. William Wells, a founding member of the Anthology Society, published the Brahmin response in the *Massachusetts Mercury*. Wells urged Bostonians not to let Morse "terrify our fellow citizens with groundless alarms, nor become the dupes of every foolish tale, which the prejudices or ignorance of Europeans may fabricate." See the *Massachusetts Mercury* of August 3 and August 10, 1798.

56. See Conrad Wright, "The Controversial Career of Jedidiah Morse," *Harvard Library Bulletin* 31 (1983): 64–87. For more on the relationship of Morse and the Freemasons, see Steven C. Bollock, *Revolutionary Brotherhood: Freemasonry and the Transformation of the American Social Order, 1730–1840* (Chapel Hill, 1996).

57. Mott, *American Magazines*, 256.

the lucubrations of men of learning and taste."[58] As for religion, editor-in-chief Emerson wrote:

> On the solemn and awful mysteries of some of the subjects of theology, many of us are unqualified to judge. . . . We feel ourselves therefore pledged to the support of no system, and when any theological work passes under our examination, it will only be in the regular survey of the literature of our country.[59]

"Theology," Joseph Stevens Buckminster declared in a later issue, "is the subject upon which much of our genius and learning has always been employed, and not seldom wasted." How remarkably this reveals the general trend of the Brahmins toward literary culture and away from strictly religion. The founding of the *Monthly Anthology* and the society's editorial policies reflect the secularizing trend transforming Boston's Congregationalist churches. Self-consciously nonsectarian, the *Monthly Anthology* editors never contended that they were undertaking religious work.[60] They promoted themselves as New England's cultural gatekeepers and the *Monthly Anthology* as a "significant venture in cultural pioneering." The anthologists' "design," declared John Thornton Kirkland, was to foster "useful knowledge and harmless amusement, sound principles, good morals, and correct taste."[61]

The pages of the *Monthly Anthology* reveal just how seriously the anthologists took their role as cultural critics. Convinced of the notion of the western movement of culture, they believed Boston to be the rightful and sole heir of Athens, Rome, Florence, and London. Typical was the anthologist who asked where could be found "the legitimate successors of Selden, Grotius, Le Clerc, Vossius and Bayle?"[62] In a *Monthly Anthology* essay en-

---

58. *Monthly Anthology* 5 (1808); 2 (1805): 333.
59. *Monthly Anthology* 2 (1805): 678.
60. James King Morse, *Jedidiah Morse: A Champion of New England Orthodoxy* (New York, 1939), 76.
61. See John Thornton Kirkland, "The Anthology: Objects and Principles," *Monthly Anthology* 4 (1807): 1; *Monthly Anthology* 5 (1808): 56.
62. Anonymous, "The Degeneracy of Modern Scholars," *Monthly Anthology* 3 (1806): 175. Neither M. A. DeWolfe Howe nor Larry Buell have been able to identify the author of this article. See Buell's "Identification of the Contributors to the *Monthly Anthology and Boston Review*, 1804–1811," *ESQ* 23 (1977): 99–105.

titled "The Dangers and Duties of Men of Letters," Joseph Stevens Buckminster specifically called upon his colleagues to defend the literary republic. Paraphrasing the Roman historian Sallust, Buckminster declared:
"Darent operam censores, ne quid respublica (literum) detrimenti caperet.
[That the censors should take heed that the republic of letters should not
suffer harm]."[63] Interestingly, Buckminster deliberately changed Sallust's
phrase and its meaning, substituting "censors" for "consuls" and "republic
of letters" for "republic." By analogizing the anthologists' role as censor
with that of the Roman consul, he revealed the Brahmin conviction that
the function of clerical intellectuals like himself was undergoing an important transformation. The clergy was proceeding to exchange its predominantly religious and civic roles for literary and cultural ones. Devoting less
time and energy to exclusively religious issues, the Brahmin ministers of
the Anthology Society anticipated a generation of New England intellectuals who insisted on measuring the success of society by its contribution to
Western culture.[64]

For generations, to be sure, Congregational clerics had dabbled in science and the arts. A century earlier, New Light ministers had accused their
colleagues of an increasing sacerdotalism and of stressing the intellect over
the heart.[65] Yet, these Brahmin ministers were moving far afield from the
John Cottons and Cotton Mathers, or even from the inclinations of a Solomon Stoddard or Charles Chauncy. For leading Congregational ministers
to claim to be "unqualified to judge" issues pertaining to "the Subject of
theology"—even in their role as journal editors—was nothing short of
revolutionary. It signaled not only a change in their intellectual sensibilities
and self-conception, but also the fact that the Brahmins now sensed the
opportunity to explore more literary, artistic avenues.

This shift, encouraged by wealthy patrons, by no means signified the

---

63. Joseph Stevens Buckminster, "Polity of Letters," *Monthly Anthology* 3 (1806): 19; Sallust
    was Gaius Sallustius Crispus.

64. It is worth noting that Ralph Waldo Emerson, who was preeminent in advocating the
    evaluation of society by its high culture, proved to be very critical of the preceding
    generation's efforts on that score. He cited only "the Anthology and the Athenaeum" as
    worthy of approbation in "that early ignorant & transitional *Month-of-March*, in our
    New England culture." See his letter to William Emerson, February 10, 1850, in *Letters of
    Ralph Waldo Emerson*, ed. Ralph Rusk (New York, 1939), 4: 178–79.

65. See James Schmotter, "The Irony of Clerical Professionalism: New England's Congrega-
    tional Ministers and the Great Awakening," *American Quarterly* 31 (1979): 148–68.

abandonment of religion altogether. To read the non-Christian elements of twentieth-century Unitarianism and Universalism back into the early nineteenth century would be erroneous; ministers like Buckminster and Channing were deeply spiritual men. Nonetheless, while Brahmin ministers had committed their lives and professional careers to the service of God, they found diminishing intellectual nourishment in rehashing stale theological issues. Boston society, however, proved a distinct distraction from otherworldly concerns. For many ministers, the call to a Boston church meant welcome relief from having to sermonize on, as Joseph Stevens Buckminster stated, "man as a fallen and apostate creature."[66] Instead, they could publish in the *Monthly Anthology*. The ministers of the Anthology Society and their colleagues had commenced a steady, if slow, process toward the urbane secular intellectual.

The anthologists campaigned mightily for support of the *Monthly Anthology*, and the arts generally, arguing that their encouragement was "essential to the protection of the wealthy class from barbarity."[67] The editors appealed directly to the affluent on several levels: self-interest, social responsibility and duty, as well as civic pride.[68] These various appeals were often mixed together with a healthy dose of admonitions, as they warned that the pursuit of riches alone was a sure sign of degeneracy. When "the passion for wealth," warned Theodore Dehon in his 1807 Phi Beta Kappa oration, "is the absorbing passion of the people, when it is pursued only for itself, and the extent of possessions is the measure both of merit and influence, there will be little emulation of superior attainments. The soul, intent upon acquisition of sordid wealth, as the only means of power and distinction, will have for intellectual pursuits neither time nor regard."[69] The anthologists revealed in the pages of the *Monthly Anthology* how well they understood Boston merchants' and bankers' sensitivity to the charge of philistinism. The anthologists shrewdly played on this sore point. In a

---

66. Buckminster to Morse in a 1799 letter, as quoted in Lee, *Memoirs of Rev. Joseph Buckminster,* 327.

67. *Monthly Anthology* 6 (1809): 91.

68. A striking contrast can be made between the production of Brahmin culture in Boston and that of the so-called Second Great Awakening in Rochester. Paul Johnson's study of Rochester, *A Shopkeeper's Millennium* (New York, 1978), portrayed the awakeners as creators of a culture of the petite bourgeoisie. It seems clear that intellectuals were at the center of a number of projects of class consciousness.

69. Theodore Dehon, *Monthly Anthology* 4 (1807): 471.

piece called "American Literary History," Buckminster warned readers that "avarice, and the extraordinary opportunities we have for making money, as it is termed, are at least some apology for our immoderate love of gain. This is the sin that most easily besets us, and debases much of the native generosity to literature."[70] What the anthologists issued as a warning, the Philadelphia *Port Folio* printed as an accusation. In a piece of verse entitled "A Picture of Boston," purposely reprinted in the *Monthly Anthology,* the *Port Folio* asked whether the "Christian Jews" and "tradeful sons of Boston" had not succumbed to the headlong pursuit of riches:

> Does rich reward their mental wealth repay?
> Or Phantom honours, and reluctant praise
> Light without warmth the desert of their days?[71]

The anthologists chose pieces that often repeated this theme, albeit without the sententiousness of the *Port Folio,* because it struck such a resonant chord with their patrons.

In stark contrast to the money-mad, acquisitive trader of the *Port Folio* verse, stood the socially responsible and civic-minded Boston man of wealth who, the liberal ministers of Boston emphasized, demonstrated his interest in and love for the nascent high culture. The Boston Brahmin distinguished himself by his generous support of cultural institutions and literary intellectuals; "we should allow to men of talents a little of their leisure," an "Address by the Editors" urged, "for unless we will endow colleges, or unless we will give encouragement to literature as a profession, there seems to be no other means of forming among us a body of men of learning."[72] "Very great, we are persuaded," wrote Theodore Dehon, "would be the advantage to the literature of our country, if the meritorious editors of these works were enabled by the generous patronage of the rich, and the liberal contributions of the learned, so to conduct them that Minerva would not blush to find her image in the frontpiece."[73]

In the first decade of the nineteenth century, men of learning meant specifically Boston's emerging Brahmin clergy. One "Address by the Editors" of the *Monthly Anthology* went so far as to make a direct pitch for the

---

70. See Buckminster, "American Literary History," *Monthly Anthology* 5 (1808): 56–57.

71. *Monthly Anthology* 4 (1807): 289–90.

72. *Monthly Anthology* 5 (1808): 5.

73. Theodore Dehon, *Monthly Anthology* 4 (1807): 473.

ministry. "In a country like ours, where there are so few men of literary leisure, and where there is so little reward for literary exertion, the clergy should be allowed, I speak coldly, they should be encouraged to exert their talents for the purpose of diffusing general instruction, and in the cause of general literature."[74] In other words, give generously to the liberal clergy so that they might bring literary fame and renown to Brahmin Boston. "It is ardently expected of all lovers of VIRTU," another article in the *Monthly Anthology* declared, "that the youth of this country may be able to pursue studies to advantage under the patronage of the rich and powerful."[75] In essence, anthologists told the merchants that what differentiated them from avaricious parvenus was their conspicuous funding of projects like the *Monthly Anthology*.

The anthologists believed civic pride and patronage to be distinct virtues, but virtues with tangible rewards. Cultural institutions brought notice, commendation, and respect from many quarters. "The time will arrive," wrote William Tudor,

> when the contention will be not which state has the best soil, which has the largest city, and which city has the best market; but which state had made the most eminent discoveries in science, which has produced the most eloquent divines and orators, which the ablest statesmen; where have the muses been propitiated to shed inspiration; which cherishes the artists, whose names are to be enrolled with those of Phidias and Apelles, of Michael Angelo and Raphael.[76]

Patronage of the arts legitimated the public authority of the civic-minded mercantile elite.

Calling patronage a "VIRTU" and alluding to the great figures of classical Greece and the Renaissance proved a common device of the contributors to the *Monthly Anthology*. Conspicuously contrasting with the Reformation allusions so characteristic of articles in the *Panoplist*, its orthodox counterpart, *Monthly Anthology* essays betrayed the Brahmins' classical and Renaissance sensibilities. In Boston, the republicanism initiated by the "Machiavellian moment" manifested itself more in Brahmin patronage of

74. *Monthly Anthology* 5 (1808): 4.
75. John Williams, "Desultory Remarks on the Fine Arts in the United States," *Monthly Anthology* 1 (1804): 109. "Virtu" is a Latin reference, not a misspelling or typo of "virtue."
76. William Tudor, *Monthly Anthology* 9 (1810): 159–60.

the arts—à la the Medici princes—than in politics or political ideology.[77] Mercantile support of the arts, whether in endowing professorships at Harvard, buying shares in the fledgling Athenaeum library, or supporting the clerical intellectuals of the Anthology Society, proved to be a uniquely Bostonian brand of civic duty.[78] In a burgeoning democratic society, in which all-too-often claims of "Gold is thy GOD" rang true, the Boston Brahmins sought to put their wealth and cultural taste to use.[79] They adopted patronage of the arts as their civic virtue.[80]

In addition to the *Monthly Anthology*, the main object of Brahmin patronage, insisted the anthologists, ought to be Harvard College, "our literary parent."[81] When Anthologist John Thornton Kirkland became Harvard president in 1810, the college, like the *Monthly Anthology*, became a Brahmin stronghold. In the succeeding years, the Boston elite were not shy

---

77. See J. G. A. Pocock, *The Machiavellian Moment: Florentine Political Thought and the Atlantic Republican Tradition* (Princeton, 1975).

78. Tamara Plakins Thornton suggests that the Boston elite's "rural and agricultural" pursuits served a similar function. She goes on to suggest that keeping estates helped offset their reticence about engaging in "amoral market relations." See Thornton, *Cultivating Gentlemen: The Meaning of Country Life among the Boston Elite, 1785–1860* (New Haven, Conn., 1989), 7.

79. Joseph Dennie's *Port Folio* published a "Picture of Boston." See *Monthly Anthology* 4 (1807): 289–90.

80. Historians have portrayed the mercantile elite's patronage of the arts as a self-conscious push for cultural hegemony. In this case, the "cultural hegemony" interpretation proves overly reductive on two levels. Firstly, historians arguing for cultural hegemony, following Antonio Gramsci, do not give intellectuals their due, considering them to be merely "organic intellectuals." One historian asserts that the Brahmin intellectuals in the Anthology Society and at Harvard "functioned as cultural ornaments to mercantile society." Intellectuals, as a constituent class of society, have their own interests to protect and advance. In the case of turn-of-the-century Boston, they cannot be relegated to the role of ideological cheerleaders doing the bourgeoisie's bidding. Secondly, the motives of the Brahmin merchants of Boston cannot be reduced to crass material interest. At least in this case, the mercantile elite's support of highbrow culture proved to be the result of rather complex motivations. On "organic" intellectuals, see Antonio Gramsci, "The Formation of Intellectuals," in *The Modern Prince and Other Writings* (New York, 1957), 118–25. On the Boston bourgeoisie, see, for example, Story, *Harvard and the Boston Upper Class* and Thornton, *Cultivating Gentlemen*, 16.

81. Andrews Norton said in his address at the inauguration of Kirkland to the presidency of Harvard that "all of us regard [Harvard] with high respect, and most of us acknowledge with gratitude as our literary parent." Address reprinted in the *Monthly Anthology* 9 (1810): 350.

about patronizing their alma mater. Like the efforts of the anthologists, Kirkland's exertions on behalf of Harvard revealed the Brahmin drift away from religious culture toward more catholic, literary tastes.

Conceived and published by a Brahmin "society of gentlemen," the *Monthly Anthology* represented the Brahmins' changing cultural and class interests. The *Monthly Anthology* demonstrated their progression from a high culture dominated by religious and theological issues toward one devoted to the liberal arts and sciences. It was only the first of many merchant-funded Boston institutions designed to provide Brahmin intellectuals an outlet for their thinking and the merchants a means of social legitimation.

Within two years of the founding of the *Monthly Anthology,* several clerical members of the Anthology Society undertook another important step in the creation of a secular high culture with the founding of the exclusive Boston Athenaeum. Conceived by the same ministers who had adopted the *Monthly Anthology,* the Athenaeum quickly became, along with Harvard, the principal institution for the intermingling of wealth and intellect. Like the *Monthly Anthology,* the Athenaeum promised to promote the union of money and minds; but, unlike the Boston periodical, the Athenaeum, as a social library, required a very large capital investment both to purchase the books and miscellany needed to fill its shelves and to provide the growing collection with a permanent home. None of the founders harbored any illusions as to what the sole source of these funds would be. From its inception, the Athenaeum depended on the mercantile elite of Boston and its pecuniary generosity. It was their money and largely their institution.

Founded in 1807, the Athenaeum was not the first social library in Boston, nor even the first founded in that year. Under a Massachusetts act of 1798, the state incorporated and registered social libraries.[82] There were already four such institutions incorporated by the time the Athenaeum made its application, including the Boston Theological Library society with none other than the Reverend William Emerson serving as its president.[83] The Athenaeum, however, proved to be a new departure. Whereas the other libraries were small organizations with specific patrons and purposes—medical, legal, scientific, and theological—the Athenaeum was

---

82. *Massachusetts Acts and Resolves* (Boston, 1911), 2:221.

83. For a discussion of Boston's other social libraries, see C. K. Bolton, "Social Libraries in Boston," *Publications of the Colonial Society of Massachusetts* 12 (1908–9): 332–38.

conceived with a more general plan and far grander ambitions.[84] If the founders realized their ambitions, the Boston Athenaeum would prove to be a cultural landmark and social status symbol.

The founders of the Athenaeum were none other than "the early members of the Anthology club."[85] During their numerous and well-stocked supper meetings, it occurred to some members that of all the "obstacles to our progress in the cultivation of learning and the arts which are peculiar to our situation, . . . the first of these is the want of libraries."[86] Of the members of the Anthology Society, the ministers—Kirkland, Buckminster, and the ubiquitous William Emerson—figured prominently in the founding of the Athenaeum, as did William Smith Shaw, whose labors on behalf of the library proved so substantial as to earn him the nickname "Athenaeum Shaw." In his position as secretary for more than fifteen years and because of his "avid interest in collecting books, all of which he turned over to the Athenaeum," Shaw was responsible for procuring a large proportion of the approximately twenty thousand titles in the Athenaeum's ample collection upon his retirement in 1823.[87]

The Athenaeum founders were fully cognizant that "our government, from its nature, does not comprise within its cares" the endowment of a literary and social library, especially an institution as ambitiously conceived as the Athenaeum.[88] They well realized that "nothing but the industry and munificence of individuals will [be able] to establish and supply" such an undertaking.[89] The founders were not rich men, but they had access to affluent friends and parishioners, and they sought them out. Formally incorporated in the winter of 1807, the Athenaeum boasted a select group of trustees, including John Lowell, Judge John Davis, Robert Hallowell Gardiner, Harrison Gray Otis, James Perkins Jr., and Samuel Eliot. Of the more than two dozen persons active in the earlier stages of the Athenaeum, two-thirds had their estates valued at over twenty-five thousand dollars, placing them, according to one historian, "in roughly the top 2.1

---

84. See Proprietors' Records, Boston Athenaeum, March 18, 1826, and January 1, 1827, and Arthur B. Ellis, *History of the First Church in Boston*, (Boston, 1881), 168.
85. Josiah Quincy, *The History of the Boston Athenaeum* (Cambridge, Mass., 1851), iii.
86. Tudor, *Monthly Anthology*, 156.
87. Harrington, "'Society of Gentlemen,'" 13.
88. *Monthly Anthology* 4 (1807): 3–4.
89. Ibid.

per cent of the population."[90] The founders were a veritable "who's who" of Brahmin Boston.

By far, the majority of the finances for the nascent enterprise came from the sale of proprietary shares. The founders issued a circular—they styled it a memoir—among the wealthy parishioners of the Brahmin churches advertising their ambitions. It read, in part: "Feeling a confidence, that these objects will be thought worthy of your patronage, and hoping that from private as well as public considerations, you will be induced to give it your countenance and support."[91] It should be noted that the Athenaeum's supporters utilized the same basic arguments that the founders of the *Monthly Anthology* had several years earlier. Patronizing the high culture benefited the Brahmin elite both privately and publicly. On a personal level, "the man of business will have the means of intellectual activity and enjoyment," while he will fulfill his public, social responsibilities by plowing some of his riches back into the community.[92] Josiah Quincy, looking back forty years later, made precisely this claim: "This establishment, it was said, will confer honor on its patrons. For it must be acknowledged honorable to apply wealth to some of its noble uses; to join to a spirit of commercial enterprise a just estimate of the value of letters and arts; and to lay a permanent foundation for their cultivation and advancement through successive periods."[93]

The memoir proved extremely successful. By the end of the first year of incorporation, the Athenaeum had raised over forty-five thousand dollars, vending one hundred and fifty proprietary shares at the price of three hundred dollars each. These first thousands were rapidly dissipated together with the "annual subscription" of "one hundred and sixty subscribers at ten dollars a year."[94] As the Athenaeum expanded, the need for more funds grew apace. Accordingly, the Athenaeum sold several blocks of additional proprietary shares, the proceeds from which went primarily to the unstinting purchase of rare and valuable books and periodicals. By 1830, the li-

---

90. Ronald Story, "Class and Culture in Boston: The Athenaeum, 1807–1860," *American Quarterly* 27 (1975): 181.

91. Quincy, *Athenaeum*, 24.

92. William Smith Shaw, "The Boston Athenaeum," *Monthly Anthology* 4 (1807): 227.

93. Quincy, *Athenaeum*, 37.

94. Shaw in a letter to Buckminster, May 13, 1807, as quoted in Quincy, *Biographical Sketches* (Cambridge, Mass., 1851), 37.

brary boasted a collection exceeding 27,000 volumes, making it one of the largest holdings in the nation. At the time of the Civil War, Athenaeum shares numbered over one thousand and sold for as much as nine hundred dollars. Assets totaled over seven hundred thousand dollars.[95]

Substantial additional funding came from private donations and bequests. Wealthy trustees, such as James Perkins Jr., John Bromfield, and Samuel Appleton—merchants and bankers all—considered the Athenaeum an important enough Boston institution to bequeath very large sums for its improvement and expansion. John Bromfield, grown wealthy in the lucrative China trade, donated $25,000 to the Athenaeum, while Samuel Appleton gave an equal amount.[96] James Perkins Jr. and the entire Perkins clan, who "engaged extensively in the trade to the North-west coast and to Canton," proved to be by far the most generous benefactors.[97] Not only did the family donate some $40,000 in cash, but in 1821, "when the need arose for more spacious quarters, the society took advantage of [Samuel] Perkins' gracious offer of his mansion on Pearl Street, valued at twenty thousand dollars."[98] Whatever their motivations, the merchant princes of Boston fulfilled the wildest ambitions of the clerical intellectuals of the Anthology Society.

One of the means of attracting support for both the *Monthly Anthology* and the original Athenaeum subscription had been the appeal to wealthy Bostonians' sense of social responsibility; yet the Athenaeum hardly served any public function at all. Unlike the *Monthly Anthology*, which any literate Bostonian could read, the Athenaeum was exclusive. From the first, it effectively excluded all but the wealthy and their intellectual associates. Rule number eight of the Athenaeum charter explicitly stated that "no inhabitant of Boston, who is not a subscriber to the institution, shall be allowed to have access to the library and reading-room."[99] This policy of exclusion came under fire, particularly when the institution, fast becoming the largest private library in the country, emerged as an important center

---

95. Cleveland Amory, "Boston's Old Guard," *Harper's* (October 1947): 321, and Story, "Class and Culture," 180.

96. Charles K. Bolton, "The First One Hundred Years of Athenaeum History: A Chronological Sketch," in *Athenaeum Centenary* (Boston, 1907), 26–30.

97. *Monthly Anthology* 4 (1807): 293.

98. Quoted in Harrington, "'Society of Gentlemen,'" 221–22.

99. "Rules and Regulations," in Quincy, *Athenaeum*, 15.

for research. One irate writer in the *Boston News Letter and City Record* complained that, "When the poor are favored with permission to study the neatly fitted up shelves of books which adorn the Athenaeum, we shall be convinced of the necessity as well as the worth of it, and not before."[100] The Athenaeum grew in membership, acquisitions, and status, but it did not change its exclusive, and ultimately elitist, policies in the course of the entire nineteenth century. So when Buckminster praised the Anthology Society for founding "an institution in the metropolis of New-England, which will be useful to various classes of our citizens," he meant only those classes with money or connections.[101] The Athenaeum excluded the less fortunate.

Even the exceptions to the Athenaeum's strict rules demonstrated its exclusivity. Rule eleven of the charter stated that "Judges of the Supreme Court and the Judges of the Circuit and District Court" as well as the "President and Professors of Harvard College . . . shall be considered honorary members of the institution."[102] The succeeding regulation extended to all full members the privilege of inviting one guest per month into the Athenaeum, provided he or she resided outside of Boston. The most intriguing exception to the Athenaeum's restrictive policies had to be the one adopted in 1819, when the Standing Committee authorized the institution to admit "any of the regular clergy of Boston to the privileges of the Athenaeum."[103] In addition to the original founders—Emerson, Kirkland, Buckminster, and Charles Lowell, whose brother, John Lowell, had purchased him a share—all members of the Boston clergy were now entitled to enjoy Athenaeum society.[104] It should be noted, however, that admission for members of the clergy was at "the discretion" of the Standing Committee.[105] Only the Brahmin Unitarian clergy perused the collections and engaged in social conversation with the membership. Significantly, the sole exceptions to the Athenaeum's restrictive admission policies were for the few Boston clerical intellectuals, for whom the purchase of a membership

100. *Boston News Letter and City Record,* February 25, 1826, cited in Bolton, *Athenaeum Centenary,* 30.

101. Joseph Stevens Buckminster, *Monthly Anthology* 4 (1807): 601.

102. Quoted in Quincy, *Athenaeum,* 15.

103. Ibid., 67.

104. See Ferris Greenslet, *The Lowells and Their Seven Worlds* (Boston, 1946).

105. Quincy, *Athenaeum,* 14.

was beyond their means. Boston's ministers might not be rich, but they were surely welcome in the highest circles. Like the *Monthly Anthology,* the Athenaeum represented the meeting of "great minds" and "great wealth," the signature of Brahmin Boston.

The few exceptions notwithstanding, the exclusivity of the Athenaeum's rules and regulations betrayed the institution's nature. While the proprietors could buy or sell shares freely, very few shares actually changed hands. Proprietors enjoyed lifetime memberships, which they almost uniformly bequeathed to their heirs. In addition, the shares proved to be prohibitively expensive, costing as much as "five to thirty times as much as other social libraries in America charged."[106] Restrictive in membership and extremely well endowed, the Boston Athenaeum proved to be a Brahmin institution through and through.

Not only did the admission standards reflect the mercantile backing of the society, but Athenaeum policies did as well. The Athenaeum opened its doors to Hannah Adams, a poor but pedigreed widow and historian, as well as an enemy of the orthodox Jedidiah Morse, so she could conduct her research, while it excluded others.[107] During the Athenaeum's second decade, among the most noxious contemporary issues to the elitist membership was antislavery and the activities of the nascent abolitionist movement. Accordingly, New England abolitionist Lydia Maria Child had her right to use the collections revoked as soon as she published her first abolitionist pamphlet. The Athenaeum had not accumulated its unparalleled collections, exclaimed the outraged membership, so that Child or anyone else could research and write radical antislavery tracts within its walls.[108] The Athenaeum was an exclusive, genteel, private institution, funded by Boston businessmen and governed by their Brahmin sensibilities.

---

106. Story, "Class and Culture," 195.

107. The Brahmins championed Hannah Adams in no small measure as a result of a bitter fight she had with Jedidiah Morse. What turned out to be, like so many of Morse's dealings, a foolishly and overly drawn-out feud over an abridged history reader, pitted the widow Adams against Charlestown's abrasive minister from 1804 until 1815. See Morse's account of the controversy, published at his own expense: *An Appeal to the Public on the Controversy Respecting the Revolution in Harvard College* (Charlestown, Mass., 1814).

108. See Deborah Pickman Clifford, *Crusader for Freedom: A Life of Lydia Maria Child* (Boston, 1992), 47–51. See Walter Muir Whitehill, "Three Letters of John Quincy Adams," in *Athenaeum Items* 62 (July 1955).

The Boston Athenaeum and the *Monthly Anthology* proved to be two of the first institutions of exclusive high culture in Massachusetts and the United States. The Anthology Society, the outgrowth of a small coterie of young, literary ministers founded both. Boston's wealthy men had engaged them for their cultural virtuosity and freed them from traditional pastoral duties. Like the affluent Congregational churches where the ministers preached, the *Monthly Anthology* and the Athenaeum reflected the increasingly class-based nature of American cultural institutions. Both avowedly flaunted their exclusive class membership and cultural tastes.

The relationship between the democratization of politics, as demonstrated by the Bay State's vote for Thomas Jefferson's reelection in 1804, and the establishment of these most "undemocratic" private institutions is unmistakable. The sea change in the status of a political career, the diminution of opportunities to serve in the national government—which Massachusetts Federalists had been instrumental in creating—and the popularization of American political culture fundamentally altered the Boston Brahmins' vision of their political obligations and possibilities without eradicating their sense of civic responsibility.[109] Unwilling to retreat entirely, yet reluctant to engage in popular politics, the Boston Brahmins pursued an alternative, and altogether predictable, course. The ministers and merchants, barristers and bankers, created institutions of high culture, at once exclusive and "useful." Excluded from the public arena, they sought private means to fulfill their sense of social responsibility. Patronage and philanthropy supplanted politics.

---

109. Again, David Hackett Fischer's insights in *The Revolution of American Conservatism: Federalist Party in Jeffersonian Democracy* (New York, 1965) notwithstanding, the older generation, at the very least, realized and lamented these democratic changes in the polity. I find Fischer's claims about a new generation only partially convincing. Whatever Jeffersonian techniques they eventually adopted, the Federalists never regained anything approximating an equal position in national politics. Whether this was simply because the stigma of Federalist elitism was too great to overcome, or whether the electorate understood that popular politics was, in the end, anathema to Federalists, old school and new, is open to debate. It seems to me that Fischer is right to a point. If the significance of Jeffersonian politics was its embrace of campaigning and electioneering, then Fischer seems convincing. But if one considers a truly national political organization to be Jefferson's great innovation, then Fischer's idea that Federalists embraced Jeffersonian political methods proves unconvincing. No matter how the so-called young generation of Federalists changed, they never managed to create any kind of inter-regional coalition.

State Street merchants supplied the patronage and Brahmin ministers supplied the intellect and initiative. While condemning the democratization of politics and the profound want of culture in New England society, the Brahmin clergy openly advocated and actively encouraged mercantile promotion of the elite cultural institutions it championed. The ministry effectively convinced the mercantile elite—or at least reinforced its belief—that philanthropy, by necessity, was the sole means of cultivating taste, nurturing the intellect, and giving something back to society. Civic pride and social responsibility obligated philanthropic support of artistic and literary undertakings; "the Saint of the Nineteenth century is the Good Merchant," because he is a patron of the arts,[110] wrote Rev. Theodore Parker, hardly an elitist like Kirkland or Emerson.[111] Convincing the bourgeoisie of the propriety of philanthropy, Boston's Brahmin ministers assured themselves a position of status and power within their own circles. In undertaking this transformation, the ministers in effect renounced once and for all the two-century-old Puritan notion of a national covenant. Emerson, Kirkland, and Buckminster could hardly feel themselves shepherds of all their people when they spent their days and nights preaching solely to those who could afford to purchase pews in their exclusive churches, instructing those who could afford Harvard tuition, writing for the few who read the *Monthly Anthology,* and socializing with those who bought proprietary shares in the Athenaeum. In short, the Brahmin clergy of Boston had transformed God's covenant with the Puritan nation into a class compact with a privileged elite.

---

110. The national fast day was called by President Adams in response to events surrounding the XYZ affair.

111. Theodore Parker as quoted in Freeman Hunt, *Worth and Wealth* (New York, 1857), 253–54.

CHAPTER 4

Harvard and the Brahmin Class

*One of the most charming characteristics of the Proper
Bostonian is his regard for something which is not lo-
cated in Boston at all but a few miles up the Charles
River in Cambridge, and which he calls Hahvud.*

—CLEVELAND AMORY

O N NOVEMBER 23, 1793, the West Boston Bridge was completed. By
joining Boston and its upriver neighbor, the bridge brought Harvard
into the orbit of the state capital's growing mercantile elite at the very moment when its economic fortunes were ascendant. Before long, the bridge
served as a conduit for a continuous flow of Boston money and influence
in one direction and a steady stream of Harvard-educated young men—
"the scholar and the gentleman united"—in the other.[1] Within a few decades, so historians have argued, rich Bostonians "owned" Harvard.[2]

Harvard was central in the forging of a Boston aristocracy.[3] The tremen-

---

1. Attributed to "Silva" in the *Monthly Anthology* 3 (1806): 18. "We seldom meet here with
   an accomplished character, a young man of fine genius and very general knowledge, the
   scholar and the gentleman united." "Silva" was John S. J. Gardiner.
2. Historian Richard Brown uses this word in a review essay. See his "Who Should Rule at
   Home? The Establishment of the Brahmin Upper Class," *Reviews in American History* 9
   (March 1981): 58.
3. See Ronald Story, *Harvard and the Boston Upper Class: The Forging of an Aristocracy, 1800–
   1870* (Middletown, Conn., 1980). The title of this work is misleading insofar as it claims
   to span the years 1800 through 1860; yet the author does not examine Harvard in the age
   of Washington and Jefferson.

dous influx of "upper-class" money into the college's coffers on the one hand, and the proliferation of Harvard-educated lawyers and businessmen on the other, provides ample proof of that. But far more was involved in the transformation of Harvard than merely the grand bourgeoisie's push for cultural hegemony.[4] The fight for Harvard represented a turning point in the culture of eastern Massachusetts. Bitterly contested by those involved, it exacerbated the emerging bifurcation of the Standing Order into hostile camps of orthodox and Brahmin ministers. In the aftermath, the Brahmin clergy, freed up from clerical duties by generous salaries and acquiescent churches, began in earnest to apply its cultural virtuosity toward the production of a high culture with great literary pretensions. The takeover of Harvard proved a critical first step in a long process.

Orthodox observers most certainly did not consider the West Boston Bridge and the subsequent challenge to their authority a boon to Harvard. Timothy Dwight, president of Yale University and close associate of many Bay State orthodox ministers, remarked that "the greatest disadvantage, under which this seminary labours, is the proximity to Boston. . . . The erection of the West Boston Bridge has rendered this evil still greater."[5] Dwight was particularly solicitous of Harvard students, for whom the "allurements of the metropolis have often become too powerfully seductive to be resisted."[6] Others expressed alarm at encroaching influences of a different nature: the latitudinarian creed espoused by Boston's elite, proto-Unitarian ministers.[7] Foremost among those who objected to the Brahmins were several prominent professors and members of Harvard's Board of Overseers. They feared for Harvard the same fate that had befallen the Congregational churches of Boston, where just across the West Boston Bridge wealthy merchants and bankers had used their money and power to remake church, parish, and ministry in their own image. This transfor-

---

4. See Robert Rich, "A Wilderness of Whigs: The Wealthy Men of Boston," *Journal of Social History* 4 (Spring, 1971): 263–76; Cleveland Amory, *The Proper Bostonians* (New York, 1947); Frederic Jaher, *The Urban Establishment* (Urbana, 1982); and Paul Goodman, "Ethics and Enterprise: The Values of a Boston Elite, 1800–1860," *American Quarterly* 18 (1966): 437–51. See above for a discussion of the meaning and use of cultural hegemony.

5. Timothy Dwight, *Travels in New England and New York* (New Haven, Conn., 1821–22), 1:487.

6. Ibid.

7. "Unitarian," although the chosen term of most historians, is inaccurate. There was no real Unitarian designation until William Ellery Channing's Baltimore Sermon of 1819.

mation, derisively called Unitarianism for its disavowal of the trinity, entailed far more important social and intellectual changes than doctrinal ones. In the middle of the first decade of the nineteenth century, eight of the nine Congregational churches in Boston had embraced the Brahmin creed. The orthodox vowed to stop this arrogant assault, as well as the growing elitism and exclusiveness of the Brahmins, by any means and at all costs.[8]

The opponents of the Unitarian onslaught, coalescing into a formidable bloc in defense of Harvard, had good reason to fear the encroachment of Brahmin Boston. At the turn of the century, the Brahmins had not only taken control of Boston's oldest and most venerable churches, but also had shown themselves to be interested in extending their influence. With the largesse from Boston's lucrative overseas trade, they had already begun to create novel cultural outlets in order to demonstrate their affluence as well as their burgeoning civic pride.[9] Finding the political culture and its democratic tendencies increasingly alien and more difficult to manage to its advantage, the Boston elite sought to gain control of Harvard, the leading force in the production of high culture. Little wonder, then, that the orthodox braced themselves for the Brahmin assault on Harvard College.

The Brahmin play for Harvard was precipitated by the death of three prominent university figures within the span of a year. While the controversy centered around the replacement of David Tappan, Hollis Professor of Divinity until his decease in August 1803, the virtually simultaneous deaths of President Joseph Willard and Rev. Simeon Howard turned the consequential but regular selection of a new faculty member into the fight for Harvard. Since both Willard and Howard were members of the Harvard Corporation, the choice of their successors went a long way in determining the future of the six-man body that effectively controlled the school, while the Hollis Professor of Divinity, occupying the most prestigious and influential chair in the university, determined to a large extent

---

8. My discussion of the West Boston Bridge derives in part from a brief article by Lewis P. Simpson called "The Intercommunity of the Learned: Boston and Cambridge in 1800," *New England Quarterly* 23 (1950): 491–99.

9. After the adoption of the Jay Treaty in 1795, the American maritime industry, concentrated in eastern Massachusetts, flourished. Exports alone grew from $33 million in 1794 to $94 million in 1801, nearly a 300 percent increase. See Curtis Nettels, *The Emergence of a National Economy, 1775–1815* (New York, 1962), 395–96. For Boston, see Samuel Eliot Morison, *A Maritime History of Massachusetts, 1783–1860* (Boston, 1921).

the religious tenor of the institution. So it is not surprising that John Eliot, minister at New North Church in Boston and Howard's successor in the corporation, asserted that the campaign for the presidency and the professorship was conducted "with as much intrigue . . . as was ever practiced in the Vatican."[10]

The Harvard conflict with its intrigue and acrimony ultimately precipitated a schism in the Standing Order, serving as the culmination of a growing rift between the Brahmin clergy of Boston and the Bay State's other Congregational divines. Samuel Eliot, upon reviewing the controversy a generation later, made precisely this point. "The election [of Henry Ware as Hollis Professor] should not," wrote Eliot, "be regarded as a cause, so much as it was an effect, of a change of public opinion in the neighborhood; which for many years had been silently going on, and of which the evidences are to be sought in the character, and manner of preaching, of the clergy of this part of the Commonwealth, and the spirit of investigation and of independence of mere authority, which were conspicuous in their congregations."[11] It is worth noting that Eliot makes no reference to theological beliefs or creeds. Many subsequent historians, particularly those sympathetic to the orthodox side, have insisted that the Unitarian controversy, as it was called, centered around religious matters. Because the Brahmins had renounced the key tenets of Calvinism, even doubting the trinitarian nature of the Christian deity, none of them could be trusted in the key religious office at Harvard. Eliot and his cohorts contended that "character and manner of preaching" as well as "political considerations" were more relevant than doctrine to the dispute.[12] Eliot betrays his sympathies by neglecting to mention at any point the growing discrepancy in status and income between the Brahmin ministers occupying the prestigious pulpits in the "neighborhood" of Boston and those divines not so fortunate.[13] The resentment of the less well-settled ministers to a large extent fueled the fires of the Unitarian controversy.

As early as 1793, when Tappan was installed as Hollis Professor, there

---

10. Rev. John Eliot quoted in Samuel Eliot Morison, *Three Centuries of Harvard* (Cambridge, Mass., 1936), 188.

11. Samuel Eliot, *Sketches of the History of Harvard College* (Boston, 1848), 99.

12. William Wells, "Religion and Learning," *Monthly Anthology* 2 (1805): 152.

13. For figures on the disparity in income between Boston's "pew proprietorship" pulpits and the remainder, see chapter 2.

was disagreement over the appointment between orthodox and Brahmin ministers. Harvard chose Tappan, the favorite of the orthodox Jedidiah Morse, minister at Charlestown and thus a Harvard overseer, in part because the Brahmins were not yet organized and their merchant allies had not yet supplanted the state as the primary financial contributor to the university. Only after the merchants had commenced to pour money into the school's coffers, did they more forcefully assert themselves. The Brahmins accepted—even welcomed—Tappan in spite of his religious orthodoxy. Tappan's "doctrinal thermometer," wrote John Gorham Palfrey, "fell within the somewhat vague range of what had already begun to be called *moderate Calvinism*."[14] William Bentley, minister at Salem, called his views "Calvinistic," while Jedidiah Morse maintained that Tappan was imbued with "the highest degree of orthodoxy."[15] Tappan's election demonstrates the relative indifference to creed among the Brahmins, who concerned themselves more with behavior than dogma. Increasingly latitudinarian, the Brahmins assented to Tappan's selection because of his upright character and earnest compassion for his students. "In piety, knowledge and Christian zeal," wrote Josiah Quincy, "he was exemplary."[16] Tappan generated almost a cult following among his students, whom he persuaded "to love religion."[17] Ironically, his most affectionate pupils became Boston's leading Brahmin ministers, including William Emerson, Joseph Stevens Buckminster, and John Thornton Kirkland, the last to become Harvard president. Tappan's students respected and emulated him not for his beliefs—with which they came to disagree—but for his reasonableness and tolerance in matters of doctrine. Professor Tappan "scarcely intimated his own opinions, but gave impartial views of the best arguments on opposite sides, and led his pupils to weigh and balance the evidence for themselves."[18]

During the years of Tappan's tenure as Hollis Professor "the general atmosphere at Cambridge had been greatly changed"; the position of the Brahmins, several of whom Tappan had mentored, had been significantly

---

14. John Gorham Palfrey notes this of Tappan in his essay on Henry Ware in *American Unitarian Biography*, ed. William Ware (Boston, 1850), 1:236–37.

15. William Bentley, *The Diary of William Bentley* (Salem, 1905–14), 3:38.

16. Josiah Quincy, *The History of Harvard University* (Cambridge, Mass., 1840), 2:262.

17. Bentley, *Diary*, 3:38.

18. J. W. Alexander, *Life of Archibald Alexander* (New York, 1894), 254.

strengthened in the university and in the community generally.[19] Brahmin ministers were now ensconced in the major pulpits in Boston, positions which also entailed the "big six" pulpits' membership on Harvard's Board of Overseers.[20] Most importantly, with the replacement of Simeon Howard by John Eliot, the six-member corporation boasted four Brahmins. Besides Eliot, Brahmin members of the corporation included Dr. John Lathrop, minister of the Second Church of Boston; Ebenezer Storer, wealthy merchant and treasurer of the university since 1777; and "the learned and upright" Judge John Davis, member of Federal Street Church and Harvard Corporation Fellow.[21] Control over university concerns was clearly passing into the hands of the Boston Brahmins.[22]

Although the Brahmins outnumbered the orthodox in the corporation, the leadership of that body devolved to Eliphalet Pearson, Hancock Professor and member of the corporation since 1800. As the senior member of the faculty, Pearson was chosen acting president by the overseers upon the death of President Willard. With Judge Oliver Wendell, the father-in-law of the orthodox Rev. Abiel Holmes, Pearson led the fight against the appointment of Henry Ware to succeed Tappan as Hollis Professor.

The enigmatic Pearson circumspectly kept his precise religious views obscure. According to John Pierce, Professor Pearson was "ultra-liberal," at least for a time, while Sidney Willard, son of the Harvard president, noted that prior to "the long controversy about the choice of a Hollis Professor of Divinity, I was not aware of the sternness of Dr. Pearson's orthodoxy, so called."[23] Pierce also notes that Pearson's theological commitments underwent some sort of metamorphosis at about the time he assumed the presidency of Harvard. "Upon the death of President Willard, [Pearson] then suddenly claimed to be orthodox; & the change was so sudden &

19. James King Morse, *Jedidiah Morse: A Champion of New England Orthodoxy* (New York, 1939), 86.

20. The "Big Six" towns whose teaching elders were made overseers of Harvard were Boston, Roxbury, Dorchester, Charlestown, Newtown, Watertown, and Cambridge. The inclusion of the "Big Six" reflected the correlation of religious culture and higher education in the minds of Massachusetts's divines.

21. Sidney Willard, *Memories of Youth and Manhood* (Cambridge, Mass., 1855), 2:195.

22. For a list of the corporation fellows and their tenures in office, see Evelyn Walsh, "The Effects of the Revolution on Boston" (Ph.D. diss., Brown University, 1964), 437.

23. Willard, *Memories*, 2:175, and John Pierce, "Memoirs and Memorabilia," in *Proceedings of the Massachusetts Historical Society* 7 (1891):308.

thorough, without the appearance of better motives, that a large proportion of his old friends considered him merely acting a part."[24] Whatever
his "true" religious sentiments, Pearson spearheaded the attempt to block
Ware's appointment.

The corporation met five times in December 1804 in an effort to choose
a new Hollis Professor.[25] At the first meeting, the dynamics of the situation
became apparent. The Brahmins had their candidate in the person of
Henry Ware. Forty years old and sixteen years the minister of the Congregational church at Hingham, Ware had "acquired so high distinction in his
profession," that his colleagues thought he was all but assured election to
the Hollis Professorship.[26] "Certain it is," wrote John Gorham Palfrey,
Ware's biographer and colleague, "that he was conspicuous in the first rank
of the clergymen of the day in all the accomplishments and graces that
become the character. His services as a preacher were held in the highest
esteem."[27] Brahmin, learned, and loquacious, Ware was in position to become the next Hollis Professor. The problem was Pearson. Under pressure
from the Brahmins as well as of the Board of Overseers to make a prompt
decision, Pearson "was loath to proceed to the election of a Prof. of Divinity," because he knew that Ware was the odds-on favorite.[28] At the corporation meeting of December 7th, when "it was urged to choose a Professor
of Divinity immediately," Pearson threw down the gage, declaring that
Ware was unacceptable because he did not meet the requirements demanded by Thomas Hollis when he endowed the chair in 1720.[29] According
to John Eliot, Pearson, or "Megalonyx,"[30] as he dubbed him,

---

24. Pierce, "Memoirs," 7:308–9.
25. Minutes of the meetings of the corporation are in Harvard's Pusey Library archives; the
    notes of Fellow John Eliot and the accounts of Eliphalet Pearson appear in Conrad
    Wright, ed., "The Election of Henry Ware: Two Contemporary Accounts," *Harvard Li-
    brary Bulletin* 17 (1969): 245–77; they can also be found in the Harvard University Ar-
    chives in Pusey Library.
26. Palfrey, "Henry Ware," in William Ware, *American Unitarian Biography*, 235.
27. Ibid.
28. Eliot's diary, in Wright, "The Election of Henry Ware," 261.
29. Several newspaper articles took up the issue of the delay in appointing a successor to
    Tappan. One went so far as to suggest that the money dedicated to the professorship
    had been misused. See consecutive issues of the *Columbia Centinel* and the *New England
    Palladium* for November and December 1804.
30. The term "Megalonyx" is, of course, a hilarious, satirical usage of Thomas Jefferson's
    appellation of the animal with the "Great Claw" he described in his famous foray into

made a most solemn speech in which he told us how much he had thought & prayed upon this matter—that we were under the necessity of Electing a Calvinist—from the Records of the *College,* the public mind, the character of the former professors &c. . . . He pleaded argued, scolded—discovered himself so much a Jesuit as to bring a wonderful revolution in my own mind.—Not that a Calvinist should be chosen![31]

Pearson continued his histrionics into the succeeding meetings in which he "was treating us as children"; at one point, claims Eliot, Pearson "threw the foam of billingsgate upon me, thinking he had a right to abuse me as I was a new member."[32] Eliot and several of the more senior members insisted that Pearson spell out his evidence for insisting that only a Calvinist could assume the Hollis chair. To this challenge, Pearson replied, "that the will of the Founder was for a Calvinist—that 19 out of 20 were Calvinists who wished the prosperity of the College. That None but a Calvinist was good enough, That they were better men than Arminians &c."[33] This tack of insisting that neither Ware nor any Brahmin met Thomas Hollis's requirements because they were not of "sound and orthodox principles" was utilized by Pearson's ally, Jedidiah Morse, at the Board of Overseers meetings as well.[34] It rested on the dubious contention that the phrase "sound and orthodox" in the original contract entailed the selection of a nineteenth-century orthodox Congregationalist. In order to ensure that this criterion was met, Pearson and Morse adamantly maintained that the selection of the Hollis Professor necessitated a thorough examination of the candidates' theological commitments. Not surprisingly, this demand

---

paleontology. See his essay in the American Philosophical Society *Transactions* 4 (Philadelphia, 1799), 246–60. Federalists were wont to engage in this type of satire, as Linda Kerber points out in *Federalists in Dissent: Imagery and Ideology in Jeffersonian America* (Ithaca, 1971).

31. Eliot's diary, in Wright, "The Election of Henry Ware," 261–62.

32. Ibid., 262.

33. Notes of John Eliot as given to Harvard University Archives by Joseph McKean, minister in Milton, Massachusetts; printed in Wright, "The Election of Henry Ware," 262–63.

34. Text of Hollis endowment is in Jedidiah Morse, *The True Reasons on Which the Election of a Hollis Professor of Divinity in Harvard College was Opposed at the Board of Overseers, Feb. 14, 1805* (Charlestown, Mass., 1805), 10–11. Harvard-Andover Theological Library's copy is bound incorrectly; page 11 follows page 14.

for religious conformity and "insistence on first principles" proved anathema to the Brahmin clergy and its allies.[35]

Having reached an impasse, the six members of the corporation at their fourth meeting on December 26 decided to submit the matter to the Board of Overseers. Scheduled to meet on January 3, 1805, the board could make several nominations for the corporation to consider. Fully aware that there were no orthodox candidates comparable to Ware and that Brahmin influence was greater on the Board of Overseers than in the corporation, Pearson, "immediately aroused," refused to allow any such appeal be drafted. Although the corporation yielded to the acting president's wishes, the Board of Overseers nonetheless took up the issue—in the end, making the sensible suggestion that the corporation decide on a new president first, who would then be able to cast the deciding vote for the Hollis Professorship.

At the corporation's next meeting in the first week of February, Judge Wendell proposed, and the fellows accepted—with Pearson "violently opposed"—to vote simultaneously for the vacant president's chair as well as the Hollis professorship.[36] It was hoped, it seems, that a compromise could be reached in which the Brahmin Ware might be chosen president (where there was no creedal contract to debate) and an orthodox clergyman, likely Jesse Appleton of Hampton, New Hampshire, could be selected for the Hollis chair. Appleton, according to Samuel Eliot Morison, was Pearson's "own candidate for Divinity professor."[37] Significantly, Pearson, for whom this compromise was crafted, dissented immediately. When "one gentleman" proposed "to elect Mr Ware president and Mr Appleton professor—Megalonix [was] violently opposed to either."[38]

In accounting for Pearson's opposition and general irascibility, most historians have followed the explanation given by Fellow John Eliot,[39] who noted in his journal that "a great secret was communicated [after one meeting] wh[ich] . . . will account for much of the strange conduct, & the inconsistency of *Megalonyx*."[40] Eliot was referring to Pearson's "so sud-

---

35. Morison, *Three Centuries,* 187–88.
36. Eliot's diary, in Wright, "The Election of Henry Ware," 263.
37. Morison, *Three Centuries,* 189.
38. Ibid. Eliot spelled *Megalonyx* with both a "y" and an "i."
39. The three major historians of Harvard all agree: see Josiah Quincy, Samuel Eliot Morison, and Conrad Wright.
40. Eliot's diary, in Wright, "The Election of Henry Ware," 262.

den & thorough" embrace of orthodoxy as well as his precipitous rejection of any nominations for the vacant Harvard presidency.[41] Both Eliot and John Pierce concluded that Pearson had ambitions for the Harvard presidency himself. Pierce decided that "without appearance of better motives," it was clear that Pearson was "merely acting a part" in order to realize his objective.[42]

It seems altogether likely that Pearson and Jedidiah Morse conspired. They resolved that Pearson would keep the Hollis chair vacant long enough for Morse to be nominated at the meeting of the Board of Overseers, while Morse would actively promote Pearson for president among the overseers. That Pearson kept Morse informed of the machinations of the corporation meetings is evident from the contents of several letters Morse wrote to his friend Dr. Joseph Lyman of Hatfield.[43] One letter in particular, dated December 27, 1804, the day following the first full corporation meeting concerning the Hollis appointment, betrays Morse's knowledge of the proceedings, information he must have obtained from Pearson. Morse offered striking details to Lyman about "the violent struggle to elect an Arminian Professor and President for our university, and avowedly make it the Arminian College. . . . I fear and deprecate a revolution in our university more than a political revolution. I pray God in mercy, to prevent both."[44] Evidently, a number of overseers divined that "Morse himself would have liked to have the opportunity of teaching at Harvard."[45] In his *History of the Harvard Church in Charlestown, 1815–1870*, Henry Edes notes that several members of the Harvard board had the "resolute and successful purpose that [Morse] should not fill the Hollis Professorship of Divinity at Cambridge, nor even dictate who should fill it."[46]

Realizing that the Brahmins would not brook his appointment, Morse sacrificed his personal ambition at least for the moment and assented to Pearson's promotion of Jesse Appleton, who was less controversial and

---

41. Pierce, "Memoirs," 7:308.
42. Ibid.
43. Yale University has numerous letters between Morse and Lyman from December 1804 through June 1805 that deal directly with the Hollis fiasco.
44. Jedidiah Morse to Dr. Lyman, December 27, 1804, Yale University Archives (copy).
45. Morse, *Jedidiah Morse*, 88.
46. Henry Edes, *History of the Harvard Church in Charlestown, Massachusetts, 1815–1870* (Boston, 1879), 54.

even "loved" by at least some members on both sides.[47] Nonetheless, Appleton garnered only two votes for the professorship, so the compromise failed even though Ware received four votes for the presidency.[48] By this, the sixth meeting concerning the Hollis chair, it was clear that Pearson could not be mollified. "To candidates for the President's chair, [Pearson's] opposition was uniform, [while] his attempt to introduce a categorical examination into the creed of a candidate" was unacceptable to the majority, which they styled "a barbaric relic of Inquisitorial power."[49]

Frustrated and tired after the compromise measures had failed, the fellows determined to bring the debate to a head and offer up a candidate. "It was then agreed," an exasperated John Eliot wrote, "to vote for the professor of divinity, and that the gentleman who received the most votes should be sent up to the Overseers—Mr Ware had four votes Mr A. two."[50] So on February 1, 1805, "by a change of one vote," the corporation chose Henry Ware, Brahmin minister from Hingham, Harvard's Hollis Professor of Divinity.[51]

The corporation's nominee had to be confirmed by the Board of Overseers. That the nomination of Ware occasioned a great deal of interest is manifest by the unusually large attendance at the Board of Overseers meeting convened expressly to act upon his appointment. The February 14 meeting, assembled at the council chambers of the Massachusetts State House, was attended by approximately twice the normal number of overseers. Whereas most meetings drew fewer than thirty laymen and no more than six ministers, this meeting attracted fully fifty-seven individuals, including twelve ministers.[52] When the secretary read Ware's nomination to

---

47. John Eliot states, "I loved Appleton," in his notes; he lamented not selecting him for the Hollis position, "for which I am now sorry." *Eliot's Diary*, 263.

48. The actual trial ballots were saved and are in the Harvard University Archives.

49. Quincy, *History*, 2: 285–86.

50. Eliot's diary, in Wright, "The Election of Henry Ware," 263.

51. Subsequent testimony reveals that John Lathrop was the deciding vote, having switched his allegiance from Appleton to Ware. The voting reveals that creed and religious conviction were not the overriding concerns of the corporation, the vitriolic harangues of the Professor Pearson notwithstanding. Conrad Wright concludes exactly this, writing that "it is clear that non-theological and nonecclesiastical factors played a large role in the outcome." See Wright's commentary in "The Election of Henry Ware," 256. The two critical factors, it seems to me, were the personal ambitions of Pearson and the partisan concerns of the orthodox.

52. Forty-five out of forty-seven lay overseers comes out to 96 percent attendance! The

the gathering, Newburyport senator Enoch Titcomb, who had been "carefully briefed in advance by either Morse or Pearson," inquired whether Ware could assume the Hollis chair without examination.[53] He demanded to know: "Does the candidate possess the qualifications required by the founder: Is he of *sound and orthodox* principles? Did the electors, previous to their choice, examine the candidate, as was done in the case of the first two Professors, as to his *orthodoxy?*"[54] Jedidiah Morse, quickly following up on Titcomb's query, "dared to object in the most open manner" to the nomination of any but an orthodox minister to the Hollis chair.[55] Taking the "same ground as Dr. Pearson had assumed in the Corporation," Morse insisted on two main items:[56] it was "necessary and proper [to] inquire" whether the nominee was "a man of solid learning in Divinity" and of "*sound* or *orthodox* principles;"[57] and, if "the Prof-elect was not a Trinitarian, as the foundation required," his nomination should be defeated.[58]

The crux of the debate for Morse and the orthodox members of the board came down to the phrase "sound and orthodox principles" in the Hollis contract of 1720. Morse insisted, as Pearson had earlier, that the word "orthodox" meant something very specific, namely, adherence to the Westminster Confession. If Ware did not subscribe to the Westminster Confession then he was "a disciple of the new school, an enemy to Calvinism in every form," and his election would transgress the terms laid down by Thomas Hollis.[59] This "appeal to the Hollis statutes" is remarkable, considering that easily a majority of those present, from whom Morse needed at least some support, no longer subscribed to the Westminster Confession themselves.[60]

Samuel Dexter Jr., son of the wealthy merchant and founder of the Har-

---

numbers are based on Morison, *Three Centuries,* 189, and Wright, "The Election of Henry Ware," 257.

53. Wright, "The Election of Henry Ware," 257.

54. Morse, *True Reasons,* 19.

55. Bentley, *Diary,* 3:141.

56. Quincy, *History,* 285. Wright says virtually the same thing in "The Election of Henry Ware," 257.

57. Morse, *True Reasons,* 10, 19.

58. Bentley, *Diary,* 3:141.

59. Yale letter to Joseph Lyman, February 9, 1805, Morse Family Papers, Yale University Archives.

60. Pierce, "Memoirs," 3:225.

vard Dexter Lectureship, issued the Brahmin response. According to the notes of John Pierce, Dexter "turned the councils of this busy heresiarch into foolishness."[61] Dexter noted that Hollis himself, "notoriously not a Calvinist," did not subscribe to the Westminster Confession, nor did his own pastor, the Reverend Mr. Hunt.[62] In fact, Hollis stated that the sole subscription to be demanded of the divinity professor was that "the Bible is the only and most perfect rule of faith and practice."[63] Josiah Quincy, upon studying the contract between Hollis and the college, exposed just how untenable the orthodox argument was when he noted that the key phrase, "sound and orthodox" of Article 11, had not been in Hollis's original document. Not Hollis, but the orthodox members of the Harvard Board of Overseers had added it to the final draft. Equally as significant, Quincy found that while Hollis had no objection to the phrase, he pressed his conviction that the only "form of a declaration to be made by the professor [was] that the Scriptures were to be accepted as the only rule of faith."[64] As a member of the state Senate, Quincy was a member of the Board of Overseers. He attended the February 14 meeting, but there is no evidence that he revealed his findings at that time, likely because it proved unnecessary.[65] At the meeting, the board concluded that Ware's election would breach neither the letter nor the spirit of the Hollis contract.

The orthodox position undermined and Morse's objections rebuked, the Board put the nomination to a vote. "The question then taken," writes Morse, "*thirty three* were in favor of approving the choice of the Corporation, and *twenty three* against; and so the choice of the Rev. HENRY WEARE [*sic*], as Hollis Professor of Divinity in Harvard College was confirmed."[66] In spite of the "vigorous efforts ... to prevent these evils" by Pearson in the corporation and Morse in the Board of Overseers, the Brahmins prevailed. Thus, the way was cleared for a Brahmin to assume the most prestigious chair in America, as "the oldest theological department in New England went Unitarian."[67]

---

61. Ibid.
62. Morse, *True Reasons*, 25, and Quincy, *History,* 2:285.
63. Quincy, *History,* 1:538.
64. Quincy, *History,* 1:230–34, and Wright, "The Election of Henry Ware," 259n.
65. See Conrad Wright, "The Election of Henry Ware," 259n.
66. Morse, *True Reasons*, 27.
67. Morison, *Three Centuries,* 189.

No sooner was the fight over the election of Henry Ware settled than both sides rushed into print, the Brahmins to defend themselves from charges leveled during the controversy, and the orthodox to warn that Harvard was "most imminently threatened with a revolution which will deeply & lastingly affect the cause of evangelical truth."[68] Jedidiah Morse immediately "put himself off as the head of the opposition among the clergy," publishing "within a matter of weeks" a pamphlet entitled *The True Reasons on Which the Election of a Hollis Professor of Divinity in Harvard College was Opposed at the Board of Overseers.*[69] Benjamin Welles, a member of the Anthology Society, penned the Brahmin defense of Ware's election; entitled "Religion and Learning," it appeared in the *Monthly Anthology.* Additionally, members of both parties published caustic articles in the various area newspapers. Yet, one of the most revealing accounts of the controversy, penned by Pearson himself, never reached public scrutiny, as it was not published. It now rests in the Harvard University archives.

These works, as polemical as they are, reveal two camps with remarkably different outlooks. Both sides understood the importance of the election of Henry Ware, but for dissimilar reasons. For Morse, the issue hinged upon belief; Ware was "a rational Christian," "an enemy of Calvinism in every form," and therein lay the "revolution."[70] Morse insisted that the Brahmins, secretly Unitarians, threatened to undermine the religious fabric of society. "Unitarianism," wrote Morse, "dissolves all the bonds of Christian union, & deprives religion of all its efficacy and influence upon society."[71] Pearson echoed these sentiments, repeatedly emphasizing the creedal innovations of Ware and the Brahmins. He was adamant that, by elevating "a person to be a Professor of Divinity, who is an *Arminian, Arian,* &c" the Brahmins were undermining "the religious character of the University."[72] The Ware appointment for both Pearson and Morse was "a revolution of sentiment in favor of what is called *rational* in opposition to *evangelical* religion"; it was a "revolution in religion."[73] "[F]rom such

68. Morse to Lyman, February 9, 1805, Yale University Archives.

69. Bentley, *Diary*, 3:149.

70. Morse in the *Columbian Centinel*, November 24, 1804; Morse to Lyman, February 9, 1805, Yale University Archives.

71. Morse to Joseph Lyman, June 15, 1805, Yale University Archives.

72. Pearson, "Intended Publication Relative to Choice of Professor of Divinity," in Papers Relating to the Election of Hollis Professor, Harvard University Archives.

73. Ibid.

liberality, from such sentiments, from such *Presidents & Professors*," wrote Pearson, "all pious Christians, who believe the Divinity of Christ, will devoutly pray, 'good Lord, deliver us.'"[74]

The Brahmins insisted that the issue was not religion, but erudition. That Ware disbelieved in Trinitarianism was not relevant; they would have elected an orthodox divine, they maintained, had there been one suitable, and there seems little reason to doubt their contention. Writing under the pseudonym "Constant Reader," an advocate of the Brahmin cause proclaimed that "whether the candidates for the *Presidential* & *Theological* chairs be Calvinists, Arians, Socinians, or Latitudinarians, is not of so much importance, as whether they are learned, pious, moral men; capable of diffusing instruction; and anxious to discharge their duty with fidelity."[75] Ware was just such a man, "with singularly blended sweetness of temper, austere integrity of conscience and a touching humility of spirit."[76] The Brahmins rejected any and all proposals to examine the doctrinal beliefs of the candidates, so they argued, not because they feared Ware would betray any heterodox opinions, but because such scrutiny was irrelevant. Similarly, the Boston Association of Ministers had decided to forgo the examination of new candidates for their pulpits altogether. The Brahmins sought the same qualities in the Hollis Professor that they had been seeking in the ministers of Boston: literary talent, a pleasing manner, and eloquent but measured oratorical virtuosity.[77] In a sense, Pearson and Morse were right; the Hollis appointment was a revolution. Yet, they revealed the difference between their agenda and that of the Brahmin movement by reading this transformation as a shift from one set of religious beliefs to another. That the Brahmins rejected orthodoxy, whether Calvinist, moderate Calvinist, Hopkinsian, or whatever, was true, but irrelevant in the case of Ware's appointment. The real revolution in the Brahmin transformation at Harvard, as well as in Boston's churches, was their conscious movement from strictly theological concerns toward literary, high-cultural preoc-

---

74. Ibid.
75. *Columbian Centinel,* January 16, 1806.
76. Quoted in Joseph Allen and Richard Eddy, *History of Unitarians and Universalists,* 187.
77. In an essay on Ralph Waldo Emerson, Loren Baritz notes that Emerson "was preparing to turn from theology to literature." In this chapter, I argue that the generation of William Emerson, Ralph Waldo's father, inaugurated this "turn," of which the appointment of Ware is one example. See Loren Baritz, *City on a Hill: A History of Ideas and Myths in America* (New York, 1964), 215.

cupations. The Brahmins were becoming New England's cultural gate-keepers.

No sooner had Ware been installed in the Hollis chair than the corporation sought to fill the vacant presidency. As if to prove that religious creed mattered less than social and cultural factors, the corporation extended an offer to Fisher Ames, an Episcopalian.[78] When Ames politely declined the appointment, the college found itself without a president as the year 1805 came to an end.[79] With the choice ultimately between professors Pearson and Webber, the corporation decided on the latter, offering him the presidency on the last day of February 1806. As a result, Eliphalet Pearson promptly proffered his resignation not only as acting president, but as Hancock Professor as well. In his letter of resignation he lamented that "there remained no reasonable hope to promote the reformation of the society he [had] wished."[80] Without the possibility of "rendering any essential service to the interest of religion by continuing his relation to it," Eliphalet Pearson quit Harvard for good.[81]

With Brahmins installed as Hollis Professor of Divinity and as president, the orthodox all but retired from Cambridge. When John Thornton Kirkland, minister of New South Church and beloved of the Boston elite, became Harvard president in 1810, a position he held for eighteen years, he and his associates undertook the internal transformation of Harvard into a great, catholic university. During Kirkland's reign, Boston money and Brahmin cultural virtuosity transformed the institution. The Harvard leadership founded schools of law and theology, endowed fifteen new professorships, sent a host of scholars to Europe to bring back knowledge, and overhauled the college curriculum. It was called the Age of Kirkland, but in reality it was the age of the Brahmins. With the takeover of Harvard—combined with the *Monthly Anthology* and the Boston Athenaeum—the Brahmins established a powerful alliance of literary intellectuals and merchant princes, a cultural aristocracy.

Unlike the *Monthly Anthology* and the Athenaeum, Harvard was a public institution with legal and financial ties to the state. More than that, Har-

---

78. Equally as revealing, J. S. J. Gardiner, rector at the Episcopalian King's Chapel, was the first president of the Brahmin Anthology Society.
79. Morse to Dr. Green, no date, Yale University Archives.
80. Quoted in Quincy, *History*, 2:287.
81. Ibid.

vard was the crown jewel of New England culture. Founded in the midst of the Great Migration of the 1630s, Harvard was the oldest educational institution in America. While the West Boston Bridge and the expansion of the capital city brought Cambridge into closer proximity, Harvard proved a far more daunting challenge for Brahmin power than either the *Monthly Anthology* or the Athenaeum had been. The combination of the extensive erudition of Boston's Brahmin clergy and the ever-increasing financial resources of its merchant allies had made the takeover of the faltering periodical and the creation of the elitist social library relatively easy undertakings. With the single exception of obtaining a state charter for the Athenaeum, the Brahmins did not have to confront or contain any competing interests as they built their institutions. The vast majority of Bostonians neither read the *Monthly Anthology* nor set foot in the Athenaeum.

Harvard proved a far greater challenge for several reasons. It was already established and therefore had many vested interests connected with it. Unlike the *Monthly Anthology* or the Athenaeum, Harvard was a quasi-public institution. Since its inception, it had been New England's premiere institution charged with the training of Congregational ministers. If Harvard went Unitarian, the new leadership could undermine the "sacred tenets" of the Standing Order of Massachusetts. Its symbolic importance alone was enough to make it contested terrain. For all parties, then, more was at stake than just the future of Harvard.

The first decade of the nineteenth century proved a propitious time for the Boston Brahmins to use their wealth and influence to acquire control of Harvard. Virtually since the Battle of Lexington and Concord, Harvard had tottered on the brink of insolvency. The school itself was closed for "an early summer vacation" in April 1775, while the following year barely one hundred students attended class in temporary facilities at Concord. At the same time, much to the chagrin of the faculty and overseers, the "College buildings were appropriated to the needs of the militia who poured into Cambridge, the headquarters of the revolutionists."[82] By war's end, many of the college buildings were in ruins, while the several members of the faculty who had chosen the wrong side in the war had hastily removed themselves to safer shores.[83] In addition, Harvard's meager endowment,

---

82. Samuel F. Batchelder, *Bits of Harvard History* (Cambridge, Mass., 1924), 19–21.
83. Quincy, *History*, 2:166–67.

invested in continental currency, had all but evaporated. Inflation proved so problematic that students in arrears were compelled to pay the difference in the price of provisions between the time their fees were due and the time they were paid. The college was on the verge of bankruptcy.

Harvard did find a promise of relief from its dire financial straits in the Massachusetts Constitution of 1780. Appropriately enough, the constitutional convention, which included several prominent Harvard alumni, assembled in the Cambridge meetinghouse within view of the campus. At the insistence of John Adams, an entire section of the Bay State constitution was devoted to the "University at Cambridge."[84] Chapter 5, section 2, entitled "The Encouragement of Literature, etc.," stated that "it shall be the duty of Legislatures and Magistrates, in all future periods of this Commonwealth, to cherish the interests of literature and the sciences, and all seminaries of them; especially the University at Cambridge."[85] The inclusion of Harvard in the body of the state constitution, like the extension of state support to "publick Protestant teachers" in Article 3 of the bill of rights, seemed to represent a commitment of public funds, in this case to the support of Harvard. In addition, the constitution went on to declare that "the President and Fellows of Harvard College, in their capacity, and their successors in that capacity, their officers and servants" were granted these "Powers, authorities, right, liberties, privileges, immunities and franchises . . . forever."[86] According to one historian, "any anxiety that the College may have had as to its future status under a republican government was removed in 1780. . . . John Adams thought of everything."[87]

The inclusion of Harvard College in the Bay State constitution had precedent in New England history. In colonial times, the school had expected and received public financial support. By law, every household "had given the college twelvepence, or a peck of corn, or its value in unadulterated wampum peag."[88] This public patronage was considered obligatory, because by furnishing Puritan New England with educated magistrates and ministers, Harvard provided a vital resource to the community. By the

---

84. See *Acts and Laws of the Commonwealth of Massachusetts* (Boston, 1780–81), 1:26–27.
85. Ibid.
86. Ibid.
87. Morison, *Three Centuries*, 160–61.
88. This rather literary description is from Van Wyck Brooks, *The Flowering of New England, 1815–1865* (New York, 1936), 33.

1780s, however, while in short supply, ministers found themselves not in such great demand as in previous decades. New Englanders were not building so many new churches, so they needed fewer ministers.

If Adams had hoped that the legislature would prize the university and bless it with patronage, he was mistaken. Adams efforts notwithstanding, Harvard derived little immediate benefit from the Massachusetts legislature. Whatever its "duty," the legislature made little effort to fulfill it, particularly as it found itself in the same financial difficulties as Harvard in the aftermath of the war. The state was broke.

Cognizant of the financial straits of the state, yet in dire need of funds itself, the Harvard Corporation and Board of Overseers, the two governing bodies, sought a more suitable and regular means of receiving state money. The salary of the president and some of the faculty had traditionally been paid by annual grants from the legislature. The corporation reasoned that it would greatly add to the prestige and stability of the Harvard presidency, and the institution as a whole, if this "uncertain and precarious" annual grant could be transformed into a fixed annual subsidy independent of the whims of the legislature. In January 1781, the most influential members of Harvard's two governing bodies presented a petition to the legislature requesting "that a fixed salary might be annexed to the Office of the President of the College."[89] Yet, even though such outstanding men as future governor James Bowdoin, the Reverend John Lathrop, and State Treasurer Ebenezer Storer signed the petition—with the implied threat that without state support it would be very difficult to lure a suitable candidate to fill the vacant post of college president—the Massachusetts legislature turned down the request, not wanting to obligate itself to specific annual funding for Harvard. It suited the legislature to keep the institution dependent.

During the next few years, relations between Harvard and the legislature deteriorated almost to the breaking point. Just as the corporation had feared, for several years the legislature decided to forgo the annual grants of some four hundred pounds for the salaries of the president and the Hollis Professor of Mathematics and the Hancock Professor of Hebrew and Oriental Languages. The college itself lent money in the interim to its officers, who were "of consequence embarrassed in the extreme."[90] The

---

89. Quincy, *History*, 2:243.
90. Ibid., 246.

corporation reminded the legislature "that from the first foundation of the College, the President had received his support from the public by an annual salary granted by the General Court," as had the Hollis and Hancock professors. In addition, the Board of Overseers petitioned the state "to make provision for the honorable support of the President." Finally, after complaining that "the failure of these annual grants" had rendered the president's pecuniary situation "distressing," and that the professors "could not find ways and means to support their families," the legislature relented, granting £480 to President Webber and £200 each to the professors.[91] This proved to be the last monies paid to Harvard officers from the public coffers of Massachusetts for many years.

The problems between Harvard and the state were not limited to the president's salary. The Massachusetts legislature undermined the interests of Harvard in two other areas in the 1780s. In 1784, the legislature saw fit to divest the school of its right to the Boston and Charlestown ferry, "the most ancient of colonial grants," for a paltry two hundred pounds per annum, "no fair equivalent in value for the rights devested."[92] Three years later, the state took possession of some six thousand acres of Maine woodland, "which had been previously granted by the provincial General Court."[93] By means of these acts, as well as the systematic rejection of several "memorials" for funds for a botanical garden and the establishment of an infirmary in Cambridge, the legislature made clear to Harvard that henceforth it should not expect public money. As one Harvard president put it: "the temper of the times was unfavorable to the patronage of institutions, destined for instruction in the higher and more abstruse branches of learning."[94]

The state virtually abandoned Harvard for two interrelated reasons. Part of the explanation was that Massachusetts faced a very difficult financial situation. The legislature had to slash much of the annual budget. Secondly, as the temper of the times turned increasingly democratic, legislators came to view Harvard as an increasingly elitist institution of only marginal importance to their constituents. Several Baptist-dominated towns

---

91. Ibid., 248–49.
92. Ibid., 271. This was the famous Charles River Bridge over which the great Supreme Court battle was waged.
93. Quincy, *History*, 2:270.
94. Ibid., 248–49.

insisted that no public support be given to Harvard until "ministers other than Congregational be eligible as Overseers," a provision finally adopted more than half a century later.[95] The town of Petersham expressed a distinct class hostility in suggesting that "it may be possible that the Legislature may find it necessary to curtail that Rich and Growing Corporation lest it soon Endanger the Liberties of the Commonwealth."[96]

The constitution of 1780 notwithstanding, the well of public support upon which Harvard College had long depended was drying up. Harvard's leadership understood that the new political climate precluded renewal of state support in the near future. The "altogether new and ominous" wording of the last grant from the Massachusetts legislature clearly articulated the state's position.[97] Previously referred to as "gratuitous," the 1786 funds were "in consideration of services done, and to be done."[98] Members of the corporation and board, realizing the hopelessness of the situation, assumed that they could no longer count on state funds. Accordingly, within a few years the college had written off all arrears against the state. Harvard had to seek some alternate means of funding beyond that of the public treasury. At the turn of the nineteenth century, the commonwealth virtually cast adrift this quasi-public institution.

Harvard's Board of Overseers and members of the corporation, whatever their disappointment, were not taken unawares by the indifference and hostility of the Massachusetts legislature. For the previous several years, they had begun preparations to tap other sources of funds. The leadership understood that situated as Harvard was in Cambridge, only one alternative means of financial support appeared feasible. And in 1793 it was made much more proximate by the completion of the new West Boston Bridge. Like the founders of the *Monthly Anthology* and the Boston Athenaeum, Harvard would have to seek the private patronage of Boston's mercantile elite.

Massachusetts men of means had never been averse to bequeathing money to Harvard College, the donation of John Harvard's library and the generous endowment of the Hancock professorship a century later being the most notable examples. Now that Harvard was becoming an entirely

---

95. Ibid., 161.
96. Ibid.
97. Ibid., 247.
98. *Acts and Laws*, 2:124.

private institution, or "university," as John Adams referred to it in the constitution, it needed significantly larger and more regular donations. In recognition of this fact, the corporation leadership undertook a number of changes at the opening of the nineteenth century to attract and hold the allegiance of this new source of funds: Boston's emerging merchant class. With Brahmin support, the corporation transformed the government, the teaching faculty, the curriculum, and the overall mission of Harvard from that of a primarily religious institution—Harvard was still often referred to as a seminary—to that of a secular university.

The most important change promised to be that of the immediate governing body, the Harvard Corporation. For many generations the Corporation had comprised the president, five fellows, and the treasurer, the last being the only lay member of the body. Fellows were selected from the faculty of the college, some combination of professors and tutors. In essence, Harvard was run by its teachers, who were paid in large measure from the public coffers. As private support replaced public funding, the corporation became the province of wealthy patrons and their servants. No tutor was elected to the corporation after the 1780s, while in 1800 Eliphalet Pearson, professor of Hebrew, was the last professor selected to that body. His reign proved brief.

The elite of Brahmin Boston replaced the clerical faculty in the corporation; in turn, they encouraged the professors and instructional staff to spend more time on teaching their pupils and on their own scholarship. Prominent Bostonians joined the Harvard Corporation, including John Lowell in 1783, Thomas Cushing, James Bowdoin Jr., Judge John Davis, Chief Justice Theophilus Parsons, Jonathan Jackson, and John Lowell Jr. in 1810. Clearly, these men were chosen not for their knowledge of or involvement in the day-to-day affairs of the college. The president saw to all those matters. The corporation's new role in the private institution proved to be general oversight, political protection, and, most importantly, promotion of Harvard's pecuniary interests. The corporation ensured that "every first family in Boston" contributed something "into Harvard's coffers."[99] The generosity of this small group of families largely supplanted the legislature, while private donations and bequests constituted better than nine of every ten university dollars.[100] Like the Boston Athenaeum and the *Monthly An-*

---

99. Amory, *Proper Bostonians*, 173.
100. Story, *Harvard and the Boston Upper Class*, 26.

thology, whose members were to a man Harvard graduates, "the University at Cambridge" became a Brahmin institution.

Harvard's new patrons and governing bodies harbored grand ambitions for the school. The corporation sought to fulfill Adams's hope of transforming a smallish seminary into a major university. They envisioned an institution with a wide-ranging, modern curriculum that would reflect the needs and desires of the dominant mercantile elite. As early as 1783, the corporation began searching for donors for the establishment of a medical faculty, resulting in the private endowment of three professorships. Private funds were solicited and received for a professorship in natural history and thirty thousand dollars was raised for the creation of a botanical garden, after the state legislature had spurned a request for public assistance. During the administration of John Thornton Kirkland, the Boston Brahmin minister who presided over Harvard from 1810 to 1828, both the law and divinity schools were established, all by means of private patronage.

Private patronage notwithstanding, Harvard was not quite a private institution. It was contested terrain, and therefore could not be tailored to serve the interests of the Brahmins as readily as a congregation or a private social library. Some of those interests deplored the direction of the college; westerners called it eastern and elitist, Republicans believed it Federalist, while many clergymen proclaimed it to be Unitarian. These groups refused to relinquish control of Harvard without a fight, especially to elitist easterners of dubious religious sentiments. The ensuing controversy, which lasted for a decade, was fought on two fronts. In Boston, antithetical factions in the legislature contested the desirability of political control over the college Board of Overseers. Across the Charles River in Cambridge, the corporation and the faculty battled over the secularization and liberalization of the curriculum and the overall direction of the institution. With mercantile backing, the Brahmins eventually prevailed.

The political fault lines over Harvard extended back to the constitution of 1780 and the subsequent disputes over public support for Harvard. Supporters of public funding tended to be Brahmins from the eastern part of the state—Federalists all—while critics were principally Republicans and religious dissenters from the western counties. With Brahmin support, Federalists pursued a policy of laissez-faire with regard to Harvard, as they felt little trepidation at the growing influence of Boston within the Yard. While not willing to risk their political fortunes on such dubious measures as continued public support of Harvard's president and professors, which proved increasingly insignificant as Brahmin support blossomed, Federalist politicians protected the interests of the college against would-be attackers. As a result, the college administration, well aware precisely where its support lay, "became definitely partisan" during the first decade of the nineteenth century.[101] The appointment of the arch-Federalist chief justice, Theophilus Parsons, to the corporation in 1806 and the attempt to make Fisher Ames Harvard president in 1805 amply demonstrated the college's political prejudices.[102] William Bentley, minister at Salem and one of the few openly Republican members of the Congregational clergy, charged Harvard with favoritism and "snobbery" in its selection of candidates for honorary degrees.[103] Morison points out that "none but a Federalist" was so honored "from 1802 to the 'era of good feelings.'"[104]

Republican dislike of Harvard became evident in two incidents relating to the college: the first of only symbolic importance, over a student "rebellion," and the latter, of greater significance, over the composition of the Board of Overseers. The "Bread and Butter Rebellion" of 1805 occurred when students "walked out of Commons" in protest over what they contended was the all-but-inedible food served there.[105] After some typical adolescent "halooing and disorder," including the setting of several bonfires in Harvard Yard, the college administration cracked down by suspending over half the student body.[106] While these events proved similar to an earlier rebellion a decade prior to the revolution and analogous to those of 1807–8 and 1823, there was one distinct difference.[107] The Bread and Butter Rebellion took on a "political twist," when the expelled students appealed

---

101. Morison, *Three Centuries,* 187.

102. Quincy, *History,* 2:286.

103. Bentley, *Diary,* 3:38.

104. Morison, *Three Centuries,* 187. I believe James Monroe, during his triumphal tour through New England, was the first Republican since 1802 granted an honorary degree.

105. James R. McGovern, "The Student Rebellion in Harvard College, 1807–1808," *Harvard Library Bulletin* 19 (1971): 351.

106. *Records of the [Harvard] College Faculty (1806–1814),* 8:27–34, Harvard University Archives. For a different view, see "Anti-Quixotism: A Vindication of the Students with Respect to the Late Occurrences in Harvard College, by Bartholomew Bystander," manuscript in Harvard University Archives, without pagination.

107. See McGovern, "Student Rebellion," and Samuel Eliot Morison, "The Great Rebellion in Harvard College and the Resignation of President Kirkland," in *Publications of the Colonial Society of Massachusetts* 27 (1928): 54–112.

to Republican state senators, who sat ex officio on the Board of Overseers, for reinstatement and a general hearing of their grievances.[108]

The Republicans jumped at the chance of undermining the Federalist-dominated corporation. Levi Lincoln, the Republican lieutenant governor, chaired a committee of overseers commissioned to look into the matter. Its final report, which found for the students and "reported in favor of reforming the Commons, and pardoning the offenders," was defeated by the entire board by the most slender of margins. Voting along strict party lines, the total was twenty-nine opposed to the report and twenty-six in support.[109] That the Republicans lost the vote proved irrelevant, as they had undertaken the inquiry not out of sympathy for the plight of the teen-age student body, but in order to blacken the eye of the Federalist corporation. In this they succeeded.

The Lincoln report and the closeness of the final vote so outraged the Brahmin Harvard leadership that it resolved to alter once and for all the composition of the Board of Overseers.[110] To forestall any further political intrusion into the governance of the college, the corporation sought legislation that would effectively change the 1780 constitution. "The prospect of a 'Jacobinical' Board of Overseers," writes Samuel Eliot Morison, "was so unpleasant that early in 1810, when the Federalists had recovered control of the state government, they pushed through a law altering the constitution of the Board of Overseers."[111] As a result, the state Senate was expunged from the board, reducing the number of ex officio members to eleven, while providing for the eventual replacement of clerical board members by laymen.[112] By these actions, the corporation hoped to ensure Brahmin control of Harvard.

Most members of the corporation were well pleased with their political maneuvering, convinced that Republican political influence was at an end. Not everyone was so sanguine, however, particularly James Thornton Kirkland, Harvard's newly elected president, who was most sympathetic with

---

108. See *A Narrative of the Conduct of the Corporation of Harvard College Relative to the Late Disorders Perpetrated by the Students* (Cambridge, Mass., 1807) in the archives of Harvard University; McGovern, "Student Rebellion," 351.

109. *Conduct of the Corporation*, 34.

110. *Historical Register of Harvard University* (Cambridge, Mass., 1937), 25–43.

111. Morison, *Three Centuries*, 212.

112. *Historical Register*, 34.

the intentions of the corporation and their Federalist allies in the legislature. As expressed in the Corporation records, Kirkland feared that the act of 1810 would set a double-edged political precedent. It was entirely possible, if not likely, argued Kirkland, that "the example of change will do more to hurt than the nature of [the act] will do good."[113] While Kirkland understood that "by this law, Unitarianism was virtually enthroned at Cambridge," he knew that if a Federalist-dominated legislature could alter the governing bodies of the university, then any other legislature, Federalist or Republican, could change them too, quite possibly at Brahmin expense.[114]

Kirkland proved to be an accurate prognosticator, as he discovered "that what the legislature could do, the legislature could undo."[115] Republicans won a majority of seats in the very next general elections in the spring of 1811.[116] No sooner had they convened, than they sought to redress "the relinquishment, by the Senate, of the right to sit as members of the Board of Overseers," which Republicans had "opposed as unconstitutional, and as a disenfranchisement of the Senate of the Commonwealth."[117] Accordingly, "the governor's friends," wrote the Reverend William Bentley, shepherded a bill through the House and Senate repealing the action of March 1810.[118] This new bill, passed in February of 1812, not only reinstated the "now thoroughly gerrymandered State Senate" to the Board of Overseers, but did so effective immediately upon its signature by Gov. Elbridge Gerry.[119] Indeed, this proved to be, from the corporation's point of view, the most dangerous and the most dubious aspect of the Republican statute. Unlike the Federalist-inspired 1810 act, which "provided for its own suspension until and unless accepted by [Harvard's] Governing Boards," the 1812 version explicitly avoided seeking the approval of the Brahmin leader-

---

113. Kirkland quoted in Morison, *Three Centuries,* 212.
114. "Introduction and Progress of Unitarianism in New-England," *Spirit of the Pilgrims* 2 (September 1829): 478.
115. Ibid.
116. Results of May 1811 elections in Ephraim M. Wright, ed., *Tabular View of Representation in the Commonwealth of Massachusetts, from 1780 to 1853* (Boston, 1854). A good discussion of the "Republican Offensive" is Ronald Formisano, *The Transformation of Political Culture: Massachusetts Parties, 1790s–1840s* (New York, 1983), 112–17.
117. Quincy, *History,* 2:301.
118. Bentley, *Diary,* as quoted in Morison, *Three Centuries,* 213.
119. Morison, *Three Centuries,* 213.

ship of the college, which it knew it would not receive.[120] In short, the Republican legislature was vying to exert direct influence on Harvard by bypassing the Board of Overseers.[121]

Not surprisingly, President Kirkland and the corporation were outraged by this abridgment of their traditional prerogative. If the legislature could determine the composition of the Board of Overseers independently of the corporation and the sitting board, then nothing could stop it from exerting, sooner or later, effective control over Harvard in its entirety. In a carefully worded memorial to the legislature written by Kirkland, the corporation claimed that the act of 1810 had not been an attempt to deny the legislators of their "just participation in the Government of the University"; rather, it had solely been drafted for the express purpose of making the Board of Overseers more manageable by shrinking the number of ex officio members.[122] "The Memorialists," the record continued, "are convinced that the University has been conducted with liberality and impartiality and a steady view to the public good. In regard to the political divisions of the times they believe that persons best acquainted with the Course of Instruction and discipline in that place will acquit the College of any attempts to prejudice or unduly excite the youthful mind."[123] This dubious appeal notwithstanding, the legislature, once the act became law, demanded that the corporation turn over "all documents relating to Harvard and the state."[124] Failing to convince the politicians that they could change the governance of the college only with the consent of the board, there was precious little the president and corporation could do. In a meeting on April 15, 1812, the corporation voted against repeal of the 1810 act, asserting that it "derived its ultimate authority from the assent of the Corporation and Overseers thereto given."[125] Therefore, the corporation "voted, the Act last passed can have no legal effect or operation until the

---

120. Ibid.

121. A fair comparison might be made with the Dartmouth College case at the same time. As in the Dartmouth case, the issue was just how independent of the legislature a chartered college was. See Whitehead, *The Separation of College and State; Columbia, Dartmouth, Harvard, and Yale, 1776–1876* (New Haven, Conn., 1973).

122. Harvard College Minutes, February 24, 1812, in *Harvard Corporation Records* (1810–19), Harvard University Archives, 5:64.

123. Ibid.

124. Ibid.

125. Ibid.

provisions thereof be assented to by the Overseers and the Corporation."[126] One month later, a committee of overseers chaired by Christopher Gore recommended that Harvard surrender no records for the moment, while the overseers sought a ruling by the Massachusetts Supreme Court on the legality of the legislature's actions. The Gore report urged that "some measures should be devised and adopted for procuring, agreeably to the Constitution of the Commonwealth, the opinion of the Supreme Judicial Court on the validity of the act of 1812."[127]

The issue reached a climax of sorts on June 2, when two competing Boards of Overseers met simultaneously in two separate chambers in the Boston State House.[128] Unsure of exactly what to do, but urged by the ever-prudent President Kirkland to avoid a crisis which might undermine the authority of the Federalist-dominated corporation as well as the Board of Overseers, the 1810 board backed down. The board "voted, that the Secretary be directed to carry the records and proceedings of the college, as specified in the said act, before the new board, being held this day in the Senate Chamber."[129] Nonetheless, in a final act of defiance, the 1810 board stated its "opinion" that giving up the college records as requested "is not obligatory on this board without their express assent, and that it is not competent to the legislature to make any laws affecting the visitorial powers of the Corporation, or changing its government, unless such consent be obtained."[130] A month later the corporation, "guided by faithfulness to the best interests of the University," assented to the new Board of Overseers, thinking it "expedient . . . to waive all opinion on the validity of the Act of 1812." Thus, the confrontation passed.[131]

Kirkland and the corporation shrewdly avoided a direct showdown with the Republican politicians. They did not have long to wait for their party to return to power. By early the next year, the Federalists were back in control of the State House. The legislators promptly turned their attention to redressing their problems with Harvard, repealing the 1812 act and rescuing the college from the fiscal and political uncertainty from which it

---

126. Ibid., 69.
127. Ibid., May 12, 1812, 85, and Quincy, *History,* 2:303.
128. *Historical Register,* 34.
129. Quincy, *History,* 2:303.
130. Ibid.
131. Harvard College Minutes, vol. 5 (April 15 and June 17, 1812).

had been suffering for the previous several years. In a further attempt to make up for past problems, the Federalist-dominated legislature passed an act in February 1814 "for the encouragement of Literature, Piety, Morality, and the useful Arts and Sciences," providing Harvard, as well as Williams and Bowdoin, "having also petitioned for pecuniary aid," with substantial state funds virtually without restrictions.[132] Ironically, the funds appropriated to the Bay State colleges had their origin in the blatantly partisan Republican "bank tax" passed in 1813. Rather than repeal this 1 percent tax, the Federalist politicians simply applied the proceeds to higher education, with not less than 25 percent of the total earmarked for scholarships "toward the partial or total reduction of tuition fees" for needy students.[133] With proportional distribution ratio at 10:3:3, Harvard's share came to a total of some ten thousand dollars per annum.[134] Lasting for ten years, this act "for the Encouragement of Literature" proved to be a timely and significant boon to Harvard's pecuniary fortunes.

It seems clear that these disputes—from the Bread and Butter Rebellion to the composition of the Board of Overseers—had distinct similarities. In none of the events, which spanned the ten years from 1805 to 1814, were the issues raised of any grave or lasting impact upon the growth and governance of Harvard. These disputes shared a distinctive political character; Republican reaction was the inevitable outgrowth of Brahmin Boston's encroachment upon what had always been a public institution.[135] Harvard's growing elitism, out of step as it was with the spirit of the times, engendered a political response in the increasingly democratic polity in a way that the entirely private Anthology Society and Boston Athenaeum never did.

The internal controversy over the Hollis professorship of divinity between the Brahmin and orthodox parties proved far more significant for Harvard's future. It dealt with the makeup of the Corporation and the mission of the college. The "revolution at Harvard," then, turned not on the external quarrel between legislators and overseers, but the "bitter

---

132. Quincy, *History,* 2:307.
133. Ibid., 397.
134. Whitehead, *Separation of College and State,* 20.
135. Several observers intimated that Republican antipathy toward Harvard stemmed from its liberal tendencies. M. A. DeWolfe Howe claims that they "objected to the very name Unitarianism." See *Boston: The Place and the People* (New York, 1903), 201, 203.

power struggle" within the Yard between the Brahmin and orthodox camps of the Congregationalist clergy.[136] This, the so-called Unitarian controversy, not only transformed Harvard into a more secular, Brahmin institution, but precipitated the bifurcation of the Standing Order into competing, contentious, and seemingly irreconcilable factions. The 1805 fight over the religious and intellectual future of Harvard, and the subsequent installation of the Brahmins Henry Ware and Samuel Webber as Hollis Professor and university president, respectively, "a college revolution that has influenced the university to this day," can fairly be called the turning point for the Standing Order of Massachusetts.[137]

---

136. Daniel Walker Howe, *The Unitarian Conscience: Harvard Moral Philosophy, 1805–1861* (Cambridge, Mass., 1970), 4.

137. Morison, *Three Centuries,* 187; He also calls the eventual choice of Henry Ware "one of the most important decisions in the history of the University" (190).

CHAPTER 5

Orthodoxy in Massachusetts

New England was itself divided between two intellectual
centers—Boston and New Haven. The Massachusetts
and Connecticut schools were as old as the colonial exis-
tence; and in 1800 both were still alive, if not flourishing.

—HENRY ADAMS

IN THE FIRST DECADE of the nineteenth century, the Standing Order of
Massachusetts divided into two camps—the Brahmins and the orthodox. This schism centered around far more than belief, encompassing social class, educational institutions—Harvard and Yale in particular—as
well as geography. The Brahmins controlled Boston and Cambridge while
the orthodox settled in the smaller, less prestigious pulpits that flanked
Boston to the west and north. "It is confidently believed," wrote one divine,
"that there is not a strict Trinitarian clergymen of the Congregational order
in Boston."[1] Orthodox ministers called themselves by many names—Consistent Calvinists, Hopkinsians, Moderate Calvinists, Trinitarians, Orthodox Congregationalists—but whatever their many ascriptions, they united
to beat back the fearful growth of the irreligious and dangerous heterodoxy
of the Boston Brahmins. They fought to preserve orthodoxy in Massachusetts.

The preservation of orthodoxy entailed a number of objectives, only

---

1. Citation from Joseph Allen, "Historical Sketch of the Unitarian Movement," in Joseph
Allen and Richard Eddy, *History of Unitarians and Universalists in the United States* (New
York, 1894), 181.

some of which were strictly religious. Besides concerning themselves with rigorously doctrinal issues such as the continued adherence to the belief in the divine nature of Christ, orthodox ministers addressed a number of pressing social issues. Unlike their Boston brethren, the orthodox ministers found their social status in decline. Naturally, they sought to reverse this trend, which they contended was in large measure the result of the "silent but rapid and irresistible progress . . . of the inquisitive and liberal spirit" of their erstwhile Boston colleagues.[2] Much of the bitterness that the orthodox displayed toward the Boston Brahmins resulted less from jealousy, although that was an important element, than from the conviction that their declining status within the community as a whole could be reversed solely by purging heterodoxy. The preservation of orthodoxy was a concerted attempt to reassert the traditional, prominent position of the Standing Order in the Bay State.

As early as 1804, Jedidiah Morse, orthodox minister of Charlestown, remarked on the incipient fissure in the Congregational ranks. "I am apprehensive," he wrote to an associate, "that things are tending to a schism in the congregational interest."[3] As pastor in Charlestown and member of Harvard College's Board of Overseers, Morse was in as good a position as anyone to perceive the grave problems that threatened to undermine the Standing Order. Morse's apprehension stemmed most directly from the installation of Henry Ware over himself as Hollis Professor of Divinity at Harvard, an event which led him to lament that "the seal of the College, whose motto is 'Christo et ecclesiae' had better be broken, and a more appropriate one be substituted."[4] With the resignation a few months later of the orthodox Eliphalet Pearson as president, as well as Hancock Professor, and the subsequent appointment of Samuel Willard, one of Massachusetts's most venerable institutions and its principle source of Congregational clerics had gone Brahmin.[5]

---

2. Jedidiah Morse, Thomas Belsham's "American Unitarianism: Or a Brief History of the Progress and Present State of the Unitarian Churches in America" (Boston, 1814), 6.

3. Morse to Dr. Joseph Lyman, December 27, 1804, Morse Family Papers, Yale University Archives.

4. Morse to Reverend Green, December 21, 1805, Morse Family Papers, Yale University Archives.

5. While the Hollis chair was the most important religious position in the Congregationalist universe, it was less the appointment of Henry Ware than the installation of John Thorn-

Following Morse, historians have generally viewed the fight over the Hollis professorship in 1805 as the cause of the bifurcation of the Standing Order.[6] This is only partially the case. While the Ware appointment served as a call to arms for the various orthodox groups, neither it nor the "revolution in our University," as Morse styled it, can be said to have caused the controversy.[7] Rather, the appointment signaled a culmination of sorts in the rising power of the Brahmin alliance of merchants and ministers. Indeed, it is clear that the differences dividing the Brahmins from the orthodox dated back many years.[8] In a humorous and acerbic reply to a letter from Morse, former President John Adams insisted that the debate between those who favored "rational religion" and those who subscribed to "revealed religion" could be traced back nearly a century. "I can testify as a witness to its old age," he assured the "Rev. Dr."[9] As for the Unitarian doctrines whose promulgation Morse so lamented, Adams claimed that "65 years ago, my own minister Dr L. Bryant, Dr John Mayhew of the West Church in Boston, the Rev Mr Shute of Hingham, the Rev Brown of Cohasset, and perhaps equal to all, if not above all, the Rev Mr Gay of Hingham, were Unitarians."[10] The Ware nomination was no more than the immediate precipitant of a schism that had been growing for some time. The underlying cause must be sought elsewhere.

---

ton Kirkland to the presidency in 1810 that signaled the transformation of Harvard into the elitist, private institution of the Unitarian merchant princes of Boston.

6. See, for example, Frank Luther Mott, *History of American Magazines, 1741–1850* (New York, 1930), 262; "The revolutionary appointment . . . of Henry Ware to be Hollis Professor of Divinity in Harvard College in 1805 caused . . . the bitter dispute"; and more recently, Charles Forman, "'Elected Now by Time': The Unitarian Controversy, 1805–1835," in *A Stream of Light: A Sesquicentennial History of American Unitarianism*, ed. Conrad Wright (Boston, 1975), 3; "[T]he election . . . precipitated the Unitarian Controversy."

7. Morse to Joseph Lyman, December 4, 1804, Morse Family Papers, Yale University Archives.

8. See Chapter 1 for documentation of the origins of this split as early as the Great Awakening.

9. John Adams to Morse, May 15, 1815; copy in Charles Follen Papers, Collection 2, Massachusetts Historical Society.

10. Ibid. For an intriguing portrait of Ebenezer Gay, see Robert J. Wilson III, *The Benevolent Deity: Ebenezer Gay and the Rise of Rational Religion in New England, 1696–1787* (Philadelphia, 1984).

The most dramatic changes in the first decade of the nineteenth century proved to be political. For generations, similar political sentiments and institutional affiliations of both liberal and Calvinist, Brahmin and orthodox, had served as the Congregational clergy's common bond, a bond that remained intact throughout the Federalist administrations of Washington and Adams. "Many things linked the minister of the standing church to the statesmen of the ruling party," concludes James Banner; but the crucial factor was that "virtually all Congregationalist ministers were Federalists."[11] A number of developments during the 1790s engendered mutual concerns. The democratic transformation of the political culture, its manifestation in the emergent Republican party and in the person of Thomas Jefferson, as well as the dangerous notions of the French revolutionaries and their American sympathizers disgusted Brahmin and orthodox alike. While Deists and Brahmins shared a degree of latitudinarianism, Deists' apparently radical social agenda ensured that all members of the Congregational clergy would find it anathema. On account of these collective anxieties, political considerations overshadowed the growing divergence over religious doctrine and practice. When the rise of Jeffersonianism threatened Federalist political domination, the coalition commenced to fracture along social lines. Previously quiescent tensions below the surface sprang into the open.

It is no coincidence that Massachusetts voted Republican in the same year that the Unitarian controversy erupted. A decided correlation emerges between the changing political culture and the growing schism in the Standing Order between the Brahmins and orthodox. The decline of the Federalist party in national politics, the rise of spirited two-party competition in the Bay State, and the democratization of political culture had a marked effect upon the Standing Order, as historians Henry Adams, James Truslow Adams, and Harry Stout have documented.[12] What these histori-

11. James Banner, *To the Hartford Convention: The Federalists and the Origins of Party Politics in Massachusetts, 1789–1815* (New York, 1970), 152.

12. See Henry Adams, *The History of the United States of America during the Administrations of Jefferson and Madison* (New York, 1921; reprint, Chicago, 1967), 76; James Truslow Adams, *New England in the Republic, 1776–1860* (New York, 1926); and Harry Stout, "Rhetoric and Reality in the Early Republic: The Case of the Federalist Clergy," in *Religion and American Politics*, ed. Mark A. Noll (New York, 1990), 62–76.

ans and others have neither examined nor explained is the markedly distinct, even opposing, reactions to the success of the Jeffersonian politics of the two cliques within the Standing Order. The Brahmin response was to quit politics, create elite and exclusive institutions of high culture, and eschew popular culture generally. They circled the wagons and withdrew into the exclusive churches of Boston and the classrooms of Harvard College.

The orthodox party, while equally dismayed by the democratization of the political culture, interpreted these developments very differently. In contrast to their Brahmin colleagues, they refused to retreat, choosing instead to oppose vigorously this unfortunate turn of events with the intention of restoring the clergy to its rightful position of leadership in New England society by any means necessary. The orthodox threw themselves into the effort with a sense of desperation brought about by a conviction that their traditional prominence in society was in grave danger. In the community as a whole they were becoming just one denomination among many, while within their own church they were forced to witness the hated Brahmins benefiting—at their expense, so it seemed—from the benign indulgence of the mercantile elite of Boston, who lavished upon their ministers fat salaries and endowed benefices. Not surprisingly, the orthodox blamed the Brahmins for their plight, which they tied to the general religious declension within society at large. To restore ministerial standing in the community and recoup their place within the Congregational church, the course was clear; the orthodox had to expose the Brahmins.

The orthodox clergy sought to vanquish the Brahmins from the Standing Order by a series of endeavors, including the founding of a periodical, the *Panoplist,* which provided a "most effective" means of expressing their views, the formation of a theological seminary to train new ministers, and the creation of an orthodox church on Park Street in the heart of Brahmin Boston. As it turned out, the twin aims of exposing the heterodoxy of the Brahmins and restoring the Congregational clergy to its position of preeminence within Massachusetts society proved to be mutually exclusive. In exposing the Brahmins for what they were, mouthpieces for a distinct class of interests, the orthodox betrayed the self-interest behind their own ideology and actions.

Smarting from his 1805 defeat at the hands of the Brahmin Harvard Board of Overseers, Jedidiah Morse selected for himself the role of vanquisher of the Brahmins, a function for which he seemed particularly fitted and to which he devoted himself during virtually his entire tenure in the Bay State.[13] By 1820, Morse's "total suspension of intercourse with the clergy of Boston," his "engagements in, and encouragement of controversies," as well as his "indiscriminate distribution of contradictory pamphlets and tracts" had engendered so much ill will that even his own congregation had tired of his partisan machinations.[14] Morse's enemies, all "obviously Unitarians," forced him to resign his pastorate in the summer of 1820.[15]

When the young Jedidiah Morse first ventured to Boston in 1788, he appeared to fit the ideal of the new generation of Congregational ministers being called to Boston. Like Jeremy Belknap, who initially sought Morse's services for the First Church at Charlestown, Morse's literary reputation outshone his theological achievements.[16] His *Geography Made Easy* and soon to be published *The American Geography* had come to the attention of Belknap, "with whom he had much in common in his taste for geographical and historical studies."[17] When the pastorate at Charlestown became available, Belknap asked his friend and fellow geographer, Ebenezer Hazard, about Morse's suitability for the position. Typical of the Brahmins, the correspondence between the two barely broached the potential candidate's religious convictions. More important were his intellectual and personal traits "as a man."[18] Hazard noted to Belknap that "I like him [and] . . . am charmed with him. He is judicious and sensible, decent and modest in his comportment, a cheerful companion, who prettily supports the dignity of the clergyman in the midst of friendly affability."[19] On the basis of Morse's literary reputation, his well-received guest pastoring, and Hazard's recommendation, he was offered, and subsequently accepted, Charles-

13. The most complete and least flattering recent portrait of Morse is surely, Conrad Wright, "The Controversial Career of Jedidiah Morse," *Harvard Library Bulletin* 31 (1983): 64–87.

14. Josiah Bartlett to Morse, February 18, 1817, Morse Papers, Massachusetts Historical Society.

15. Morse to his son, May 13, 1819, Samuel F. B. Morse Papers, Library of Congress.

16. Hamilton Hill states that Morse was called to Charlestown "through the influence of Mr. Belknap." See Hill, *History of the Old South Church* (Boston, 1889), 2:245.

17. Belknap had, of course, only heard of *The American Geography*, because it was not published for another several months. Morse's reputation as a geographer stemmed primarily from his 1793 *The American Universal Geography*.

18. Ebenezer Hazard to Belknap, April 16, 1788, Belknap Papers, *Collections of the Massachusetts Historical Society*, 5th ser., 3 (1877): 31.

19. Ibid., 30–31.

town's call. It is revealing to note that while Morse's *Geography* helped to secure him his position in Massachusetts, it simultaneously stood him in the bad graces of his father, Jedidiah Morse Sr., deacon of the Congregational Church of Woodstock, Connecticut.[20] Deacon Morse repeatedly remonstrated with his son for ignoring his pastoral responsibilities, "which is the whole duty of man," in order to gain literary notoriety.[21] Significantly, Belknap and the Brahmins sought Morse because they thought him to be one of a growing band of clerical literati devoted to culture, while Jedidiah Morse Sr. desired his son to be a literate cleric unstintingly devoted to his pastoral duties. With the founding of the *Panoplist,* Morse most emphatically had to come to heed his father's admonitions.

The first years of Morse's tenure at Charlestown proved rather benign. His congregation treated him with "affection and generosity," while the nascent Massachusetts Historical Society invited him to become a member.[22] Richard Cary, a Charleston entrepreneur and distiller, thanked his friend Belknap for recommending Morse, whose "amiable, prudent, benevolent temper will always command him affection & esteem."[23] As minister of one of the "big six" pulpits of greater Boston, Morse assumed his place on the Board of Overseers of Harvard College and shortly thereafter became a member of the Boston Association of Ministers, where his colleagues "received him with great cordiality."[24] Within a few years, Morse was elected secretary of the Boston Association, an office from which he began to reveal his divisive and vindictive nature.

Morse first drew critical attention to himself by an ill-advised foray into politics. While Massachusetts ministers had long betrayed their political sentiments from the pulpit and in traditional election sermons, which were often published, most divines by the middle of the 1790s had begun to

---

20. Hazard remarked to Belknap that the Presbyterians in New York City, where Hazard heard Morse, considered Morse's *Geography* a distraction. Writes Hazard: "his Geography employed so much of his time, that he could not devote himself to his theological studies, and thus injured himself in the opinions of some." Hazard to Belknap, November 15, 1788, reprinted in Belknap Papers, 3:72–74.

21. Deacon Morse to Jedidiah Morse Jr., October 7, 1792, Morse Family Papers, Yale University Archives.

22. Quoted in William Sprague, *Annals of the American Pulpit* (New York, 1857), 1:22.

23. Richard Cary to Belknap, November 11, 1788, Belknap Papers, *Collections of the Massachusetts Historical Society,* 6th ser., 4 (1891): 427.

24. William Sprague, *The Life of Jedidiah Morse* (New York, 1874), 13, 22.

eschew political sermonizing. Morse, on the other hand, in addressing a 1796 Boston town meeting concerning the Jay Treaty "by noisy acclamations disturb[ed] the intended order of the meeting" to such a degree that it earned him the rebuke of the Boston *Independent Chronicle*.[25] The good reverend, the paper's editors acidly noted, should "attend more to the duties of the clerical office, and not attempt to interfere in the proceedings of other towns."[26]

Morse failed to heed the *Independent Chronicle*'s admonitions and within twenty months was embroiled in another controversial political issue, this time with far greater personal consequences. The so-called "Illuminati" controversy stemmed from a fast-day sermon that Morse delivered in May of 1798 to Boston's New North congregation.[27] In this sermon, inspired by the publication of John Robison's *Proofs of a Conspiracy Against All the Religions and Governments of Europe, Carried on in the Secret Meetings of the Free Masons, Illuminati, and Reading Societies*, Morse claimed to have unearthed "the causes which have brought the world into its present state."[28] Masons in Europe—and America, by implication—were undermining religion and society, Morse declared to this predominantly Brahmin congregation. "I hold it a duty," he went on, "which I owe to God, to the cause of religion, to my country, and to you, at this time, to declare to you, thus honestly and faithfully, these truths. My only aim is to awaken in you and myself a due attention, at this alarming period, to our dearest interests. As a faithful watchman I would give you warning of your present danger."[29] The "Illuminati" speech drew a great deal of attention to Morse, putting him squarely in the center of a political maelstrom.[30]

Morse's warning should not have fallen on deaf ears. After all, here was an arch Federalist suggesting a vast and sinister French intrigue to a friendly congregation during the period of the quasi-war. Yet, while some Federalist clergy from outside Boston cheered Morse's speech and repeated

---

25. *Boston Independent Chronicle*, April 25, 28, 1796.

26. Ibid.

27. The national fast day was called by President Adams in response to events surrounding the XYZ affair.

28. Jedidiah Morse, *Sermon on the National Fast, May 9, 1798* (Boston, 1798).

29. Ibid.

30. For the larger political context of the Illuminati controversy and its relation to the internal machinations of party politics, see Vernon Stauffer, *New England and the Bavarian Illuminati* (New York, 1918).

his accusations, his sermon had a contrary, dissonant effect on his Boston audience. Those who heard his charges against Masonry thought them unfounded, while subsequent readers of his pamphlet quickly became convinced that they were nothing but a scurrilous attack, based solely on personal prejudice and ignorance.[31] William Wells penned Brahmin Boston's response in a review in the *Massachusetts Mercury*. Wells, a man of catholic tastes and soon to be a member of the Anthology Society, urged Bostonians not to let Morse "terrify our fellow citizens with groundless alarms, nor become the dupes of every foolish tale, which the prejudices or ignorance of Europeans may fabricate."[32] Other critics came forward to claim that Morse had egregiously overstated the present danger of the Illuminati. William Bentley, Jeffersonian minister at Salem, dressed down his colleague from Charlestown in several articles, which in itself was not surprising insofar as Morse and Bentley had opposing views on virtually every topic from politics to theology. Far more remarkable was the fact that many Boston Brahmins sympathized with the ardent Democratic-Republican Bentley, when he publicly rebuked Morse, a Federalist to the core.[33] Morse responded to Bentley in the *Mercury* a few weeks later with an unseemly personal attack, which implied that Bentley "himself has been illuminated,"[34] a charge that Conrad Wright styled "roughly the equivalent of calling an ardent New Dealer a Communist agent."[35] That the Brahmin clergy of Boston sided with Bentley, a Republican, over Morse is highly significant, particularly since Bentley was a Harvard-educated cleric with a growing literary reputation. The Brahmins' favoring of Bentley at the expense of the partisan, Yale-educated Morse presaged the shift from Federalist against Republican to Brahmin versus orthodox.

In the 1790s, virtually all the ministers of the Standing Order decried the dreadful turn in French politics as well as the growing popularity of the Jeffersonian Democratic-Republican societies, which Morse proclaimed

---

31. Stephen C. Bullock has persuasively argued that Morse actually had meant no discredit to Masonry, per se. See his *Revolutionary Brotherhood: Freemasonry and the Transformation of the American Social Order, 1730–1840* (Chapel Hill, 1996).
32. William Wells in *Massachusetts Mercury*, August 3, 10, 1798.
33. See William Bentley, *A Charge Delivered before the Morning Star Lodge* (Worcester, Mass., 1798).
34. Bentley in *Massachusetts Mercury*, September 21, 1798.
35. Wright, "The Controversial Career of Jedidiah Morse," 72n.

"the genuine offspring" of the atheist Bavarian Illuminati.[36] Yet Morse clearly went much further than other Federalist clergy in both his public declarations and his adamant resolution that it was "necessary to exterminate" these "dangerous enemies."[37] In a ploy remarkably similar to Senator Joseph McCarthy's infamous Washington's Birthday speech nearly two centuries later, Morse proclaimed that he had in his possession "an official, authenticated list of the names, ages, places of nativity, professions, &c. of the officers and members of a Society of *Illuminati* . . . consisting of one hundred members."[38] This reference to the Wisdom Masonic Lodge in Portsmouth, Virginia, proved an entirely bogus charge for which Morse either could not or would not produce any evidence when called upon to do so. Unlike McCarthy, whose Republican colleagues refused to disassociate themselves from the Senator's fabrications, Morse, finding himself "repeatedly and unjustly attacked," was forced to weather a barrage of criticism from both Republicans and Federalists.[39] In his biography of Harrison Gray Otis, Samuel Eliot Morison notes that "neither Otis nor any other prominent Federalist subscribed to the theory."[40] Morse's charges proved so vacuous that the Masonic editors of the Federalist *Columbian Centinel* joined their counterparts at the *Chronicle* in denying Morse access to their pages. Embarrassed by his recklessness, they shut Morse out.

Morse failed to convince his fellow ministers of the grave threat posed to the Standing Order by the Bavarian Illuminati and their American allies. Convinced, nonetheless, that New England religion and its defenders were under siege, Morse soon found what he believed to be the true source of the declension. That source was none other than the enemy within, the growing Brahmin element of his own denomination, which had betrayed its waning religious commitment by its disdain for his Illuminati admonitions. Commencing with the fight over the Hollis appointment at Harvard, Morse succeeded where he had failed in the Illuminati controversy. By the end of the first decade of the nineteenth century, Morse had been instru-

36. Morse, *Sermon*, November 29, 1798, 72.
37. Jedidiah Morse to Oliver Wolcott Jr., July 13, 1798, Wolcott Papers, Connecticut Historical Society.
38. Jedidiah Morse, *A Sermon, Exhibiting the Present Dangers, and Consequent Duties of the Citizens of the United States of America* (Charlestown, Mass., 1799), 15.
39. Morse in the *Massachusetts Mercury*, August 31, September 18, 1798.
40. Samuel Eliot Morison, *Harrison Gray Otis, 1765–1848: The Urbane Federalist* (Boston, 1969), 118.

mental in ensuring that the growing rift in the Standing Order would not be repaired.

Morse's role in the controversy surrounding the appointment of Henry Ware to the Hollis professorship at Harvard, particularly the publication of his partisan and polemical pamphlet, *The True Reasons,* irrevocably set him against Boston's Brahmin ministers.[41] Yet, it was not until Morse undertook the publication of the *Panoplist* in the spring of 1805 that he effectively publicized the disaffection between the Brahmins and "a holy confederacy" of orthodox ministers.[42] It is not clear where Morse got the idea of starting a periodical, but his efforts a few years earlier on behalf of the *New England Palladium* proved very helpful.[43] Like the *Palladium,* which boasted the likes of Timothy Dwight and Warren Dutton, the *Panoplist* had a distinctly evangelical, Yale-educated board. Morse's father, Deacon Jedidiah Morse Sr., always pressing his son to devote more of his editorial skills to matters of theology instead of geography, might well have proposed such an undertaking. In one missive to his son, he noted that "our [Connecticut] Evangelical Magazine seems to be a great means & help to carry on the good work; as some parts of them are read in the weekly conference."[44] Whatever the source, with the publication of the first edition of the *Panoplist,* Morse and the orthodox ministers commenced a relentless assault upon the "unprincipled and designing men" of Boston's churches.[45]

The orthodox board of the *Panoplist* included the most strident ministers in the Commonwealth.[46] In addition to Morse, the "Association of Friends to Evangelical Truth," as they called themselves, boasted Leonard Woods, pastor at Newbury and soon to be, with Morse, a leading figure in the formation of the Andover Theological Seminary; Abiel Holmes, intimate of Morse and the "studiously polite" evangelical minister of the First

---

41. See Morse, *The True Reasons on Which the Election of a Hollis Professor of Divinity in Harvard College was Opposed at the Board of Overseers, Feb. 14, 1805* (Charlestown, Mass., 1805).

42. *Panoplist* 2 (March 1807): 506.

43. See Richard J. Moss, *The Life of Jedidiah Morse: A Station of Peculiar Exposure* (Knoxville, 1995), 83–85.

44. Deacon Morse to Jedidiah Morse Jr., December 9, 1800, Morse Family Papers, Yale University Archives.

45. *Panoplist* 1 (June 1805): iv.

46. For biographical information on Woods, see E. A. Lawrence review of Woods in *Congregational Quarterly* 1 (April 1859): 114; for Evarts, see Sprague, *Annals.*

Church at Cambridge;[47] and Moses Stuart, successor of Eliphalet Pearson as professor of sacred literature at Andover.[48] In addition, Morse soon brought in Jeremiah Evarts, his close friend and for years a leading polemicist. Under Evarts, who wrote many of the most "militantly controversial" pieces to appear in the journal,[49] the *Panoplist* "received for a time the almost undivided support and confidence of evangelical Christians throughout the country."[50] While Leonard Woods was nominally the editor for much of the first decade, Morse made the major decisions and, with Evarts, contributed the most copy to the fledgling publication.[51] As the pages of the *Panoplist* revealed, these ministers harbored a great deal of resentment for the Boston Brahmins, whose heterodoxy they condemned in every issue.

From its inception, the "Association of Friends to Evangelical Truth" utilized the *Panoplist* to achieve a number of related objectives. In addition to "the important design in maintaining and disseminating evangelical truth,"[52] the *Panoplist* apprised the faithful of the serious declension in religion, warned them of the dangers of an unconverted ministry and conveyed the urgent need for "a judicious, firm, and active co-operation of all the friends of truth."[53] "The Panoplist," Morse explained in a letter to his Connecticut friend and orthodox colleague, Dr. Joseph Lyman, "is the only channel through which we can, with effect, communicate such information to the public from time to time, as may be necessary to our pur-

---

47. See Sprague, *Annals*, 1:240–46 for biographical information; William Jenks to Sprague in same.

48. Sprague, *Annals*, 1:475–78; Mott fails to mention Stuart as a member of the Friends of Evangelical Truth, but does note that "we are nowhere informed" just who composed this body. See Mott, *American Magazines*, 263.

49. Mott, *American Magazines*, 262.

50. "Review of Sketches of the Life of Jeremiah Evarts, Esq.," *Spirit of the Pilgrims* 6 (1831): 602. See also John A. Andrew III, *From Revivals to Removal: Jeremiah Everts, the Cherokee Nation, and the Search for the Soul of America* (Athens, Ga., 1992).

51. Morse was instrumental in securing not only the *Panoplist* post for Evarts, but the Cambridge call for Holmes and the Andover professorship for Stuart. William Sprague erroneously states that Morse "was sole editor for five years." See E. A. Lawrence's review of Woods in *Congregational Quarterly* 1 (April 1859): 114–15.

52. *Panoplist* 1 (June 1805): iii.

53. *Panoplist* 5 (June 1809): v.

pose. . . . 'Tis the only weapon of the kind which our opposers fear."[54] The *Panoplist*'s "opposers" were the Brahmin ministers of Boston, who several months earlier had begun publication of their own journal, the *Monthly Anthology*. The Friends to Evangelical Truth made clear in their first number that the *Panoplist* would serve as an antidote to the "poison" put forth by the *Monthly Anthology*, which the Friends to Evangelical Truth dubbed the "offspring of worldly ease and affluence."[55]

Superficially, it appears that the *Panoplist* and the *Monthly Anthology* had much in common. Both were the product of Congregational ministers, both issued from the Boston area, and both commenced publication within a year of each other.[56] In addition, both the *Panoplist* and the *Anthology* reflected the particular outlook of their respective editorial boards. Yet there the similarity ends. In their respective subject matter, goals, circulation, and overall tone the *Monthly Anthology* and the *Panoplist* were poles apart. The *Monthly Anthology* was an avowedly literary journal run by clerical intellectuals, whereas the *Panoplist* proved to be a doctrinaire, theologically partisan publication edited by militant ministers.[57] The *Monthly Anthology* addressed the growing schism in the Congregational churches only on occasion and obliquely. In contrast, the *Panoplist* was founded in response to the crisis engendered within the Standing Order by the emergence of the Brahmins and its pages were singularly devoted to attacking this new breed of clerical intellectuals. Indeed, it may fairly be said that the *Panoplist* proved to be the wedge Morse and his cohorts drove between themselves and the Brahmins.

The preface of the first issue of the *Panoplist* distinguished the aims and mood of its editors from those of the anthologists. "While one species of these publications," it stated, "conducted by unprincipled and designing men, have administered poison to the publick faith and morals; another, conducted by the wise and the good, have circulated the antidote."[58] Here,

---

54. Jedidiah Morse to Joseph Lyman, April 22, 1806, Morse Family Papers, Yale University Archives.

55. *Panoplist* 1 (June 1805): iv.

56. Mott, *American Magazines*, 263–65.

57. For a discussion of the aims and editorial policies of the *Monthly Anthology*, see chapter 3.

58. *Panoplist* 1 (June 1805): iv.

as in succeeding issues, the editors gave evidence of both their objective—to attack the other "species of publication" by articulating "evangelical truth"; and of their tone—aggressive, admonitory, and intensely polemical.[59] Morse looked forward to the day when he could write that "the opposition feel and dread its effects, and know not how to counteract them."[60] In sum, the pages of the *Panoplist* were nothing short of a "call to arms" against the Brahmins.[61]

In its strident and provocative manner, the *Panoplist* repeatedly addressed three basic issues. First, each number contained articles decrying the general decline of religion in New England society as manifested in the lack of respect paid to religion and, above all else, in the slipping prestige of the ministry. A second prominent topic concerned the dangerous intimacy between the growing bourgeoisie of Boston and its Brahmin ministers, who "prostituted [themselves] for the most unworthy purposes."[62] The third and most frequently addressed set of issues—and the major source of the other concerns—proved to be the latitudinarianism, tolerance, and generally irreligious tone of the Boston clergy. "Liberty," wrote one author, "means licentiousness."[63]

Fear of and belief in Puritan declension harkened back to the first generation of New England divines. It was expressed in the form of jeremiads delivered from New England pulpits. In the first decades of the nineteenth century, Brahmin ministers wrote virtually none of these admonitory speeches, the vast majority penned instead by the orthodox who, like Jedidiah Morse, warned that it was "a time of great declension both in morals and sentiments."[64] Not surprisingly, the *Panoplist* contained numerous jeremiads decrying Congregational abandonment of orthodox theology. The *Panoplist*'s annual "Address of the Editors" conspicuously imitated the lamentation of the prophet. For example, in the third volume, "the editors" foretold imminent catastrophe:

---

59. Ibid., iii.
60. Morse to Reverend Green, December 21, 1805, Morse Family Papers, Yale University Archives.
61. Jedidiah Morse's term, as used in a letter to Leonard Woods, October 21, 1806, in appendix to Leonard Woods, *History of the Andover Theological Seminary* (Boston, 1885), 463.
62. *Panoplist* 2 (January 1807): 365.
63. Ibid.
64. Morse in *Columbian Centinel*, November 24, 1804.

from the *alarming events, which are taking place, both in Europe and America.* How numerous and multiform are the errors of the Day. . . . The Panoplist rises to counteract prevailing evils, and to prevent their increase; to stem the torrent of vice; to point out disorders and dangers of the times; and earnestly to call men to withdraw their affections from the uncertain changing interest of this world, and set them on that kingdom, which never can be removed.[65]

Similarly, an article signed simply "Pastor" asked:

Should it please the exalted Redeemer to address the churches in New England, especially in this Commonwealth, we have reason to conclude, that his language would not be unlike that, which he addressed to the Asiatic churches. He would certainly find as little to approve, and as much to condemn, as he found there. Not a single erroneous practice or opinion existed among them, which does not, in substance, exist among us.[66]

These writers concurred with one another that religion in New England was in decline. The Friends to Evangelical Truth placed the blame for this disturbing religious degeneration firmly at the feet of the Congregational ministry; not at their own feet, of course, but at those of their erstwhile Brahmin colleagues. The Boston Brahmins were clearly the culpable party.[67]

The second repeated theme in the pages of the *Panoplist*, intimately related to the first, was the dangerous liaison between Boston merchants and

---

65. "Address of the Editors," *Panoplist* 2 (May 1807): iii.
66. *Panoplist* 1 (May 1806): 541–42.
67. Ann Douglas, for example, writes that "the case of the ministers is clear-cut; they lost status and respect," while historians from David Donald to Stanley Elkins have sought the origins of benevolent reform and abolitionism in ministerial "status anxiety." The significance here is that the *Panoplist* was the product of only one side of a debate that split the Congregational church. That the *Monthly Anthology* never once broaches the issue is significant. Equally important is the fact that the orthodox blamed the decline in their status on their supposed colleagues of liberal persuasion. This suggests that not everyone's status declined, or even remained stable. See Ann Douglas, *The Feminization of American Culture* (New York, 1977), 11; see also, Stanley Elkins, *Slavery: A Problem in American Institutional and Intellectual Life* (New York, 1959); Clifford S. Griffin, *Their Brothers' Keepers: Moral Stewardship in the United States, 1800–1865* (New Brunswick, N.J., 1960); and David Herbert Donald, "Toward a Reconsideration of the Abolitionists," in *Lincoln Reconsidered: Essays on the Civil War Era* (New York, 1989).

ministers. Religion lost prominence because the Brahmin minister "flatters the great and the rich."[68] "Be they ever so irreligious," Boston's Brahmin merchants were lauded by their self-serving preachers who "in order to get preferment, courts their patronage by soothing them in their vices, by espousing their political measures, or by mean compliances that are utterly inconsistent with the dignity of his office."[69] The author of this article, entitled "The Unfaithful Minister," continued by reminding his readers that the rich all too often attained their wealth through un-Christian means and should be rebuked accordingly. The Brahmin minister was far too solicitous when he welcomed into the church the rich merchants "as if they were real Christians and heirs of heaven."[70] The orthodox editors of the *Panoplist* felt it was the role of the minister to issue stern warnings to the successful merchant. "Worldly grandeur is very ready to inspire the mind with pride and self-sufficiency," stated one writer, "which is, of all things, the most destructive of real religion."[71] A letter from a "Christian" businessman entitled "A Good Hint for Men in Business" echoed a similar theme in remarkably Weberian language. "I endeavor to follow my business because it is my duty rather than my interest; the latter is inseparable from a just discharge of duty; but I have ever looked at the profits in the last place."[72] The letter concluded with a statement unlikely to be issued from a Boston pulpit and calculated at a minimum to tweak Boston merchants; the truly Christian businessman was unstintingly pious and humble, "knowing that there was a Hand which could easily overthrow every pursuit of this kind, and baffle every attempt either to acquire wealth or fame."[73] In the orthodox view, ministers offered merchants "the true riches," and not the inverse.[74] Accordingly, Brahmin ministers, like the children of the rich, had to choose between being the heirs of fortunes or the "heirs of heaven."[75] Small wonder, then, that the orthodox so frequently

68. *Panoplist* 3 (August 1807): 364.
69. Ibid.
70. Ibid.
71. *Panoplist* 4 (June 1808): 406–7.
72. *Panoplist* 5 (June 1809): 28.
73. Ibid. This sermon would hardly appeal to a rational, long-range planning, financially secure, insured mercantile elite.
74. *Panoplist* 4 (March 1809): 407.
75. Ibid.

accused the Brahmin minister of surrendering conviction to the allure of a privileged social status. *Panoplist* writers regularly concluded that like their mercantile patrons, the prospect of "carnal security" had corrupted Boston's ministers.[76]

In a long series of articles entitled "Survey of the New England Churches," Jedidiah Morse and Leonard Woods developed the theme of a ministerial sellout. In the October 1806 issue, the authors claimed that because of "the loose conduct of the ministers, multitudes of nominal Christians have taken license to cast off the restraints of the law and gospel, and to live according to the course of this world."[77] They warned that the weak and depraved "character of these men, whom many writers and the world in general treat with the highest respect and honour," would lead to dangerously heterodox views "respecting good and evil."[78] Like other orthodox ministers, Morse and Woods adopted a rhetorical posture strikingly reminiscent of Richard Hofstadter's notion of American anti-intellectualism. "Men of subtle minds," they warned, "can, by the assistance of perverse misstatement, very easily distort and entangle a moral or theological subject."[79] These distortions resulted from "the subtleties and absurdities of what is called *rational Christianity.*"[80] In ways reminiscent of the New Lights of the religious awakenings a century earlier, the *Panoplist* Friends often castigated their Brahmin opponents by calling them, of all things, "learned." The evolving and diametrically opposed views of higher education so clearly contrasted in the pages of the *Panoplist* and the *Monthly Anthology* proved to be at the center of an often vitriolic debate that continues until today, especially in American religious culture.

Embittered and still enraged by the "recent revolution at Harvard College," in which the Brahmins had wrested control of the institution from the orthodox, Morse and the Friends to Evangelical Truth saved their most venomous attacks for the Harvard faculty. In a piece published barely a year after the controversy, Morse asserted that "the bulk of the professors, lukewarm and degenerate, prefer their own interests before the interests of

---

76. *Panoplist* 1 (June 1805): iv.
77. *Panoplist* 2 (October 1806): 212.
78. *Panoplist* 3 (August 1807): 354.
79. Ibid, 106.
80. *Panoplist* 2 (May 1807): 50.

Christ, and so are little affected with the boldness of his enemies, the wounding of his cause, or the triumph of his grace."[81] Harvard professors, members of the Anthology Society, as well as the Brahmin ministers of Boston, were all vilified for succumbing to the secular seduction of the mercantile elite, grown rich in the postwar prosperity. Morse and the orthodox, "heirs of heaven," stood, so they believed, in stark contrast; "precluded from wealth and power, we have no opportunity . . . to obtain any influence, but that of truth and goodness."[82]

Of all the issues addressed by the editors of the *Panoplist*, none recurred more often or with more intensity than that of the dangers of an unconverted ministry. No articles took the aggressive and uncompromising tone of Gilbert Tennent's famous "Unconverted Ministry" sermon of the Great Awakening; yet, the *Panoplist* contained the most strident critiques leveled by one Congregationalist against another in the early republic. "The Ruler of the Universe," wrote Morse to a friend, "appears to be preparing us and other parts of Christendom for trying conflicts. The world is peculiarly convulsed and will not I believe be calmed till it shall have been purified by fire."[83] For Morse and the editorial board, the *Panoplist* was a critical participant in this purification.

In a most revealing article, a *Panoplist* editor writing under the pseudonym "Luther" suggested that the imposition of a rigorous examination of prospective ministers would be an excellent first step in the purification process. "At the present day," wrote Luther,

> there is as much licentiousness in religion, as in politics; and as much perhaps in the ministry, as among the people. . . . The examination of candidates previously to ordination has, of late, been not only neglected, but violently opposed; not only treated as a matter of indifference, but as a destructive evil. . . . And shall men be introduced into the ministry, an office infinitely more important than any other, with little, or no attention to their qualifications?[84]

In succeeding issues, contributors to the *Panoplist* made their answer to Luther's query abundantly clear. "As it is one great duty of a minister to

---

81. *Panoplist* 2 (December 1806): 317.
82. *Panoplist* 2 (March 1807): 511.
83. Morse to Joseph Lyman, October 11, 1803, Morse Family Papers, Yale University Archives.
84. *Panoplist* 1 (April 1806): 480–81.

explain and enforce the doctrines of salvation," the *Panoplist* stated, "a church may reasonably require that he whom they receive as their minister, should believe those doctrines."[85] To come to know a prospective candidate's beliefs mandated that he undergo a thorough examination.

The lack of effective examinations and creedal uniformity had caused "an evil of great magnitude . . . in many of our churches."[86] Without careful enforcement of doctrinal rigidity, ministerial "liberty, free inquiry, [and] private judgement" had become "instruments of infidelity, and a fair mask, under which apostasy from Christianity and hatred of all goodness have disguised themselves."[87] These tendencies, the delight of Brahmin Boston, insidiously undermined the basic tenets of the faith and, if not checked, would destroy New England religion. Already, Boston churches embraced ministers, who "bring in damnable heresies," while "large numbers of nominal Christians among us are not washed from their sins."[88] In order to protect the remainder of the churches of the commonwealth, Boston churches had to be isolated and their ministers ostracized. "The welfare of Zion requires," wrote Morse and Woods in their ongoing "Survey" of the Congregational churches, "that the character of nominal Christians, in general, be reformed, and that more care be used in the admission of church members; that faithful discipline in its various branches be revived; that churches exercise proper vigilance respecting the religious character and sentiments of their ministers."[89]

The editors of the *Panoplist* went beyond simply pointing out the grave difficulties plaguing Congregationalism in Massachusetts. They offered a host of suggestions to vanquish the Brahmins and sweep the churches clean of their "moral disorders."[90] The cause of orthodoxy demanded, above all else, unity, "an army of banners, which its enemies cannot subdue."[91] Some specific articles of faith, or creed, had to be adopted "as the basis of union."[92] It was incumbent upon those "in the cause of evangelical truth," wrote the *Panoplist,* either to undertake a "counter revolution in our Uni-

85. *Panoplist* 2 (January 1807): 361.
86. *Panoplist* 1 (October 1806): 211.
87. *Panoplist* 2 (January 1807): 365.
88. *Panoplist* 1 (April 1806): 486; *Panoplist* 2 (June 1806): 17.
89. *Panoplist* 2 (March 1807): 504.
90. *Panoplist* 2 (August 1806): 173.
91. *Panoplist* 2 (March 1807): 506.
92. Ibid., 510.

versity" or, failing that, to create a new institution for the training of orthodox ministers.[93] "And if, in many churches, of which we had hoped better
things," a *Panoplist* writer stated, "divine truth has lost much of its purity
and lustre; we should reckon it the more indispensable duty, openly to
maintain evangelical principles."[94] "Maintaining" evangelical truth meant
several things: espousing orthodoxy, exposing heterodoxy, and enforcing
doctrinal uniformity. In short, maintenance entailed aggressive action.

It is worth comparing more closely the distinct approaches taken by the
members of the Anthology Society and the Friends to Evangelical Truth.
While the anthologists at least claimed to be "pledged to no party in religion and politics," the *Panoplist* Friends never missed an opportunity to
trumpet their partisan objectives.[95] The *Panoplist* was created to counter
the *Monthly Anthology,* and its editors openly professed their intention to
highlight the unmistakable differences separating the two groups, as well
as the all-but-unbridgeable chasm between them. Their aim was explicitly
religious: to expose Brahmin heresies and save the church from "an increasing declension."[96] The anthologists, on the other hand, eschewed confrontation and the opportunity to distinguish themselves from their clerical brethren. In fact, the anthologists, ministers included, virtually ignored
doctrinal issues and the "metaphysical subtleties" of religion. The "Society
of Gentlemen" self-consciously undertook the creation of a "genteel" and
literary journal. When one historian wrote that "it is surprising to find that
religious writings were practically negligible" in the pages of the *Monthly
Anthology,* he, like the staff of the *Panoplist,* misunderstood the motives of
its editors, who were in the process of creating a literary high culture.[97]
The *Panoplist* and *Monthly Anthology* articles did not take the form of a
debate over the tenets of New England theology, or even about the doctrines of Calvinism, which even the orthodox jettisoned within a few decades.[98] The orthodox were in the business of engaging in doctrinal hair-

93. Morse to Leonard Woods, October 21, 1806, in Woods, *Andover,* 463.

94. *Panoplist* 2 (December 1806): 316.

95. *Monthly Anthology* 5 (1809): 122.

96. *Panoplist* 2 (June 1806): 173.

97. Richard Parker Harrington, "The *Monthly Anthology*: Literary Excellence as Interpreted
by 'A Society of Gentlemen'" (Ph.D. diss., University of Texas, 1964), 100.

98. See Chapter 7 on Lyman Beecher and voluntarism for a extended discussion of this
point.

splitting and stamping out heterodoxy. The anthologists had no such intentions. For them, theology was never the issue.

For the editors of the *Panoplist,* it was axiomatic that the twin issues of religious dogma and the necessity for doctrinal uniformity dominated their journal. They spent much of their time and energy putting into practice the various theological proposals articulated in the *Panoplist.* Jedidiah Morse, Leonard Woods, and Moses Stuart played vital roles in working on the major orthodox projects of the first two decades of the century. In addition to building a powerful General Association of Evangelical Ministers, they played critical roles in establishing the Andover Theological Seminary and the Park Street Church, at the same time making great efforts toward the formation of a formal consociation out of the disparate elements of the Standing Order. While they never succeeded in achieving a united front to exile the Boston Brahmins, or even to put them on the defensive, Morse and his associates did precipitate the formal splitting of themselves from their Brahmin counterparts. In this, their primary objective, they succeeded.

Brahmin ministers harbored no such intentions. Fully cognizant of the objectives of the schismatics, they sought to avoid any public bifurcation, especially over what they believed to be minor theological issues. In a pointed sermon, conspicuously entitled "But Be Ye Not Called Rabbi," Bridgewater minister John Reed told the assembled Annual Convention of Congregational Ministers that neither Brahmin nor orthodox "possessed the right of dictating to others in matters of religion, or of censuring those, who may presume to differ from [them]."[99] Attempts by one minister to persecute another or "to impose his interpretation or creed upon others," Reed continued, should be denounced for the simple reason that "uniformity of truth is not to be expected, even among Christians."[100] Rather,

> a perfect agreement with respect to those passages of scripture, which have been deemed abstruse and difficult, or of the most uncertain and disputable signification, is commonly of least importance. . . . The various commands and exhortations of Christ are

---

99. John Reed, "Annual Sermon of 1807," in *Annual Sermons Delivered to the Massachusetts Convention of Congregational Ministers* (in Andover-Harvard Library, Rare Books Division), 4.

100. Ibid.

predicated upon the supposition, that there would be a *diversity* of opinions and practices among Christians.[101]

Reed was not alone. His sermon received universal commendation from the Brahmin brethren present. John Pierce, minister of Brookline was favorably impressed, noting in his "Memoirs" that "Dr Reed of Bridgewater delivered a very ingenious discourse. . . . He showed the absurdity of the pretension in any minister of the gospel to dictate to his fellow men their religious belief."[102] It was, the Brahmins agreed, a timely oration. For the orthodox, to whom the "Rabbi" oration was clearly addressed, Reed's sermon made little impression', except to demonstrate the Brahmins' drift toward heterodoxy. Morse and his associates did not pause in the pursuit of their ambitions.

In addition to condemning Harvard, the editors of the *Panoplist* called for the creation of a competing institution for higher education. Accordingly, the orthodox next undertook the formation of a theological seminary. They founded Andover Theological Seminary largely in reaction to the Brahmin "takeover" of Harvard. "A phoenix might arise," wrote the irrepressible Morse, "out of the ashes of the ancient seminary."[103] In fact, the *Panoplist*'s Friends to Evangelical Truth conceived of the seminary as "a religious institution [established] on principles and for purposes similar to those on which Harvard College was founded."[104] Morse, Woods, and Stuart provided virtually all the initial impetus in garnering support and financial backing for the undertaking. Significantly, the two major donors behind the project, Samuel Farrar and Samuel Abbot, had, before the "Unitarian" takeover, proposed to make bequests to Harvard, the primary source of Bay State ministers for 150 years.[105] Abbot, in fact, changed his will in 1805, redirecting his large bequest to Phillips Academy for the appointment of a professor of theology with "sound and orthodox, Calvinis-

---

101. Ibid., 7.
102. John Pierce's remarks are from his manuscript "Memoirs," Pierce Papers, Massachusetts Historical Society. The manuscript dates from 1803–11. See "Memoirs," 65.
103. Morse to Reverend Green, December 21, 1805, Morse Family Papers, Yale University Archives.
104. Ibid.
105. Daniel Day Williams, *The Andover Liberals* (New York, 1941), 4.

tic principles of divinity."[106] Andover Theological Seminary met these requirements precisely.[107]

Jedidiah Morse proved to be the main force behind the proposed seminary. The majority of persons affiliated with the project, including its backers, its first professors, and its Board of Visitors, had some connection to the Charlestown pastor. As early as the spring of 1806, Morse expressed the hope "of placing Dr. Eliphalet Pearson," his ally in the Hollis professorship fight, "at the head of" the nascent undertaking.[108] Morse was also instrumental in securing the post of professor of sacred literature for Moses Stuart, his friend and frequent contributor to the *Panoplist*.[109] Stuart proved to be the most prolific and erudite scholar in Andover's first half century. Among the members of the Board of Visitors who were charged with the general oversight of the seminary, the most notable was Timothy Dwight, president of Yale, father-in-law of Abiel Holmes, and Morse's personal friend. It appears that after giving the inaugural address on September 28, 1808, Dwight had little direct role in the life of the seminary. Yet his participation proved significant in several ways; he assured the involvement of Connecticut clergy, which led to the Connecticut Consociation's direct participation in the 1810 establishment of the American Board of Foreign Missions, and he bound Andover to orthodox Yale University.

Renowned in no small measure for his successful fight to save New Haven from the clutches of Deism, Dwight brought Yale's considerable prestige to the fledgling theological seminary. In this he was not alone; with the exceptions of Pearson and Woods, every other minister directly involved in the founding of Andover had graduated from Yale. In fact, the vast majority of the orthodox party in the Bay State were Yale men; in addition to Morse and Stuart, the reverends Abiel Holmes; Samuel Huntington; Edward Dorr Griffin, first pastor at the orthodox Park Street church; Sereno Dwight; Thomas Holt; Enoch Hale; Joseph Lyman; and, of course, Edward

---

106. Quoted in the Andover *Memorial of the Semi-centennial Celebration of the Founding of the Theological Seminary at Andover* (Andover, 1859), 152n.

107. Abbot's stipulations echoed almost exactly the terms of the Hollis professorship: "sound and orthodox."

108. Morse to Joseph Lyman, April 22, 1806, Morse Family Papers, Yale University Archives.

109. For biographical information on Stuart, see Sprague, *Annals*. For discussion of Stuart's years at Andover, see Jerry Brown, *The Rise of Biblical Criticism in America, 1800–1870: The New England Scholars* (Middletown, Conn., 1969), 45–59.

and Lyman Beecher—all orthodox stalwarts during the years of schism—had been educated at Yale University and primarily under the tutelage of President Dwight.[110] This remarkable correlation gives evidence to Henry Adams dictum that "two intellectual centres" divided New England: "the Massachusetts and Connecticut schools."[111] Massachusetts's Standing Order fractured along institutional lines: New Haven orthodoxy against Boston Brahminism.[112]

---

110. For biographical information, see Sprague, *Annals,* vol. 1, and Increase N. Tarbox, D.D., "The Congregational Churches of Boston since 1780," in *The Memorial History of Boston,* ed. Justin Winsor (Boston, 1881), 3:406–16. For Dwight's influence, see Louise L. Stevenson, *Scholarly Means to Evangelical Ends: The New Haven Scholars and the Transformation of Higher Learning in America, 1830–1890* (Baltimore, 1986).

111. Adams, *History,* 58.

112. Church historians have often asked why a similar schism between Unitarians and orthodox never developed in the Nutmeg State. According to Joseph Allen, Richard Eddy, Earl Wilbur, and Leonard Bacon, to name the primary authorities on the subject, the failure of Unitarianism in Connecticut may be explained in terms of church polity. Dating from the Saybrook Platform of 1708, Connecticut enjoyed a singularly strong consociational bond, which enabled the majority, overwhelmingly orthodox, to systematically examine candidates and extirpate established clergymen with controversial beliefs. More recently, Louise Chipley has offered a contrasting interpretation. She argues that Unitarianism could have overcome the Connecticut consociations, but failed to do so for "a variety of factors," most importantly because of a desire to avoid conflict within the Standing Order and a lack of support for liberal-leaning divines from their neighbors to the north. Since Chipley found no instance of the consociated clerics interceding on strictly "doctrinal grounds," she concludes that the facts "do not support the contention that the disciplinary machinery of the Saybrook Platform played a pivotal role in keeping Unitarianism out of Connecticut's established churches." While this appears true enough, it seems more plausible that it was the threat of consociated action, and not the execution, which inhibited the growth of Unitarianism in Connecticut. More importantly, as this study of the Bay State Standing Order suggests, the problem with Connecticut is that neither New Haven nor Hartford could compare with Boston. Neither city threw up a mercantile bourgeoisie with the power and prestige of the Boston Brahmins. Indeed, without mercantile backing, Unitarianism in Massachusetts would never have become the cultural force it did. It never stood a chance in Connecticut. See Leonard Bacon, "An Historical Discourse," in *Contributions to the Ecclesiastical History of Connecticut* (New York, 1861); Allen and Eddy, *Unitarians and Universalists;* Earl M. Wilbur, *A History of Unitarianism in Transylvania, England, and America* (Cambridge, Mass., 1952); Louise Chipley, "Consociation and the Unitarian Controversy in Connecticut," *Proceedings of the Unitarian Universalist Historical Association* 21 (1987): 13–31.

The reasons for founding an orthodox seminary readily presented themselves to the orthodox ministers. The "great motive for them to undertake the work of founding a Theological School," Leonard Woods wrote, was the "state of things in Boston and Cambridge."[113] Jedidiah Morse and Eliphalet Pearson felt similarly, the latter writing to Morse in September 1806 that their "pious" ends could be achieved if "even a small number of serious, pious and zealous Christians, especially ministers, combined together and mutually pledged to each other for the sole purpose of supporting, encouraging and quickening one another in every prudent exertion to save and strengthen the things which remain and are ready to die."[114] He went on to warn his friend that "time is short, the period of execution will soon close."[115] Accordingly, Morse threw himself into the project.

The major stumbling block turned out not to be Morse's Brahmin enemies, but his orthodox colleagues. For some time, it seems, the Hopkinsians, or Strict Calvinists, had harbored the idea of founding an orthodox seminary.[116] Both Samuel Spring and Nathaniel Emmons had been soliciting donations from wealthy Calvinist businessmen for such an undertaking.[117] In fact, Dr. Spring had been quite successful in his efforts, having procured from "the chamber of *orthodox commerce*" donations of some "$30,000 to a Theological Academy."[118] The obvious problem, as all knew, was bringing the two sides and their patrons together.[119] "If we can only get all calvinists together," Woods wrote Morse, "we need not fear. Hopkin-

---

113. Woods, *Andover*, 27–28.

114. Eliphalet Pearson to Morse, September 1, 1806, Morse Family Papers, Yale University Archives.

115. Ibid.

116. While the Hopkinsians called themselves—and were called—Strict Calvinists, their beliefs hardly warrant that appellation.

117. No one in the orthodox camp considered petitioning for public support. Leonard Woods noted that "such were the strifes and jealousies of political parties in Massachusetts, that the legislature could not be expected to patronize an orthodox school of divinity." See Woods, *Andover*, 86.

118. Letters of Dr. Samuel Spring to Leonard Woods, January 22 and April 1, 1807, in Woods, *Andover*. Italics in the original.

119. Morse's patrons were Samuel Abbot and John Phillips; the latter eventually underwrote the construction of the two main seminary buildings on the grounds of Phillips Academy in Andover.

sians must come down, and moderate men must come up, till they meet. Then the host will be mighty."[120]

It proved difficult to unite the two parties. Both recoiled in the face of the Brahmin takeover of Harvard and knew forceful action must be taken to counter it. "It is a day of alarm and danger," Woods revealed in a letter to Spring, "a flood of anti-Christian error and soul-destroying corruption [is] coming in upon us, and threatening to sweep away every remnant of primitive truth and goodness."[121] Yet, if differences over doctrine had caused the retreat from Harvard, then churchmen of such contrasting beliefs as Hopkinsians and Moderates would be highly reluctant to form a union with one another. As late as 1800, there was "no line of demarcation," wrote William Bentley.[122] Similarly, in his King's Chapel lectures, William Wallace Fenn noted, "Such was the condition of things at the beginning of the century—there were these strongly marked differences with the possibility of division, but in that event it was by no means clear where the line of cleavage would run—would the Moderates ally themselves with the Hopkinsians or the Liberals?"[123] Whether these orthodox factions would bridge their doctrinal differences was far from certain in 1807.

Jedidiah Morse had reason to hope for "a general union . . . to strengthen the cause of Christ among us."[124] Not only had he been urging such a "holy confederacy" in the pages of the *Panoplist,* but he had just realized a similar union with the merging of the Hopkinsian *Massachusetts Missionary Magazine* with the *Panoplist.*[125] As with that endeavor, Morse had to use all his political and diplomatic skills to secure the marriage. His evident success was duly noted by Woods, who singled out his colleague and friend for bringing the two sides together. "The happy tendency," he wrote, "towards the union among the different classes of the orthodox,

120. Woods to Morse, March 15, 1806, Morse Family Papers, Yale University Archives.
121. Cited in Williams, *Andover Liberals,* 2.
122. Bentley in Allen, "Historical Sketch," 185–86.
123. William W. Fenn, *A Religious History of New England—The King's Chapel Lectures* (Cambridge, Mass., 1917), 102.
124. *Panoplist* 2 (February 1807): 412.
125. This union occurred in the spring of 1808. Like the seminary, it did not come off without raising the concerns of the Hopkinsians, particularly those of Nathaniel Emmons. See letter of March 11, 1808, from Woods to Morse in Woods, *Andover,* 574–76.

which was manifested in the joint publication of the *Panoplist* and *Missionary Magazine,* and in the General Association, showed itself still more remarkably, during 1807 and 1808, in the founding of a united Theological Seminary." [126] To secure this "happy" union, "I had to plead as for my life," declared Morse; "and if cutting off my right hand could prevent such a disaster [as making rival institutions], I would gladly have done it on the spot." [127]

Significantly, while Morse did not have to surrender an appendage, he was forced to compromise some Moderate principles, especially in agreeing to the Edwardsian Andover Associate Creed, a pledge to which all members of the Andover Seminary community swore. The Andover oath, which William Ellery Channing called part of Andover's "espionage of bigotry," stressed "disinterested benevolence" as the key test of faith. [128] Pearson perceived as much, feeling that Morse had "sold out" the Moderates in his negotiations; in a letter to Woods, Morse was "suspicious" that Pearson harbored some ill will on account of this betrayal. [129] Woods replied by assuring him that "there has been nothing but a small bit of difference of judgment, respecting the mode of union." [130] Morse's breach of principles was great enough to prompt his biographer to write that "to Morse theology was not of primary importance, and he sacrificed his moderate views in the interest of establishing what he believed would be a bulwark against the growing Unitarian influence." [131] This assessment is at once too harsh and too charitable: too harsh because Morse did not sell out or sacrifice very much, and too charitable because Morse did not set out to establish Andover specifically because of his devotion to any specific creed or set of doctrines. Rather, he was motivated, at least in part, by personal aggrandizement or, as one contemporary acidly wrote, "to the gratification of the

---

126. Woods, *Andover,* 46

127. Morse quoted in Leonard Withington, *Contributions to the Ecclesiastical History of Essex County, Massachusetts* (Boston, 1865), 325.

128. For a discussion of the differences between "Old Calvinists," Moderates, and Hopkinsians, see Williston Walker, *A History of the Christian Church* (1919; rev. ed., New York, 1959), 466–69; William Ellery Channing, "Spiritual Freedom," *The Works of William Ellery Channing* (Boston, 1888), 180.

129. Quoted in letter of Woods to Morse, December 28, 1808, in Woods, *Andover,* 627.

130. Ibid.

131. Morse, *Jedidiah Morse,* 120.

unholy ambitions of [an] aspiring heresiarch."[132] In any case, Morse got his compromise and his seminary.[133]

When Andover Theological Seminary opened its doors on September 28, 1808, it engendered a great deal of rejoicing among the orthodox and an equal amount of ridicule from the Brahmins. No part of the orthodox constitution received more criticism than "The Confession of Faith," or, as it came to be called, the Andover Associate Creed. One writer for the *Monthly Anthology* dubbed it "an institution which would have disgraced the bigotry of the Middle Ages."[134] A graduate of Andover later remarked that the creed ensured that "conservatism and dogmatic Calvinism were written into the very structure of the new institution; for the founders believed they were defending the truth of God against evil and error."[135] Still smarting from the Brahmin's loose construction of the terms of the Hollis professorship, the founders and associates of Andover were determined to have no such problems of interpretation. Accordingly, the founders required "that every professor on the Associate Foundation shall at his inauguration make and subscribe a declaration of his belief in the doctrines of revelation, as expressed in the Associate Creed."[136] Incredibly, professors were obliged to renew their "vows" every fifth year.

Based on the Westminster Confession, the Andover creed's almost one thousand words mandated that each professor pledge his unswerving opposition, "not only to Atheists and Infidels, but to Jews, Papists. Mahomatans, Arians, Pelagians, Antinomians, Arminians, Socinians, Sabellians, Unitarians, and Universalists."[137] This rather inclusive list the founders debated at length. The Moderates eventually gave in to the Hopkinsians, whom "[n]o other Creed would have satisfied," wrote Leonard Woods; "as the oldest of them expressed it, [he] 'wished for Calvinism up to the

---

132. *Monthly Anthology* 4 (March 1809): 205.
133. On Morse's motivations, see Moss's recent biography, *The Life of Jedidiah Morse*. Moss takes a decidedly psychological approach, claiming, "We cannot fully understand Morse's Crusade against the liberals without understanding the degree to which it involved the projection onto his enemies of negative qualities Morse feared he possessed." Moss, *Jedidiah Morse*, 107.
134. *Monthly Anthology* 3 (January 1808): 30.
135. Williams, *Andover Liberals*, 7.
136. Henry K. Rowe, *History of Andover Theological Seminary* (Newton, Mass., 1933), 17–20, and Woods, *Andover*, 334.
137. Woods, *Andover*, 334.

hub.'"[138] And Calvinism he got, with the further provision that the creed "shall forever remain entirely and identically the same, without the least alteration, or any addition or diminution."[139]

At least one of Andover's first generation of professors expressed reservations about the creed and his obligation to sign it. That professor was Moses Stuart, fittingly the most cosmopolitan of Andover's young instructors and a friend of Harvard professor Edward Everett and other Brahmins.[140] At a point of marked frustration brought on by what he felt was the intellectual vacuity of Andover, Stuart confessed his misgivings: "I hope I am honest in my attachment to the Creed of this Seminary," he admitted to Everett, "but I am very far from opposing investigation and discussion."[141] Stuart's reticence on this and other matters generated "a degree of alarm" at Andover, as the strict maintenance of orthodoxy was "a matter of serious concern to them."[142] Nonetheless, neither Stuart nor any other professor or Andover official failed to sign the Andover Associate Creed.[143]

The Brahmins, particularly those in the Anthology Society, had a field day with the creed, in which they found embodied "the exclusive and denouncing spirit of Andoverian Calvinism."[144] Samuel Cooper Thacher penned a scathing critique for the *Monthly Anthology,* in the course of which he listed several obnoxious elements of the orthodox creed. It was "founded on the assumption," he wrote, "that the essential doctrines of Christianity are not *distinctly* and *explicitly* expressed in the language of

138. Ibid., 103; no attribution for the quotation.

139. Rowe, *History of Andover,* 18–19.

140. For biographical information on Stuart, see John H. Giltner, "Moses Stuart, 1780–1852" (Ph.D. diss., Yale University, 1956).

141. Letter from Moses Stuart to Edward Everett, May 14, 1814, Everett Papers, Massachusetts Historical Society.

142. Moses Stuart, "On the Study of the German Language," *Christian Review* 6 (1841): 451.

143. For a revisionist defense of the seminary, see Harold Young Vanderpool, "The Andover Conservatives: Apologetics, Biblical Criticism and Theological Change at the Andover Theological Seminary, 1808–1880" (Ph.D. diss., Harvard University, 1971). "By now it is evident," writes Vanderpool, "that both the self-image and the actions of Massachusetts trinitarians lay leagues removed from the assessments of their Arminian contemporaries as well as from much American historical scholarship" (p. 30).

144. Andrews Norton, "A Contrast Between Calvinists and Hopkinsians," *General Repository and Review* 3 (April 1813): 368.

the volume which contains them," a rather arrogant assertion.[145] On the one hand, Thacher ridiculed Andover because the "coincidence of opinion, which it is the design of these instruments to produce, can never take place," while on the other hand, he found it equally obnoxious that the orthodox founders, knowing the impossibility of giving the same opinions to every professor, established a creed "with a designed ambiguity of meaning, with the express intention of permitting men of different opinions to sign it."[146] Sensitive that this criticism not be viewed as partisan, another anthologist defended Thacher's harsh assessment of Andover's founders and their creed. "We attack them not because they are Hopkinsians, and not because they are Calvinists, but because their conduct and their principles we believe all honest Calvinists and Hopkinsians ought to unite in condemning. . . . [The *Monthly Anthology*] stands on record against the institution, and all the waters of the ocean can never wash out the stain."[147] In the same publication, Joseph Stevens Buckminster, whom the Andoverians loathed for his application of high German criticism to the Bible, stated the case against the new seminary more succinctly. "We abhor bigotry," he wrote, "whether in an Episcopalian, or a dissenter, in a Trinitarian or an Unitarian."[148] To Buckminster and all the Brahmins, the Andover creed was the quintessence of intolerance.[149]

The controversy over the Andover oath precipitated so much rancor on both sides because it stood at the core of the growing divergence between the Brahmins and the orthodox. Like the Universalists who considered tolerance both a duty and a sign of progress—and with whom the Unitarians would eventually align themselves—the Brahmins deemed the doctrinal

---

145. Samuel Cooper Thacher, "Review of 'The Constitution and Associate Statutes of the Theological Seminary in Andover,'" *Monthly Anthology* 5 (March 1808): 609.

146. Ibid.

147. *Monthly Anthology* 6 (March 1809): 205.

148. J. S. J. Gardiner review article in the *Monthly Anthology* 5 (June 1808): 340.

149. Lawrence Buell suggests that the "Arminian Ethos of Unitarianism" was anathema to creeds of any sort. "The Unitarian ethos thus was not only prepared to countenance free intellectual inquiry and expression but also, at least in theory, to give much greater encouragement to them [than the Andoverian Calvinist ethos]." He thus concludes that "all the best non-theological literary and intellectual magazines were established by Unitarians and other religious liberals." "Best" as a result of the liberals' "free intellectual inquiry and expression," it would seem. This "free intellectual inquiry" did not extend to political issues—abolitionism in particular. See Lawrence Buell, *New England Literary Culture: From the Revolution to the Renaissance* (New York, 1984), 39.

hairsplitting of the orthodox distasteful, uncharitable, and anachronistic. It was futile, the ministers argued, to think that the Standing Order would be able to exercise the domination it once enjoyed. Brahmins boasted of their growing toleration for diverse beliefs, while the orthodox declared for all to hear that the "catholicism of Boston is the most intolerant bigotry."[150]

The orthodox, Morse in particular, were overjoyed by the seeming disquietude in Brahmin circles sparked by the founding of Andover. Barely able to contain his exhilaration, Morse noted exultantly in a letter to Timothy Dwight that "the camp of the enemy is alarmed. . . . they are awake and every engine of opposition is in requisition. But we are better fortified and are stronger than they imagine. The Union in the Theological Institution and in the Panoplist and Magazine makes us powerful and enables us to look them in the face boldly."[151] Morse was well pleased with his efforts. He knew better than any of his colleagues that it was his enormous energy and unstinting effort that had made the orthodox united front a reality. Additionally, Morse also gloated over the fact that the founding of Andover, especially with the "placing of Dr. Pearson at the head of it," turned out to be ideal retribution for the "grave injustice" he and Pearson had suffered at the hands of the Brahmins at Harvard.[152] Morse was jubilant.

Brimming with confidence, the orthodox clergy quickly formulated its next move. This time the orthodox attacked the Brahmins on their own turf—in the heart of Boston. Again, the main impetus behind the undertaking proved to be the duo of Morse and Woods. As a result of a series of successful revivals at Old South Church in Boston a few years earlier, they had hatched the idea of founding what came to be known as Park Street Church.[153] The interest and general religious enthusiasm aroused by the revival seemed sufficient to support a new congregation, particularly considering that Old South was Boston's sole orthodox church.[154] As early as

---

150. Edward Dorr Griffin to James Richards, September 15, 1810, as quoted in William Sprague, *Memoir of the Rev. Edward D. Griffin, D.D.* (New York, 1839), 117.

151. Morse to Timothy Dwight, July 15, 1808, in Woods, *Andover,* 597.

152. Morse to Joseph Lyman, April 22, 1806, Morse Family Papers, Yale University Archives.

153. Ronald Formisano, *The Transformation of Political Culture: Massachusetts Parties, 1790s–1840s* (New York, 1983), 218.

154. William Bentley thought the so-called need for another orthodox meetinghouse in Boston was manufactured. He concluded "from a conversation with a candid minister of Boston, I am informed, that the overflowing of the Old South is a pretense." See Bentley, *The Diary of William Bentley* (Salem, 1905–14), 3:425.

1807, during a trip to New York, Morse made inquiries of several ministers concerning their possible interest in relocating to Boston. His second contact, Edward Dorr Griffin, Presbyterian pastor at Newark, became Park Street Church's first minister three years later.[155] Griffin was a Presbyterian, but like Morse and so much of orthodoxy in Massachusetts, he was a Yale man.

Three years is not a long time to gather a church, build a suitable dwelling, attract a congregation, and call a minister. Yet, the indefatigable Dr. Morse and his colleagues managed to pull it off, although not without a struggle. The founders encountered a multitude of difficulties, from numerous spurned offers from prospective pastors—in at least two cases from concern over "the theological warfare that was about to begin"[156]—to being cited for building too close to the sidewalk, Charles Bulfinch, architect, notwithstanding.[157] Nevertheless, the biggest hurdle to negotiate was money.

Like any other ambitious project, the founding of Park Street required substantial resources. Believing they needed a minimum of $40,000, the orthodox ministers spent the years 1807–8 searching, negotiating, and pleading for funds.[158] The initial subscription papers, signed at the end of 1808, listed twenty-three contributors promising some $16,700. With less than half the funds, Morse, Woods, and their colleagues undertook a frantic three-week effort during which they secured new pledges for contributions totaling over $33,000. Just shy of the minimum needed to begin construction, the ministers appealed anew to the wealthiest initial subscribers, who in turn promised another $8,000, bringing the total to better than $41,000.[159] Having obtained sufficient funds to commence construction,

---

155. On Morse's excursion and contact with Dr. Griffin, see Sprague, *Life of Morse*, 108–10.

156. The two divines were Dr. Eliphalet Nott, president of Union College, and Dr. Miller of New York City. Quoted in H. Crosby Englizian, *Brimstone Corner: A History of Park Street Church* (Chicago, 1968), 47.

157. Surely enough, in a letter in the Bulfinch Papers, one writer notes that "a public regard for public ornament and convenience compels me to resist such encroachments, which are daily becoming more common." Bulfinch Papers, May 5, 1809, Massachusetts Historical Society.

158. Park Street Church, *Proceedings of the Business Meetings, 1809–1834*, January 13, and *Subscription to New Church Lot*, December 5, 1808. Both items are at the Park Street Church Archives, Boston.

159. *Park Street Subscription*, December 5, 1808.

ground was broken for the first new church "on the old territory of Boston" since 1748.[160]

Park Street's ten major subscribers met with the region's leading orthodox clergy at the home of William Thurston on the afternoon of Monday, February 16, 1809. These patrons, including Thurston, Elisha Ticknor, John Tyler, and Josiah Bumstead, formed a committee to select a suitable site and begin the construction of a meetinghouse.[161] From this inaugural gathering it seems that, to a man, they were sanguine about the prospects for the church and acutely aware of the partisan, aggressive nature of their undertaking. Not only were they forming the first new church in Boston in better than half a century, but they were also doing so on terms guaranteed to set to boiling the blue blood of Brahmin Boston.

At their initial February meeting and in those that followed, the subscribers formed their society, as planned, on decidedly orthodox, evangelical terms.[162] After a brief talk with Morse, a New York minister wrote to a friend that

> some worthy and influential gentlemen, devoted to the interests of evangelical truth, propose to build a large and handsome church in the heart of Boston, and to call one, if not two, able, evangelical and devoted men to undertake the pastoral charge; and to make this, like the [Andover] seminary, a centre of orthodox operations.[163]

Gathered in reaction to the Brahmins and as the "centre of orthodox operations," Park Street Church adopted extremely exclusive terms of admission and subscribed to specific religious doctrines and church practices. While the other Boston churches professed no particular creed, Park Street "required subscription to both the general statements [of Calvinist faith— the Westminster Shorter Catechism and the 1680 Confession of Faith] and to its own particular confession, as a condition of membership."[164] Clearly, the orthodox had determined to use these confessions of faith, like the

---

160. Tarbox, "Congregational Churches of Boston," 3:403.

161. Registry of Deeds, Suffolk County, Boston, Massachusetts; copy at Park Street Church Archives.

162. The succeeding meeting, which included Morse and the Reverend John Codman of Dorchester, took place at the home of Henry Homes. *Park Street Proceedings*, 12–21.

163. Samuel Miller to Griffin as quoted in Sprague, *Edward D. Griffin*, 108–9.

164. Hill, *Old South*, 2:341–42.

Andover creed, to steel themselves against the encroachment of heterodoxy.

The strict confession aroused a great deal of controversy. In fact, Park Street's founders had hoped as much, with Morse, for one, convinced that they were "marking an epoch in the religious history of New England."[165] Accordingly, the confession and other restrictive policies were roundly condemned in the pages of the *Monthly Anthology*, whose editors ridiculed them as yet further examples of orthodox "bigotry, illiberality, [and] exclusiveness."[166] According to John Pierce, the Boston clergy proved virtually unanimous in its antipathy to Park Street from its inception, refusing to participate in any way in its organization. "Failing in their attempt to gain a party in Boston" to sanction the church officially, observed Pierce in his diary, Park Street's fathers "next applied to those who stood with open arms to receive them & who were ready to sanction all their separating principles. They applied to Dr Morse's church in Charlestown, Dr Holmes of Cambridge, & Mr Codman's of Dorchester, who gathered them into a church in Wm Thurston's house in May 1809."[167]

The exclusive and "separating principles" of Park Street did not stop with its rigid confession. Equally as restrictive, and far more problematic in the end, proved to be the rules concerning the activities of the Park Street minister both in and out of the pulpit. As a result of this doctrinal baggage, Park Street found it more difficult to attract qualified candidates than it might otherwise have been had its founders not been so obsessed with doctrinal uniformity. "[A]sked to promise, should he accept the call, not to baptize any children unless one parent was a communicant," Dr. Eliphalet Nott, president of Union College, "declined the call."[168] Park Street also required that Dr. Nott and other prospective candidates "not exchange pulpits with any minister denying the trinity as explained in the Westminster Confession."[169] As a result, the church "intended to exclude from their pulpit a large portion of the [Boston] Association, & that their minister was to hold no ministerial intercourse with them."[170] Small won-

---

165. Morse quoted in Sprague, *Edward D. Griffin*, 115.
166. Joseph Sylvester Clark, *A Historical Sketch of the Congregational Churches in Massachusetts* (Boston, 1858), 235.
167. Pierce "Memoirs," 266.
168. Englizian, *Brimstone Corner*, 46.
169. Ibid.
170. Pierce, "Memoirs," 265.

der that in addition to Dr. Nott, Dr. Miller of New York and Dr. Kollock of Georgia spurned Park Street's call.[171]

The church eventually settled Edward Dorr Griffin as pastor, but not without a great deal of negotiation. Griffin demanded as much of the church as it demanded of him. In fact, Griffin insisted that he also be made professor at the Andover Theological Seminary.[172] He "could not think of leaving Newark, either for Boston or for Andover, but that he might be willing to remove, if he could, in some suitable way, be connected with both."[173] Remarkably, Morse and Woods overcame "strong objections" to secure the "reluctant consent" of both Andover and Park Street to Griffin's highly unusual demand.[174] Griffin made their efforts on his behalf much easier by mesmerizing the Park Street congregation with his decidedly un-Bostonian brand of pulpit eloquence during a brief stay in Boston. "What a *mammouth* of an orator," exclaimed Samuel Spring.[175]

When it came to matters of creed and church discipline, Edward Dorr Griffin and the Park Street orthodox community appeared to be an ideal match. Not only did the incoming pastor accept the church's doctrinal exclusivity, he embraced it with fervor, stating in a letter to Morse "that in my humble opinion, the immediate interest of the congregation itself greatly depends on preserving strictness in these matters."[176] Griffin, like Morse, seems to have both understood and relished the contentious atmosphere Park Street was to engender. "The stand to be made in Boston," he wrote Morse, "must be on ground encircled by a very strict line of demarcation. Unless there be a visible and palpable difference between the old churches and the new ones, who will see any reason for coming over to the latter? . . . if there ever was a clear case for decision and thorough-going discipline, there is a call for both in the congregation to be formed, *at this crisis,* in Boston."[177]

If Griffin was spoiling for a fight, he was not disappointed. He commenced his ministry most contentiously with a fiery installation sermon

171. See Bentley, *Diary,* 3:425.
172. Edward Griffin to Jedidiah Morse, July 28, 1808, in Woods, *Andover,* 599–600.
173. Woods, *Andover,* 148.
174. Ibid.
175. Quoted in Englizian, *Brimstone Corner,* 44.
176. Edward Griffin to Jedidiah Morse, July 28, 1808, in Woods, *Andover,* 601.
177. Ibid.

in which he made the distinction between friend and foe absolutely clear. "Those," he told the assembled faithful, "who stand in the way and ask for the good old paths, and walk therein, will say, Peace be to this house; those only, who have abandoned the religion of their fathers, will regard it with a cold or jealous eye."[178] The *Monthly Anthology* duly noted the "technical babble" issuing from Griffin's pulpit. The pastor responded in kind, remarking to a friend that the "*Monthly Anthology* opened its mouth as wide as a shark's and devoured it at once." "They proved," he continued, "that I have made at least four or five persons in the deity."[179]

Griffin's humor proved short lived. His sermons grew more bellicose in the succeeding months, while his estimation of Bostonians dropped precipitously. "You can form no adequate idea of the strength of Satan's Kingdom in this town," he lamented to an associate.[180]

> The injury which Chauncy, and a few other men, have done to the church in this region, is incalculable. Our church has been overwhelmed with contempt. The catholicism of Boston is the most intolerant bigotry that I ever witnessed, when directed towards the religion of Christ. It is a friend which never wears a smile but when its eye is directed towards the most abominable errors.[181]

Griffin quickly lost confidence in his ability to effect change by means of exclusivity and exhortation. "Boston folks will be Boston folks still. They will not retrench a habit, nor lose a nap at church, to save their lives. Had I known as much as I do now, I would never have left the Presbyterian world."[182]

Not long into his tenure, the Park Street church began to have problems with Griffin. From the first, the church was in debt and would continue to be for a number of decades. Yet, as the months passed and pews remained empty, the church elders increasingly blamed Griffin for their growing pecuniary difficulties.[183] Griffin proved so adamant in refusing to exchange pulpits with ministers who differed even slightly with him that he and the

---

178. Edward Dorr Griffin, *A Sermon Preached, 1–10–1810* (Boston, 1810), 19–20.
179. Quoted in Parsons Cooke, *Recollections of Dr. Griffin* (Boston, 1855), 23.
180. Griffin to James Richards, September 15, 1810, in Sprague, *Edward D. Griffin,* 117.
181. Ibid.
182. Ibid., 129.
183. *Park Street Proceedings,* 41.

congregation were forced "to suffer social and clerical ostracism."[184] A church finance committee concluded that Griffin's ultra-exclusivity and caustic preaching redounded directly upon the number of pews sold. "Although other [church] Societies," the committee argued, "whose ministers have been acceptable, have met with no difficulty in their support, yet we very much fear our embarrassments will continue to increase, by the departure of many of those who at present belong to the society."[185] To fill more pews and attract new members, Park Street needed "a minister more acceptable to them."[186] Perhaps the committee found Griffin culpable because it was responding to a complaint from its embattled pastor concerning, remarkably, what he thought was a salary insufficient to his needs. What appeared to be an ideal match doctrinally proved to be a disastrous one financially. Because Boston churches, unlike the rest of the Standing Order, were on a voluntarist system, any congregation that alienated its wealthy parishioners found itself in dire straits. Park Street and Edward Dorr Griffin parted ways early in 1815.

In debt from its inception, it seems dubious that Park Street's financial problems were due to its controversial minister, no matter what the church communicants thought. While as many as half the pews remained unsold as late as 1812, Griffin and his exhilarating style of preaching were very popular. By all accounts, both partisan and neutral, his services were well attended, especially at the beginning of his tenure.[187] In addition, Griffin inaugurated a series of extremely successful Sunday evening lectures in the winter months of 1812–13, which one historian called "the high point of his entire career."[188] The problem for Park Street proved to be that while many Bostonians listened enthusiastically to Griffin's orthodox sermons, few purchased pews.

Park Street Church was suffering from grave financial maladies at the same time that its Sunday services were well attended and its minister popular. The problem was not that Griffin's evangelical style was disliked or unpopular, but that it had a distinctive class appeal.[189] Griffin's admirers

---

184. Englizian, *Brimstone Corner*, 58.
185. Park Street Committee letter, May 3, 1814, *Proceedings*.
186. Ibid.
187. Cooke, *Recollections*, 24–25, and Englizian, *Brimstone Corner*, 58.
188. Englizian, *Brimstone Corner*, 59.
189. E. D. Griffin, "Christian Boldness," in *The American Pulpit* (Edinburgh, 1852), 225–30.

apparently did not have a great deal of assets, at least not enough to make such a substantial investment in the purchase of a pew.[190] This conclusion seems to be borne out by a financial declaration dated April 1810. It attests to the fact that vacant pews could be found throughout the meetinghouse. Significantly, of the $35,000 of unrented pews, only $6,000, or less than 20 percent, of the total was from vacancies in the gallery. Almost 80 percent of the unsold pews were located on the exclusive and expensive main floor. Even with the difference of the relative costs of the gallery and lower pews factored in, the average price of a gallery pew at less than $200 and that of the main floor at $280, similar conclusions seem manifest: the vacancy rate of the main floor remained three times that of the more affordable gallery.[191]

There can be no doubt that orthodox sermonizing had a class appeal. Morse, Griffin, and their brethren knew all too well that the orthodox minister's "pure doctrines of the gospel . . . must offend and humble the worldly, proud spirit of some of his wealthiest and most influential parishioners."[192] Little wonder that Park Street Church, "deeply in debt," had trouble securing a large number of affluent parishioners in the heart of Boston.[193] As the pew vacancies at Park Street made clear, evangelical orthodoxy proved far less popular with the wealthy than with other classes. "One who was born to wealth in Boston," a saying went, "had no need to be born again."[194]

Pecuniary problems plagued Park Street for years after Griffin's resignation. These problems can be attributed, at least in part, to a fundamental miscalculation on the part of the orthodox, who failed to take into account the unique status of Boston's churches. Because they were excluded from the provisions of Article 3 of the constitution of 1780, which provided for

---

190. For some class characteristics of the various denominations in Boston, see Anne C. Rose, "Social Sources of Denominationalism Reconsidered: Post-Revolutionary Boston as a Case Study," *American Quarterly* 38 (1986): 243–64, and Allan Kulikoff, "The Progress of Inequality in Revolutionary Boston," *William and Mary Quarterly*, 3d. ser., 28 (1971): 374–412.

191. Park Street Proceedings, 33–40.

192. Jedidiah Morse, *Sermon Delivered at the Ordination of Joshua Huntington* (Boston, 1808), 9.

193. See article on Park Street in *The Spirit of the Pilgrims*, 2:221.

194. Quoted in Vernon L. Parrington, *Main Currents in American Thought* (1927; reprint, New York, 1954), 2:320.

state support of Congregational ministers, Boston churches overwhelmingly depended on their parishioners, who supported the congregation by
the purchase of pews. Accordingly, any actions that alienated parishioners,
particularly wealthy ones, no matter how popular with devout church
communicants, spelled financial distress for both church and minister. In
Boston, then, the parishioners held the bulk of the power. Such social factors greatly impinged on religious institutions and creedal doctrines.

   Park Street's financial difficulties notwithstanding, by the second decade
of the nineteenth century, the orthodox had succeeded in establishing a
new, evangelical congregation in the heart of Brahmin Boston. Together
with Andover Theological Seminary and the *Panoplist* magazine, Park
Street spearheaded the counterattack of the orthodox. Jedidiah Morse, Leonard Woods, Eliphalet Pearson, and their brethren had gone a long way
in fulfilling Morse's "comprehensive plan" of battle against the Brahmins.
"Their union calls for a union in us," he wrote in the *Panoplist*, "a holy
confederacy."[195] What Morse and his fellow schismatics did not know was
that their efforts, while successfully reinvigorating orthodoxy in Massachusetts, sowed the seeds of religious disestablishment and the terminal crisis
of the Standing Order.

---

195. Morse in the *Panoplist* 2 (March 1807): 506.

CHAPTER 6

Schism from Below

Parishioner, Communicant, and the Standing Order

Christians, instead of being arrayed as heretofore, under the different standards of little sects, are gradually gathering by large masses and with systematic order into two great divisions.

—WILLIAM ELLERY CHANNING

I N THE SECOND DECADE of the nineteenth century, the Standing Order of Massachusetts Congregational churches became a shell of its former self. Under the pressure of several self-inflicted wounds, the bonds that for so long had conjoined Brahmin and orthodox began to give way. In the course of the decade, it became apparent that both sides lacked the desire and the determination to maintain much more than the facade of union. As a result, by the end of the decade the Standing Order, established and favored by law for more than a century, dissolved into two competing and antithetical denominations.

The primary instigator of the crisis of the Standing Order proved to be the orthodox party. Acutely conscious of its declining position within society, the orthodox clergy used the institutions it created in the previous decade to mount a sustained attack on the Brahmins. Aggressive and unrelenting, the orthodox offensive sought to expose at all costs—and the costs were high—the "magnitude of the evil" perpetrated on Congregational

religion by the Brahmins.[1] To the orthodox, Congregationalism had become infected with a growing secularization that the Brahmins embraced
in the name of "charity and toleration," but which was nothing less than
rank apostasy. True religion demanded the defeat of the Brahmins, first by
exposing the irreligion they paraded as liberality, and then by expunging
the Brahmin element altogether.

The orthodox clergy had several means at its disposal to demonstrate
the heterodoxy of its enemies within the Standing Order. In the course of
the decade, orthodoxy brought to bear all the forces it could muster in
its cause. The initial direct confrontation centered around the long-
established tradition of pulpit exchanges in which ministers invited their
colleagues, and were themselves invited, to be guest pastors in neighboring
congregations. These exchanges served several important functions, not
the least of which was as a safety valve enabling parishioners with subtle
differences in doctrinal beliefs to maintain loyalty to a minister whose
views differed from their own. When John Codman, minister of the newly
established Second Church of Dorchester, refused to exchange with his
Brahmin colleagues of the Boston Association, he undermined one of the
Standing Order's most vital and important filaments. His actions, as he
and his colleagues well knew, could not help but sound a warning for
the future unity of the Congregational Standing Order.

Following on the heels of the Dorchester controversy, the orthodox
party commenced another assault in a second arena. Led by the doctrinaire
and divisive minister of the First Church of Charlestown, the ubiquitous
Jedidiah Morse, the orthodox ministers sought to exorcise Brahmin latitudinarianism and lax religiosity from the Massachusetts churches by the
creation of a presbyterian structure. By creating such a system, as Connecticut had a century earlier, Morse and his allies hoped to establish and enforce a doctrinal creed like that of the Andover Theological Seminary, to
which all members would have to swear an oath of fealty, and which would
serve as a mechanism for dismissing ministers of questionable orthodoxy
or dubious character. Remarkably, Morse justified his "Plan for Ecclesiastical Union" by citing a relatively obscure call for union issued by Cotton
Mather over a century earlier. While the doctrinally diverse Annual Convention of Massachusetts Ministers predictably defeated the plan, its pro-

---

1. Jeremiah Evarts, as quoted in Ebenezer C. Tracy, *Memoir of the Life of Jeremiah Evarts,
   Esquire* (Boston, 1845), 69.

mulgation at the orthodox General Association of Ministers in 1814 and 1815 nonetheless served to quicken the bifurcation of the Standing Order.

The orthodox party had long been infuriated by the Brahmins' refusal to articulate their seemingly significant differences in theological doctrine. Convinced that the Brahmins were simply too afraid to betray their heresies, Morse attempted to expose in print the secretive and duplicitous nature of his enemies. He and his colleague, Jeremiah Evarts, wrote several incendiary articles for the *Panoplist* on the Dorchester controversy and its aftermath, while also publishing in 1815, at their own expense, a chapter of Thomas Belsham's *Life of Theophilus Lindsay* under the title *American Unitarianism*. Belsham's own words, they were convinced, constituted indisputable proof "derived from unquestionable sources" that the Brahmin ministers had repudiated the religion of their fathers as well as that of their orthodox brethren.[2] These publications in successive years finally provoked a direct response from the Brahmin camp, whose leadership was at that moment undergoing a transformation. Most of the elder ministers of the Anthology Society had retired or died; they gave way to younger spokesmen such as John Lowell and Andrews Norton, both of Harvard, who emerged, with George Ticknor, as the intellectual princes of Brahmin Boston. Cutting their teeth on controversy, they eschewed their predecessors' attempts to avoid open controversy except when personal honor was at stake. No less than their orthodox counterparts, Lowell and Norton seemed to relish contention and conflict. Lowell's *An Inquiry into the Right to Change the Ecclesiastical Constitution of the Congregational Churches of Massachusetts,* published in 1816, was more than a direct rejoinder to Morse's "Plan of Ecclesiastical Union." It served notice that Brahmin tactics were themselves changing, becoming at once more direct and aggressive. As the crisis of the Standing Order became public, Brahmins increasingly exchanged barbs and accusations with their orthodox colleagues. Intended to discredit the enemy as irreligious on the one hand and doctrinaire on the other, the principals published pamphlets with names such as "Are You of the Christian or of the Boston Religion?" and "Are You a Christian or a Calvinist?" Morse and his cohorts had succeeded in publicizing the differences between Brahmin and orthodox. By the end of the decade, with both sides prepared to do battle, reconciliation proved impossible.

---

2. Jedidiah Morse, *Thomas Belsham's "American Unitarianism: Or a Brief History of the Progress and Present State of the Unitarian Churches in America"* (Boston, 1814), 3.

During these first decades of the nineteenth century, churches and parishes split along the same fracture lines as the clergy. By the end of the second decade, trouble was brewing in many eastern towns, as the simmering social tensions brought about by the split in clerical ranks turned into open conflict. These controversies, which culminated in the Dedham conflict in 1818–21, pitted Brahmin parishioners against orthodox church communicants in an acrimonious fight over precisely who constituted the legitimate church society as recognized by the state and who owned the church property, the meetinghouse in particular. The growing class nature of Massachusetts society may not have been the efficient cause, but it was certainly a necessary cause of the crisis of the Standing Order that culminated a decade later in formal disestablishment in Massachusetts. There were, to be sure, other important factors at work, not the least of which was the increasing universal embrace of the idea of the separation of church and state. Yet this underlying social conflict helps explain why the religious culture of the Congregationalists bifurcated the way it did, as well as why each side drew to it specific class allies.

While many local factors proved critical in determining with which party parishioners and communicants sided, some broad inferences can be drawn. For the most part, Brahmin ministers found their greatest support among the parishioners, the well-off in particular, while the orthodox relied on the backing of the church communicants. In Dorchester, as in most towns of eastern Massachusetts, church communicants had more at stake in maintaining orthodoxy than did the more diverse parishioners. Usually not as prosperous as their neighbors, communicants lived a more church-centered life. Having sacrificed the requisite long hours of study and devotion to confess their faith, they naturally gravitated toward the evangelical strains of the orthodox clergy. Like their ministers, they more often than not believed that the shrinking number of public confessions signaled a serious decline in religiosity, one that had already produced baneful consequences for the community at large.

Subtle lifestyle differences provoked bitter dispute over issues of church doctrine and polity. Dismayed over what seemed to them a needless breakup over "subtleties of metaphysic,"[3] the Brahmins were barely able to conceal their contempt for what they considered the hopelessly outmoded doctrinal hairsplitting of their opponents. The orthodox were overjoyed at

---

3. Joseph Stevens Buckminster's words while a student of David Tappan at Harvard.

the coming to pass of a clear split between the two sides, convinced that it was a necessary first step in regaining what Jedidiah Morse labeled "pure and undefiled religion."[4] These events, so welcomed by one side and seemingly avoidable to the other, brought to a boil the simmering tensions between increasingly Brahmin parishes and consistently conservative church communicants. During the first and second decades of the nineteenth century, Congregational churches and parishes split along the same lines as the clergy. But as subsequent events were to demonstrate, in exposing the Brahmins for what they were, just one sect among many, the orthodox assured the destruction of the Standing Order and their privileged place within it. "The collapse of the Standing Order had been inevitable," wrote Conrad Wright, "because the ministers could no longer be generally accepted as public teachers of piety and morality, in view of the fact that they were also the spokesmen for particular denominations of Christians."[5] Exposing the Brahmins interred the Standing Order.

When the well-to-do Brahmin parishioners of Dorchester's Second Church withdrew in 1813 "and formed the Third Religious Society in Dorchester,"[6] the conflict that had plagued the Second Church and its minister for three tedious years was finally resolved. Yet it left behind it a lasting legacy, as the Dorchester controversy marked the first overt, public refusal of Christian fellowship among the Congregational ministers in eastern Massachusetts. John Codman's utter unwillingness to exchange pulpits with the vast majority of his colleagues in the Boston Association solely because of their Brahmin sensibilities rent his congregation in two. It also effectively commenced "that great strife, in the early years of the present century," lamented Rev. Increase Tarbox in 1881, "whereby a separation took place between the Congregational Churches since known as Unitarian and those that adhered to the old New England standards of faith."[7]

The controversy erupted in November 1809, the second year of Codman's pastorate, when some forty principal parishioners of the Second Church addressed a letter to their pastor expressing concern that he was

---

4. Morse in letter to Dorchester parish committee, as quoted in William Allen, *Memoir of John Codman, D.D.* (Boston, 1853), 86.

5. Conrad Wright, "Piety, Morality, and the Commonwealth," *Crane Review* 9 (1967): 102.

6. George Willis Cooke, *Unitarianism in America* (Boston, 1902), 102.

7. Increase N. Tarbox, "The Congregational Churches of Boston since 1780," in *The Memorial History of Boston* ed. Justin Winsor (Boston, 1881), 3:407.

not making "exchanges generally with those ministers, who make the public lecture in Boston."[8] They pointed out that previous to his ordination, he had assured several of them that he anticipated joining the Boston Association and "did not see any difficulty respecting exchanges" with his colleagues.[9] Pulpit exchanges, the parishioners noted, were a long-standing and cherished practice, "which we have a just claim to expect from your own observations."[10] Codman curtly responded that pulpit exchanges were his prerogative only and not the business of lay parishioners. Therefore, he wrote, "you must leave me to say, that I never can nor never shall PLEDGE myself to exchange pulpits with any man or body of men whatever; and that I never did, from any observations previous to my being settled as your minister, give you any just claim to expect it."[11] Faced with such a harsh and resolute stance, the parishioner group sought to enlist the entire parish to beseech their minister to reverse his policy of non-intercourse with his Brahmin brethren. The parish eventually voted forty to thirty-five "that the Rev. Mr. Codman be requested to exchange with the ministers who compose the Boston association of which he is a member," or it would endeavor to make "the connexion between themselves and Mr. Codman become extinct."[12]

A number of contemporary observers noted the remarkable irony that Codman should have been the first minister so vehemently to deny Christian fellowship to his Brahmin brethren. After all, Codman was a Bostonian, the son of John Codman and Margaret Russell, the former "an eminent merchant" and the latter "connected with some to the most influential families in Boston."[13] After attending Harvard College from 1798 through his graduation in 1802, Codman set his sights on a legal career. But in the next year, a deathbed plea in which "his father intimated a wish that his son should become a minister" prompted John to abandon the law in favor of the ministry.[14] Whether the "great shock to his sensibilities"

---

8. Jeremiah Evarts, "Review of the Dorchester Controversy," as reprinted in the *Panoplist* 10 (1814): 261.

9. *Memorial of the Proprietors of the New South Meeting-House in Dorchester to the Ministers of the Boston Association* (Boston, 1813), 44.

10. *Proceedings of the Second Church and Parish in Dorchester* (Boston, 1812), 42–44.

11. Ibid., 24.

12. Ibid., 25–44.

13. William Sprague, *Annals of the American Pulpit* (New York, 1865), 2:492.

14. Allen, *Memoir*, 23.

of his father's death impelled him from the Brahmin environment of his upbringing toward the sterner and doctrinaire teachings of orthodox Congregationalism, as several writers have contended, is far from certain.[15] Codman's drift away from the more permissive, latitudinarian tenor of his Boston colleagues—in itself unremarkable since Brahmin ministers boasted a diversity of religious opinions within the Boston Association— was "strongly reinforced" during his extended stay in Scotland commencing in 1805.[16] Codman studied in Edinburgh for two years, during which time he resided in the house of Dr. David Dickson, "where congeniality of tastes and studies led a number of young men to come together in friendly conference."[17] It was here, one contemporary claimed, that Codman adopted "his serious views."[18]

When Codman returned from abroad in 1808, he was offered the pastorate of the newly formed Second Church of Dorchester. After he intimated his receptiveness to such an offer, the Second Church "unanimously elected Mr. Codman, then a licensed candidate for the ministry, to be their pastor."[19] Within a few days, as was the law and practice in the Bay State, the parish voted on the church's nomination, giving its overwhelming assent, with all but four members in favor.[20] Codman, only a few months back from Edinburgh, thus became the established minister of the Second Church of Dorchester.

Dorchester's election of Codman on the ninth day of September was made rather hastily, since he had only just returned from abroad the previous May. The members of the congregation had "enjoyed but little opportunity of becoming acquainted" with their young shepherd's "religious opinions."[21] The candidate himself was acutely aware that two Sabbaths and one lecture hardly constituted sufficient exposure for his prospective congregation to render a careful judgment concerning his qualifications.

15. Sprague, *Annals*, 498. See also Allen, *Memoir*, 23–24; Allen claims the deathbed plea was "doubtless instrumental."
16. Conrad Wright, "Institutional Reconstruction in the Unitarian Controversy," in *American Unitarianism: 1805–1865* (Boston, 1989), 7.
17. Robert Burns, D.D., to William Sprague, April 5, 1855; quoted in full in Sprague, *Annals*, 2:498.
18. Burns in Sprague, *Annals*, 2:499
19. Evarts, "Review of Dorchester," 258.
20. *Proceedings of the Second Church*, 41.
21. Evarts, "Review of Dorchester," 258.

In an attempt to ensure that Dorchester thoroughly understood his ortho-dox sentiments, which had hardened significantly while he was abroad, Codman decided to articulate his fully formed notions in a missive to the congregation. His supporters subsequently used this letter, intended "to prevent future difficulties," as proof that the minister had forewarned Dorchester as to his beliefs. With a bit more circumspection, it seems, the parishioners might have avoided the entire controversy.[22]

Codman expressed his convictions with unambiguous clarity. "Lest there should be any doubt on the subject" on the part of the parish com-mittee, Codman made sure to set down his decidedly orthodox creed. "As Arian and Socinian errors have of late years crept into some of our Churches," he asserted,

> I think it my duty to declare to that Church of Christ, of whom I may have the pastoral charge, that I believe the Father, Son, and Holy Ghost to be the one living and true God; and that my faith, in general, is conformable to the Assembly's catechism, and to the confession of faith drawn up by the elders and messengers of the Congregational Churches in the year 1680, and recommended to the Churches by the General Court in Massachusetts.[23]

The parish committee, warmly receiving his communication of "perfect frankness," responded to him in "an affectionate letter" shortly thereafter.[24] The committee noted unanimously its "general satisfaction" with its minister-designate, while not mentioning any disquietude among its num-ber with his declared orthodox sentiments. With assurances from Codman of his "earnest endeavor, as far as consistent with the faithful discharge of ministerial duty, to promote peace and friendship among the people of my charge," the council proceeded to ordain their man on December 7, 1808.

When, a year later, Codman and his church communicant allies ran afoul of the majority of parishioners, many commentators sympathetic to the orthodox cause placed the blame squarely on Dorchester's Brahmin parishioners. After all, prior to his ordination, Codman had made perfectly clear the substance of his beliefs. The Brahmins either egregiously ne-glected to read with sufficient care Codman's epistle in the mistaken view

---

22. Codman letter in *Proceedings of the Second Church*, 12.

23. Ibid.

24. Evarts, "Review of Dorchester," 259.

that the orthodoxy of the Harvard-graduated son of a wealthy merchant must be tepid at best, or, when they assented to his appointment, they were secretly itching for a fight. In either case, "Mr. Codman's opposers were carrying on their opposition with uncommon violence, and indulging in unprovoked and bitter hostility," wrote Jeremiah Evarts.[25]

This orthodox interpretation of events, while plausible, proved remarkably uncharitable. It seems unlikely that the parish committee members misconstrued Codman's orthodox beliefs, expressed so clearly in his letter; the committee subsequently volunteered that at the time of his ordination it had harbored no illusions as to Codman's Calvinist creed. Even Evarts noted that the parish had "professed no dislike of Codman's preaching," then or subsequently.[26] The parishioners, for their part, argued that Codman's Calvinism, while not to their taste, was of no great consequence and had no bearing on the controversy. They declared the correspondence between the candidate and the parish committee irrelevant because it did not address the true source of their displeasure. Brahmin ministers and parishioners alike, proclaiming their tolerance of diverse beliefs, championed the fact that they had long ago questioned the efficacy of examining candidates for the ministry as to their doctrinal convictions. To the end, the Brahmin party asserted that Codman's "religious opinions" were not relevant to the controversy.[27]

All parties agreed that the ostensible issue at the heart of the Dorchester controversy was "the question of ministerial exchanges."[28] Latitudinarian parishioners and orthodox church communicants acknowledged that Codman, since he "soon came to have scruples on the subject," had agreed to exchange pulpits with scant few ministers in the course of his tenure. In the three years after his ordination he had not exchanged "ministerial labors" with a single Brahmin among the "Rev. Clergy composing the Boston Association," not even those who had presided at his ordination.[29] The parishioners declared this to be the genuine cause of their complaints,

---

25. Ibid., 260
26. Ibid., 261.
27. Ibid., 260.
28. Ibid.
29. Liberals at his ordination included Buckminster and Channing. Tradition dictated that Codman have Buckminster, as his own pastor at Brattle Street, preach on the occasion of his settlement, but Codman chose the more evangelical Channing.

while the church, sympathetic to Codman, claimed that the flap over exchanges was nothing more than a smoke screen.

Between 1811 and 1813, the parties convened two separate councils to hear the parishioners' complaints. On each occasion the assembled councilors, consisting of one minister and elder from several neighboring towns, deliberated on the parish committee's written request that "the connexion between themselves and Mr. Codman become extinct." Significantly, while both councils understood that they must decide the fate of Dorchester's embattled minister, neither the councilors nor the principals could agree what exactly constituted the kernel of the disagreement. The parish claimed it was Codman's exclusiveness with respect to exchanges, while the orthodox insisted it was their minister's orthodox beliefs. The parishioners blamed Codman for making the Second Church "a separate religious society; cutting us off from that intercourse with the greater part of the Christian societies (and of our own denomination) with which we have been on terms of friendship and communion."[30] Mr. Codman had never suggested—explicitly or implicitly—that he believed his Brahmin colleagues, who composed the great majority of the Boston Association, were so egregiously in error that he could not sanction "as consistent with the faithful discharge of ministerial duty" their preaching from his pulpit.[31] The parishioners did not deny Codman or any minister "all discretion in the choice of those with whom he changes pulpits."[32] It was, rather, their minister's unpardonable lack of charity and tolerance, as exhibited in his refusal to accommodate their desire to hear a variety of preachers, that had instilled their displeasure and had precipitated the crisis.

The orthodox church communicants fell in behind their minister, who they were convinced had in no way brought on the controversy. It was, as all agreed, the sole right of the minister to decide with whom he would exchange. "The question of *ministerial exchanges* would have been suffered by them to sleep in silence," declared Evarts, if it were not for Codman's Calvinism.[33] "That this opposition originated, in fact, from a dislike of the *great truths* which Mr. Codman preached, and the correspondent strictness of moral deportment which he urged, we have the fullest persuasion; and

---

30. *Proceedings of the Second Church,* 65.
31. Quoted in Wright, "Reconstruction," 8.
32. *Proceedings of the Second Church,* 65.
33. Evarts, "Review of Dorchester," 260.

we think no candid man, having an intimate acquaintance with the parties and the controversy, can entertain a doubt on the subject."[34] Evarts and the communicants of the Second Church ridiculed the parishioners for their hypocrisy; professedly tolerant, they refused to countenance the rigid orthodoxy of their own mutually agreed upon pastor. They simply camouflaged their bigotry with groundless complaints about Codman's refusal to exchange pulpits regularly.

Predictably, with the precise issue in doubt, neither council could reach a satisfactory verdict. The first council met on October 30, 1811, hearing arguments from both sides for more than a week.[35] After days of debate, the council "was found to be equally divided" on the basic issue of whether the parishioners had "a just cause of complaint."[36] Codman's delegates voted that the minister had not given the parish cause for dismissal, while the parish delegation concluded that Codman had given sufficient cause. As a result, the council could do no more than urge the two parties to settle their differences with a "condescending, mild, peaceable, and charitable disposition."[37]

The second council convened in May 1812, by which time it was clear that neither side featured a "mild or charitable disposition" toward the other.[38] On the main question, whether "it is expedient, that the ministerial and pastoral relation between the Rev. Mr. Codman and the second parish in Dorchester be dissolved," the second council, like its predecessor, split along party lines.[39] The final decision devolved to West Springfield's Joseph Lathrop, the "mutually agreed upon moderator and umpire" of the coun-

---

34. Ibid.

35. Six churches were selected by each side to send two delegates each. They were the orthodox churches at Charlestown, Hatfield, Medford, Newtown, Salem, and Worcester, which sent ministers Morse, Lyman, Prentiss, Austin, Worcester, and Greenough. Liberal churches and ministers were Reed of Bridgewater, Eliot of Watertown, Thacher of Dedham, Bancroft of Worcester, Kendall of Weston, and Thayer of Lancaster. See *Panoplist* 10 (1814): 270.

36. Evarts, "Review of Dorchester," 272.

37. *Proceedings of the Second Church,* 109.

38. The delegates and churches chosen by Codman were Prentiss of Medford, Dana of Newburyport, Stearns of Bedford, and Worcester of Salem. Those of the parish were Barnard of Salem, Reed of Bridgewater, Allyne of Duxbury, and Thayer of Lancaster. See *Panoplist* 10 (1814): 294.

39. *Proceedings of the Second Church,* 102–4.

cil.[40] After careful deliberation, Lathrop resolved that the parishioners were in the wrong; he urged them to consider that with some charity, Mr. Codman might "open a more free and liberal intercourse with his brethren."[41] As far as Lathrop was concerned, pulpit exchange was the heart of the matter, so "presuming that your pastor will be disposed to pursue a liberal plan of exchanging with his brethren in the ministry . . . you may be each other's crown and joy both here and hereafter."[42] Before adjourning, Lathrop directed a caveat toward his colleague: no member of the clergy should "treat with wanton disregard the wishes of his people," or the sensibilities of his ministerial brethren. If Reverend Codman's "future conduct should be the same as in time past, in this respect [to ministerial intercourse], I should be much disappointed and grieved; and if I should find myself thus disappointed, I should certainly have no hesitancy in giving my vote for his dismission, if called in Providence to give my voice on the question."[43] At the conclusion of the second council, it seemed clear that Codman's exclusionary practices had to change or further controversy would surely ensue.

Having resolved nothing, the first and second councils only reinforced each party's conviction that it was in the right. The parish considered it grounds for dismissal that their minister "will not suffer them to hear men of their choice," while Codman and his supporters remained adamant that it was "an important privilege of the Christian minister to regulate his exchanges with his brethren according to the unbiased dictates of his own mind and conscience."[44] Accordingly, when Codman continued to refuse to exchange with more than two members of the Boston Association, believing the others to be of "the lowest grade of Socinianism, if not some grades lower," forty-six disgruntled parishioners blasted their minister in a letter dated October 27, 1812.[45] Since Codman had resisted "a more free and liberal intercourse" with his brethren, they concluded "that nothing but a separation would restore tranquillity to the church and society."[46] A month

---

40. Evarts, "Review of Dorchester," 294.
41. *Proceedings of the Second Church,* 122.
42. Ibid., 123–24.
43. Ibid., 124.
44. William Bentley, *The Diary of William Bentley* (Salem, 1905–14), 4:39, and *Proceedings of the Second Church,* 123.
45. *Proceedings of the Second Church,* 122–24.
46. Cited in Allen, *Memoir,* 94.

later, by a vote of fifty-five to forty-five, the parish voted to dismiss its pastor.

The controversy finally came to a head in the meetinghouse of the second church on the Sunday following the parish vote for dismissal. In what can only be described as a remarkably comic situation, the parishioners, "determined to keep Mr. Codman from his pulpit," stationed "eight sturdy men on the pulpit stairs, four on each side of the pulpit, in such a manner, as to obstruct the passage entirely."[47] Barred from his usual place, Reverend Codman wasted no time in beginning "public worship" from where he stood in the first seat in front of the pulpit. His manner was so "unusually solemn and affecting" that "all became quiet."[48] During his first prayer, a man identifying himself as the "Rev. Mr. Pierce," the substitute preacher arranged for by the parishioners, calmly walked into the church and past the eight "sturdy" men and up the pulpit stairs. He remained there quietly "during the remainder of the services; and strange as it may seem, he made no further disturbance till Mr. C. had pronounced the blessing."[49] When Codman was finished, he and his supporters abandoned the meetinghouse to Pierce and the remainder of the people. As for the afternoon services, both Codman's and Pierce's were conducted in their entirety without incident but in reverse order, with Pierce conducting the first service upon the completion of his dinner, which he enjoyed "without leaving the house" lest he fail to regain it after the dinner hour.[50] Thus did the religious services of the second church transpire on this particular Sunday.

The church communicants ridiculed the actions of the parishioners as "irregular and illegal,"[51] while an intimate of Codman, fond of hyperbole, called the pulpit stunt "an act of outrage which has no parallel in modern civilized Christendom."[52] In a review in the *Panoplist* magazine, Evarts alerted his readers that all the charges against the minister of Dorchester "were groundless and therefore highly slanderous and libelous."[53] Codman's orthodox brethren also came to his defense, calling his "embar-

---

47. Evarts, "Review of Dorchester," 301.
48. Ibid.
49. Ibid., 304.
50. Evarts, "Review of Dorchester," 302.
51. Quoted in Joshua Bates, *Reminiscences of John Codman, D.D.* (Boston, 1853), 230.
52. Ibid., 230.
53. *Panoplist* 10 (1814): 300.

rassments and trials . . . the fruits of his religious convictions," and urging the embattled minister to fight on.[54] "I rejoice to hear that Mr. Codman looks up and stands forth," Leonard Woods wrote to Morse. "The Lord be with him."[55] For his part, Morse entreated Codman to stand his ground at all costs, arguing that he himself would "sacrifice his life" for the cause of orthodoxy.[56] After all, he reminded his colleague, "[b]lessed are ye when men shall hate you. Rejoice in that day, & leap for joy . . . when they shall separate you from their company, & shall reproach you, and cast out your name as evil, for the Son of Man's sake."[57]

It is likely that Morse would have pursued the fight to the bitter end, as he prodded his colleague to do, but Codman had different ideas. Far less contentious than Morse, Woods, or Evarts, Codman decided to seek some sort of mutually amicable separation from his parishioners, who had gone to such lengths to disrupt the peace of his society. He had little doubt that his position on pulpit exchanges was a most justifiable one, even if "Mr. C.'s opposers had no doubt that Mr. C. would be dismissed by the supreme court, on the charges which the parish had exhibited against him."[58] Without giving up his principled stance on exchanges, Codman thought it best as "the duty of a Christian and the sacred office of a Gospel teacher" to cut loose his disaffected parishioners.[59] Codman thus entreated his people to forge a compromise, which they subsequently concluded on December 1, 1812. The following summer, the embattled minister's supporters purchased the pews of the disaffected parishioners, the proceeds going to the formation of "the Third Religious Society in Dorchester."[60] It seems unlikely that any of the principals knew at the time that the same fate which befell Dorchester's Second Church would soon come to pass in so many more churches of the Massachusetts Standing Order.

Eager to reveal the ways in which the Dorchester controversy proved

---

54. Allen, *Memoir*, 33.

55. Leonard Woods to Jedidiah Morse, March 23, 1809, Morse Family Papers, Yale University Archives.

56. Jedidiah Morse, *Annual Convention Sermon* (Boston, 1812), 21. Bound version is in Andover-Harvard Rare Books Collection, Cambridge, Massachusetts.

57. Morse cites the "declaration" of Christ in a letter to Reverend Bartlett, February 25, 1817, Morse Papers, Massachusetts Historical Society.

58. Evarts, "Review of Dorchester," 303.

59. Ibid.

60. Cooke, *Unitarianism in America*, 102, and Evarts, "Review of Dorchester," 304.

precedent-setting in relation to the ideological conflict over Unitarian doctrines and the growing divergence between church and parish in Massachusetts, historians have not adequately addressed the underlying causes of Dorchester's problems.[61] The question remains why the vast majority of parishioners chose—or at the least assented to its church's selection of— an orthodox cleric to become minister of the Second Church. Considering that candidate Codman explicitly detailed his belief that "the Father, Son and Holy Ghost to be the one living and true God," a belief that most parishioners did not share, the parish's actions become even more remarkable.[62]

From the orthodox point of view, the parishioners' machinations seemed particularly puzzling. Convinced that the parish objected not to ministerial exchanges but to "a dislike of the great truths, which Mr. Codman preached," the orthodox simply could not explain how the parishioners had so misread young Codman's missive.[63] The parishioners, for their part, argued that professions of creed "constituted no part of our complaint."[64] This fundamental disagreement reveals a great deal about the growing disaffection between Congregational Brahmins and orthodox, not so much in doctrine or creed, but in the place of religious doctrine within their respective outlooks. Religious doctrine was of paramount importance to the orthodox, especially the church communicants, who had undergone a rigorous religious examination to attain their status.[65] Convinced that the parishioners found Codman's orthodox beliefs and pronouncements anathema, they construed the controversy as a fight over doctrine. Accordingly, the church resolutely supported its minister's unyielding stance on exchanges; his conscience alone dictated who should preach from the pul-

---

61. The best recent reading of the importance of the Dorchester controversy for the future of the Standing Order is Wright, "Reconstruction."
62. Codman letter in Evarts, "Review of Dorchester," 258.
63. Ibid., 260.
64. *Memorial of the Proprietors*, 46.
65. Ann Douglas, among other historians, has noted that communicants were increasingly women, one aspect of what she called the "feminization" of the Unitarian ministry. Interestingly, of the primary supporters of the embattled Mr. Codman, the most vocal were the women. There were 181 female authors of a "masculine" note which read, in part, "we hope you will fight manfully, and come off conqueror, and more than conqueror in this important conflict." See Allen, *Memoir*, 85, and Ann Douglas, *The Feminization of American Culture* (New York, 1977), ch. 1.

pit of the Second Church, anything short of that being "inconsistent with Fidelity to our Master in heaven."[66] Furthermore, while the parishioners railed against Codman's non-intercourse, according to the church, they really resented his Calvinism, "the subject of exchanges [being] merely incidental and subservient to the true cause."[67] For the church, the fight was between "the religion of our fathers" and Brahmin heterodoxy.

Creed proved decidedly secondary to the Brahmin members of the parish. Busy with the more mundane aspects of everyday life, they were indifferent to the exact doctrinal attachments of their new minister. It was inevitable that Codman would "sometimes speak of doctrines that may not be altogether congenial to his listeners," because, after all, his listeners entertained a variety of beliefs.[68] Other aspects of the man were far more consequential to the parish committee which, as William Bentley accurately noted, "considered more important his wealth and opportunities," which appeared on the surface to be impeccably Brahmin.[69] As a Harvard graduate and a man of substantial resources and social standing, Codman's orthodoxy, like the so-called "Hopkinsianism" of Channing and the "Old Calvinism" of Eckley, would never interfere with his enjoying the best of relations with his Congregational colleagues.[70] When Bentley remarked that the parishioners "suffered for their haste and ignorance," he was only partially accurate.[71] They erroneously assumed that Codman, like the majority of the ministers of the Boston Association, subordinated creed to conviviality, and doctrinal uniformity to a catholic toleration. The controversy stemmed from this mistaken, fateful assumption.

Some of the specific conditions of the Dorchester environment facilitated the controversy. When similar circumstances came about in Princeton in 1817, Dedham in 1819, Cambridge in 1827, and Brookfield in

---

66. Dr. Samuel Miller to John Codman, November 19, 1810, in Allen, *Memoir*, 101.

67. Bates, *Reminiscences*, 186.

68. Codman letter in Allen, *Memoir*, 69–70.

69. Bentley, *Diary*, 4:64.

70. There is some debate about Channing's "Hopkinsianism," which has been ascribed to him almost exclusively on account of the fact that he attended some of that divine's services while at Newport, Rhode Island. Significant for this study is simply that both Channing and Eckley remained on the best of terms with Brahmin Boston, Channing attaining the rank of something of a cult hero. That is, until he embraced abolitionism, for years the kiss of death on State Street.

71. Bentley, *Diary*, 4:64.

1829, the same fight ensued, pitting church against parish. The crisis occurred in Dorchester first, because of its proximity to Boston, into which it later became incorporated. Two portentous interrelated conditions manifested themselves in Dorchester at the time of Codman's ordination and subsequently in the other towns: the social standing of the parishioners had clearly begun to outstrip that of the church communicants, and the parishioners wanted a church that gave them their due, as it were.[72] Parishes had disputes with their ministers for years, but could do little about it. By the second decade of the nineteenth century, the status of church communicants had declined to such an extent that parishioners, particularly wealthy ones, felt free to exert themselves to an ever greater extent in ecclesiastical affairs formerly restricted to communicants. Parishioners increasingly displaced the communicants, who had "figured so prominently in the early generations" of Massachusetts Congregationalism.[73]

In the second parish of Dorchester it was common knowledge that the disgruntled parishioners who "took the lead in this controversy" consisted of the "rich ones."[74] In an 1810 letter written to encourage Codman, Dr. Samuel Miller, Presbyterian minister in New York, urged the embattled minister to "patiently bear all the ridicule and insults of [his] proud and wealthy foes."[75] William Allen noted that Codman's opposition had "all the wit, and learning, and wealth, and power" on its side.[76] Codman's supporters convinced themselves, not without reason, that a great deal of Brahmin animosity derived from the orthodox's critical stance toward wealth and worldliness. "Had Mr. C.," argued Evarts, "countenanced such innocent amusements as playing at cards, and midnight reveling, it is altogether possible that he would have remained unmolested."[77] "That portion of his parish," Rev. Joshua Bates argued in a similar vein, "who commenced the opposition were a gay people, exceedingly fond of amusements; and there can be no doubt, that they were determined to oppose everything which

---

72. When a few members of the church proffered the parish's charges in a communicant meeting, they were overwhelmingly voted down. See *Proceedings of the Second Church*, 45–60.

73. Justin Winsor, *The Memorial History of Boston*, 4:404.

74. Leonard Woods to Morse, March 23, 1809, Morse Family Papers, Yale University Archives; Evarts, "Review of Dorchester," 260.

75. Miller to Codman, November 19, 1810, as quoted in Allen, *Memoir*, 106.

76. Allen, *Memoir*, 108.

77. Evarts in "Review of Dorchester," 260.

interfered with their opposition to week-day meetings and extra-lectures
. . . and his preaching so much on human depravity."[78] Bates's acid remark
about Codman's enemies being "exceedingly fond of amusements," demonstrates the class conflict underlying the religious controversy. In fact, of
the thirty-eight pews advertised for sale in 1810 in the *Columbian Centinel*,
virtually all were located on the main floor, the most exclusive location in
the meetinghouse.[79] When the controversy was finally settled in 1813, "Mr.
C. and his friends" agreed to purchase "the pews of all members of the
parish, "who would sign a declaration that they were disaffected towards
him."[80] The final amount of the purchase, "about $10,000," proved to be
such a colossal sum that only the personal "great wealth" of the minister
"enable[d] him to finish this project."[81] Very much like their Boston neighbors, Dorchester's wealthy parishioners had demanded a say in their
church commensurate with their status in the community at large, a demand the orthodox proved most reluctant to meet.

The events of the Dorchester controversy set the stage for a decade of
continued strife. The following year, the orthodox clergy made certain that
the smoldering conflict would not die by publishing a very long review of
the entire episode in the *Panoplist* that included the main documentation
from the orthodox side. One year later, Morse forced the growing split
between Brahmins and orthodox into public view with the publication, at
his expense, of a section of Thomas Belsham's *Life of Theophilus Lindsay*.
As a result of Codman's refusal to exchange pulpits with his brethren "of
heterodox or doubtful sentiments," as well as the active and relentless reaction of many of his parishioners, it can fairly be claimed that the Dorchester factions never reached a mutual understanding. The controversy cli-
maxed only with their mutual separation.[82]

Whether Codman intended to force the second parish of Dorchester to
split is not clear; what is certain is that Jedidiah Morse and other orthodox
stalwarts viewed the controversy as an opportunity to force a confrontation
between themselves and the Brahmins. For orthodox ministers like Morse

---

78. Bates, *Reminiscences*, 189.
79. *Columbian Centinel*, August 21, 1810.
80. Evarts, "Review of Dorchester," 303.
81. Bentley, *Diary*, 4:140; see also Evarts, "Review of Dorchester," 303–4, and Bates, *Reminis-
    cences*, 199.
82. Miller to Codman, as quoted in Allen, *Memoir*, 106.

and Evarts, who for years had argued in the pages of the *Panoplist* magazine of "the necessity of entire separation," the principles and issues at stake in Dorchester and defended by Codman were their principles, their issues.[83] What Codman's actions implied, that Brahmin ministers were beyond the pale of Congregational religion and should be denied communion, Morse and his allies made explicit.

One of the important, albeit ancillary, consequences of the controversy at Dorchester was the obvious failure of the two church councils to offer a reasonable settlement. For almost two centuries, Massachusetts Congregationalism had depended on councilors, called upon from outside parishes by mutual agreement of the interested parties, to adjudicate crises within congregations. Necessitated by the vaunted autonomy of individual churches within Massachusetts, councils adeptly handled the tasks for which they were convened. In the majority of cases, councilors were called to hear cases of local significance with no direct bearing on themselves and their parishes. As a result, there were few instances where a council could not reach a reasonable and relatively disinterested verdict. Dorchester was different. The conflict plaguing the second church between orthodox communicants and an increasingly vocal and liberal-minded parish was a microcosm of the state as a whole. Consequently, councilors from as far away as Worcester were practically direct parties in the case. They had neither the intention nor the ability to offer a disinterested hearing, and they knew it. Not surprisingly, as subsequent events made clear, the effectiveness of outside councils had reached its nadir.

The failure of the councils to resolve the Dorchester controversy was not lost on Morse. For years, he had lamented in public and private the inability of the "orthodox majority" to enforce its will over wayward ministers who went about their heretical business with impunity. Long convinced of the need for a presbyterian structure of consociation like that of the Connecticut Congregationalists, Morse manipulated the Dorchester controversy to coax his orthodox colleagues into considering the formation of a "Consociation of the pastors and Churches, and forming them into standing ecclesiastical Councils."[84] The tumult surrounding the Dorchester

83. Tracy, *Life of Jeremiah Evarts*, 70.
84. Morse, "Report to the General Association," reprinted in the *Panoplist* 11 (August 1815): 358.

controversy, Morse held, demonstrated the urgency of consociation to deal with the enemy.

The 1814 annual meeting of the orthodox General Association of Congregational Ministers—coincidentally meeting in Dorchester—provided Morse and his colleagues with their chance to convince the assembled ministers of the need for action. Dorchester had demonstrated the threat to orthodoxy and the dire urgency of collective action. A plan was necessary to unite the churches of the Standing Order, to create an effective means of enforcing doctrinal uniformity, and to examine prospective ministers and purge heterodox ones. In his position as moderator Morse proposed, and the association readily acceded to, the formation of a committee composed of Codman, Woods, and himself to fashion a plan of union. As part of their task, they undertook a study of Cotton Mather's so-called *Proposals of 1705*, which explored the need for a Massachusetts consociation a hundred years earlier, in order to determine whether "the plan of discipline there proposed, either entire, or with alterations and amendments" should be adopted.[85]

This committee of three presented its labor, the "Plan of Ecclesiastical Order," to the association at its meeting the following year and to the public in the August 1815 edition of the *Panoplist*.[86] Morse, Codman, and Woods hoped that this scheme, upon adoption, would finally establish some unassailable central authority that could check the growth of heterodoxy in Massachusetts.[87] Unite or else, they had warned in pages of the *Panoplist* for almost a decade. Here was the plan to do it.

Morse prefaced the "Plan" with a brief "Report to the General Association" in which he claimed that Bay State Congregationalism, as it was then constituted, woefully lacked the "vital principle of ecclesiastical order, discipline, and government."[88] It was crucial that "the particular churches

---

85. General Association of Ministers, "Annual Report to the Association," 10 *Panoplist* (August 1814): 236.

86. Morse had proposed a plan of union to the all-inclusive Annual Convention of Congregational Ministers, but without success. John Lowell reports that it "was thrown out, as I am told, with pretty strong expressions of general disgust." See John Lowell, *An Inquiry into the Right to Change the Ecclesiastical Constitution of the Congregational Churches of Massachusetts* (Boston, 1816), 29.

87. Jedidiah Morse et al., "Plan of Ecclesiastical Order," printed in the *Panoplist* 11 (August 1815): 359–74, and in Lowell, *Inquiry*, 1–16.

88. Morse et al., "Plan," 366.

should all be united in one federative and well ordered community,"[89] so that they would have the means to undertake actions necessary to stem "the decay in the power of godliness."[90] Anticipating the inevitable Brahmin criticism that the plan was a gross betrayal of Congregational practice, Morse noted that "such a Consociation the Platform of our church decidedly favours; the principles for it were explicitly set forth, in distinct Propositions, adopted by the venerable Synod, composed of the elders and messengers of the churches, and holden at Boston in the year 1662."[91] Cotton Mather emphatically reinforced the call for consociation in his *Proposals of 1705*, arguing that they were "not only lawful, but *absolutely necessary*."[92] Some form of central governing body, innovative or not, was essential to the well-being of Congregationalism.

"A Consociation of the churches," the Morse plan stated, promised to address a number of pressing problems within the Standing Order. The plan confronted three issues directly: the "prevailing neglect of discipline towards offending members of churches," as Dorchester had amply demonstrated; the fact that there was "no regular and acknowledged method in which congregational churches can exercise a christian watch and care" over each other; and the "want of a settled and effectual method of calling ministers to account for immorality and errour, and of protecting them against calumny and injustice."[93] A consociation, the plan promised, could settle these problems effectively and with alacrity. In doing so, the Standing Order would once again be composed of a ministry with strict, uniform beliefs, fully capable and willing to enforce its will upon would-be dissenters.

---

89. Ibid.

90. See the *Panoplist* 4 (March 1806): 455.

91. Morse et al., "Plan," 367. George Ellis in 1889 certainly agreed with Morse on this score, stating that included in the "theory and practice of Congregationalism . . . was the full and perfect right, under the New Testament pattern, for each company—of convenient size—covenanted together to choose, institute and ordain all officers, pastors, teachers, ruling elders, and deacons needed by them in a congregation or church for teaching and ordinances." George Ellis, "Channing Hall Lectures," in *Unitarianism: Its Origin and History* ed. George Ellis (Boston, 1889), 132.

92. Morse et al., "Plan," 366, 359. John Lowell ridiculed the fact that "a manuscript of Dr. Cotton Mather is brought forward with as much parade, as if he had been an apostle. This so exceedingly resembles the monastick artifices of the dark ages . . . that it excites our jealousy, if not our contempt." Lowell, *Inquiry,* 40.

93. Morse et al., "Plan," 364.

Morse, Codman, and Woods could no doubt envision themselves at the head of such a potent organization, finally able to vent their wrath against the Brahmins. From such a position, they could "hear and decide upon any complaint or allegation, touching ministerial character, against any minister belonging to it; to acquit, or to find guilty—to advise, sustain, or depose, as the case may require."[94]

It was immediately clear to the Brahmins that the proposed "Plan of Ecclesiastical Order" was designed to expose their doctrinal differences with orthodoxy in order to break all ties of Christian fellowship. Coming so quickly on the heels of the Dorchester controversy, and authored by Codman, Woods, and Morse, the "Plan" confirmed Brahmin suspicions that Codman's "refusal of communion" was part of a larger orthodox scheme to brand Brahmin latitudinarianism a heresy. The parishioners of Dorchester had been right about Codman and his intentions. "To decline so long to exchange with the members of the Boston Association was a refusal which amounted to a denial of their ministerial character, a condemnation of a respectable body of men, an impeachment of their fidelity, and tended to stigmatize them as heretics."[95]

It is little wonder that the orthodox plan of union "was thrown out with . . . general disgust" by the doctrinally diverse annual Convention of Congregational Ministers.[96] Similarly, Charles Stearns, minister of the Church of Christ in Lincoln, Massachusetts, delivered a plea for tolerance and understanding in the keynote sermon to the convention in 1815. "There is a principle which ought to be recognized by all Christians that one Christian had just as good a right to interpret the scriptures, as another, supposing them on equal ground of office, or ecclesiastical condition. Nor has any one a right to impose his interpretation on his brother disciple."[97] Orthodox insistence upon doctrinal uniformity, as in the Andover Associate Creed, was not only wrong, but if enforced by a powerful conciliar institution, would necessitate each Brahmin and orthodox "to fight in his post like hardy Trojans, or well-equipped Grecians for the fate of religion and

---

94. Morse, "Report to the General Association," 358.
95. Quoted in Allen, *Memoir,* 88.
96. Lowell, *Inquiry,* 29.
97. Charles Stearns, *A Sermon Delivered before the Convention of Congregational Ministers in Massachusetts, at their Annual Meeting in Boston, June 1, 1815* (Boston, 1815), 12.

church, as they for the fate of Helen of Troy."[98] With Morse and Codman clearly in mind, Stearns warned that "there are men who are frequently, some almost continually, dipt in controversy," men who were aiming to tear the Standing Order asunder.[99] "Is it not certain," he asked his brethren, "that *he loves fighting who always fights?*"[100]

The responsibility of writing a direct response to Morse and the orthodox "Plan of Ecclesiastical Union" fell to John Lowell, who emerged—with Andrews Norton—as the principle advocate for the Brahmin cause by the 1820s. Under the pseudonym "A Layman," Lowell published a lengthy pamphlet entitled *An Inquiry into the Right to Change the Ecclesiastical Constitution of the Congregational Churches of Massachusetts*, which included a copy of Morse's 1815 "Report to the General Association."[101] Lowell had two objectives: to show how the Morse plan was "directly opposed to the constitution of this state, if not subversive of the rights and liberties of the Congregational churches"; and to argue that any plan of consociation was "subversive of the religious liberties of the people, and tending directly to the most dreadful anarchy in the Church."[102] According to Lowell, the true ambition of Morse and his colleagues proved to be little more than a power grab at the expense of individual congregations and their parishioners.

Lowell first sought to demonstrate how the Morse plan was "an entirely new form of Church government," without precedent either in the history of Congregationalism or in that of postrevolutionary Massachusetts.[103] The venerable "British Encyclopedia, revised in this country and reprinted by Dobson" clearly stated, Lowell pointed out, that the "independence" of each congregation was a distinguishing feature of Congregationalism; "every church ... is a body corporate, having full power to do every thing which the good of the society requires, with out being accountable to any classis, synod, convocation, or other jurisdiction whatever."[104] Lowell went on to cite Mosheim's *Ecclesiastical History*, which notes "that neither Christ

---

98. Ibid., 14.
99. Ibid.
100. Ibid., 16; emphasis in the original.
101. Lowell, *Inquiry.*
102. Ibid., 18–21.
103. Ibid., 29.
104. Ibid., 30.

himself, nor any of his Apostles, have commanded any thing clearly and expressly concerning the external form of the church, and the precise method according to which it should be governed."[105] As for "the present day, it is difficult to see any reason why one or more churches, in combination, should exercise an authority in matters of faith and discipline over other churches."[106] The Massachusetts Constitution of 1780 forbade the establishment of "any precise form of church government" argued Lowell, particularly "the 3rd article, . . . which proves the absolute equality of all Christian churches."[107] Lowell thus concluded that the Morse plan was "directly opposed to the constitution of this state, if not subversive of the rights and liberties of the Congregational churches."[108] By any measure, then, "consociationism" promised to be, or would in no time prove to be, a radical innovation.[109]

Far more ominous in Lowell's view were the autocratic elements of the Morse "Plan of Union," which would "restore those hierarchical establishments which were calculated to exalt the clergy" while keeping the laity "in a state of servitude to the privileged orders of the Clergy."[110] The Morse plan was autocratic both in relation to the individual congregations from which "judicial power is taken . . . and given to the Consociation," as well as toward "the people of the parish, the sole depositaries of sovereign power in all Church matters."[111] The parish must have "a voice, and the only voice" in the "introduction, discipline and dismission of ministers."[112] "What an absurdity," wrote Lowell, to invest any single ecclesiastical body with the power "to license ministers, to settle the mode of ordinations, and to exclude improper men from the ministry."[113] Insofar as the proposed consociation "arrogates to itself" the rights and privileges enjoyed by indi-

---

105. Lowell cites Johann Lorenz Mosheim's *Ecclesiastical History: Ancient and Modern* (Boston, 1810–11), 1:97. See Lowell, *Inquiry,* 33.

106. Ibid., 38.

107. Ibid., 33–34.

108. Ibid., 18.

109. See James Roland Beasley, "The Success of the Cambridge Platform: Interchurch Communion in Early Massachusetts" (Ph.D. diss., Tufts University, 1980) for a discussion of plans of consociation in the history of Massachusetts.

110. Lowell, *Inquiry,* 22.

111. Ibid., 36–37.

112. Ibid., 45.

113. Ibid., 34n.

vidual parishes and pastors and "annihilates the power of the people," Lowell argued, it represented a grave danger to all Massachusetts Congregationalists.[114] It was everyone's responsibility not to allow "Dr. Morse, out of pure love, as he pretends, . . . to slip on this yoke again."[115]

It seems ironic to think that Lowell, a distinguished lawyer and member of the Harvard Corporation, would find himself in the position of defending the democratic rights of the people. Like his Brahmin associates in the Congregational church, Lowell, a Federalist, harbored few illusions about the "middling sorts"; with his friend Fisher Ames, he believed that "vox populi was definitely not vox dei." Yet, Lowell and the Brahmins were playing the part of religious egalitarian in the second decade of the nineteenth century. "*The People* that is, the professing christians of every distinct church and society, enjoyed and exercised all ecclesiastical powers, even those of settling questions of faith and disputes in the church, as well as those of electing and dismissing their teachers."[116] That these individuals, conservative in well-nigh everything else, espoused extremely liberal sentiments concerning church polity must be explained in terms of church-parish relations. The Brahmin clergy were not defending the rights of the people so much as the rights of the parishioners and the committees on which they served. As the Dorchester controversy made evident, the confrontation in the Standing Order between Brahmin and orthodox clerics was equally between parishioners and communicants. While the orthodox ministers found allies among the doctrinaire and exclusive church communicants who had gone through an exacting and rigorous conversion process, the Brahmins allied themselves with the parish, which was becoming more amorphous and powerful at the same time. When the parishioners came to use their strength, which derived in large measure from the Massachusetts Constitution of 1780, they did so at the expense of the orthodox communicants.

The controversy at Dorchester progressed very much along the same social lines as did the church-parish conflicts in Sandwich, Princeton, and Tyringham. The Tyringham fight was resolved finally before Massachusetts Chief Justice Theophilus Parsons, who wrote in his decision that "By the *constitution* the rights of the town are enlarged, if it choose to exercise

---

114. Ibid., 36.
115. Ibid., 36.
116. Ibid., 37.

them, and those of the church *impaired*."[117] Like Boston, many other towns of eastern Massachusetts came to witness an alliance of sorts between Brahmin pastors and parishes against orthodox clergy and churches. Parishes supported Brahmin ministers who, in turn, supported them.

A further irony emerged in the course of the debate over the orthodox's plan of consociation. The Morse Committee "Report" and Lowell's "Inquiry" revealed opposing views on the current state of affairs in Massachusetts, particularly concerning the prevailing religious climate. The orthodox report and related articles in the *Panoplist* betrayed a remarkable pessimism, even desperation. Massachusetts society was in an evil state, the orthodox argued, as evidenced by the "visible decline in the order, discipline, purity, and fruitfulness of the Churches."[118] This almost unbounded pessimism, insofar as it encouraged the orthodox to undertake the most strident efforts to save the doctrinal uniformity of the Standing Order, proved rather problematic. Already estranged from the Brahmins of the eastern part of the state, the orthodox alienated the vast majority of the middle classes who were not Congregationalist, as well as Congregationalists whose orthodoxy was only lukewarm. Orthodox Congregationalism once again became attractive to the middle classes only after it dropped its unpopular stand in defense of a powerful Standing Order. Once orthodoxy dispensed with the notion of maintaining the Standing Order in favor of the voluntarist approach of Lyman Beecher, soon to join the orthodox as minister of Hanover Street church, its age-old populist rhetoric concerning the ungodliness of the wealthy and the dangers of materialism drew a great deal of support from the middle classes. Chief Justice Isaac Parker's 1821 *Baker v. Fales* decision was all that was needed to cause orthodox Congregationalists to reverse themselves on the utility of the Standing Order.

The pessimism of the orthodox clergy, as evidenced in the Morse report, contrasted sharply with the optimistic sentiments of the Brahmins. Their more sanguine outlook contributed to their hostile stance toward their orthodox colleagues' energetic efforts to save the Standing Order. The decline of orthodoxy in Massachusetts, they argued, was not declension, and therefore did not necessitate a plan of ecclesiastical union or any other drastic measures. Lowell expressed the Brahmin view succinctly when he declared

---

117. *Avery v. Tyringham;* see Jacob Meyer, *Church and State in Massachusetts, 1740–1833* (New York, 1933), 184–99.

118. Morse, "Plan," 358.

that orthodox clamoring about the decline of religiosity "has been the prevailing one with certain men, in all ages of the church."[119] "It is," he continued,

> like the usual complaint against the seasons, the scarcity of money,
> and the general profligacy of the age in which we live. What peculiar
> evidence, or proofs the committee [which wrote the Plan of Ecclesi-
> astical Union] have on this point, we know not. We are persuaded
> of the contrary. This part of the country is unquestionably as correct
> in its morals, more disposed to publick worship, and as well inclined
> to attend the exercises of religion, to respect and honour its minis-
> ters, and to promote all publick institutions for the advancement
> and spread of christianity, as it has been in any former age.[120]

This kind of optimism informed Brahmin toleration and complacency,
while simultaneously infuriating the orthodox clergy.

Lowell's portrait of a tolerant clergy at peace with itself and given "respect and honour" from its parishioners contrasted markedly with the
"displaced elite" argument espoused for years by historians. "The clergy,"
wrote Lowell in 1816, "are much more learned and respected than they
were a century ago. The affectation of external sanctity," which for decades
mitigated against the clergy's acceptance, "has given place to a more natural and less pharisaical and assuming manner."[121] Accordingly, the Brahmins had good reason for optimism. Their salaries were the best in the
state, and would continue to be as long as they maintained their alliance
with the Bay State's wealthiest class. Their catholic interests and varied endeavors had ample opportunity for expression, their cultural institutions
were thriving, and mercantile patronage showed no signs of abating.

The position of the orthodox, approaching the third decade of the nineteenth century, proved far different and troubling. As long as they rigidly
espoused the need for a Standing Order in the face of mounting popular
sentiment against taxes in support of the clergy, they were in a quandary.
Defending their privileged position cost them support among their likely
allies, the middle classes, which were warming to the voluntarist and dem-

---

119. Lowell, *Inquiry,* 44.
120. Ibid.
121. Ibid.

ocratic sentiments of the Methodists and Baptists. Its support dwindling, orthodoxy had to embrace new methods or else witness its fortunes continue to wane. Ironically, it was a court defeat at the hands of the Brahmins in the modest little town of Dedham that simultaneously triggered their adoption of voluntarism and the renewal of orthodoxy in Massachusetts.

CHAPTER 7

Toward Disestablishment

FOR ALMOST TWO CENTURIES the Standing Order of Congregational churches was one of Massachusetts's most venerable institutions. Bound by no specific articles of faith nor by statute to any civil authority, the clergy nonetheless constituted society's most powerful voice. The sole legal status enjoyed by its members stemmed from the 1692 act requiring towns to support their ministers. Nevertheless, people took notice when such eminences as Thomas Shepherd, John Cotton, the Mathers, Henry Wise, Jonathan Edwards, Charles Chauncy, and their myriad associates spoke. In the deeply religious aural culture of provincial Massachusetts, Congregational ministers as God's messengers met vital emotional and intellectual needs of the community. As producers and transmitters of a refined strand of reformed Protestantism, the clerics utilized their cultural virtuosity to fulfill these critical functions in society. By means of several special talents, including biblical textual exegesis, the clergy's regular utterances provided nothing short of the ideological underpinning of the society. For generations, the ministers explained the nature of the world, both the permanent and fleeting; they extrapolated a set of rules of behavior on the basis of their ontological posits; and lastly, they so admirably fulfilled these functions that most members of the community largely defined themselves on the basis of their Protestant beliefs and their ties to Massachusetts Congregationalism. From John Cotton and the New England Way to Charles Chauncy and the American Revolution, the ministers of the Standing Order, "publick Protestant teachers," uniquely derived, defined, differentiated, and explained the events of the day. Richard Brown's claim that "knowledge is power" is more applicable to the Congregational clergy than any other group in American history. Supported by the state, yet without civil authority, the clergy received money, deference, and status on the basis of their cultural virtuosity well into the nineteenth century.

The ultimate crisis of the Standing Order—there had been numerous crises from which the institution had recovered—had many causes, some obvious, some more subtle. When disestablishment finally came in 1833, it proved to be little more than a formality. The General Court drafted, and the people of the commonwealth duly ratified, the eleventh amendment to the Massachusetts constitution, abolishing once and for all "the churches established by law in this government."[1] A church establishment, even in formerly Puritan New England, was considered an anachronism by the age of Jackson. Even Connecticut and New Hampshire, the last states with established churches, had dispensed with the institution more than a decade earlier. Growing numbers of Baptists, Methodists, and Universalists had transformed the religious culture of Massachusetts to such an extent that the Congregationalist majority had shrunk by some 30 percent in a generation. Yet, equally as important to the demise of the Standing Order as the growth of competing sects and the national movement toward the separation of church and state proved to be internal divisions within the Congregational ranks. The highly publicized and often bitter feud between Boston Brahmins and their orthodox opponents, dating back to the turn of the century, was the primary cause of disestablishment. On the one hand, residents who increasingly garnered information from multiple sources, most of which, like newspapers, were secular, became skeptical of the unique and high value formerly credited to the speech of their Congregational minister. How could the Standing Order claim to speak the one and only truth when its own ministers battled so bitterly among themselves? For their part, the ministers—Brahmin and orthodox alike—found little rationale for maintaining an antiquated institution that was but a shell of its former self. In the end, Congregational infighting killed the Standing Order.

For the first two decades of the nineteenth century, Brahmins and orthodox alike advocated the maintenance of established religion in Massachusetts. Continually at odds with one another, each party believed it benefited from the Standing Order, although on different and often divergent grounds. Both material and ideal interests informed orthodox support of

1. *Acts and Laws of the Commonwealth of Massachusetts* (Boston, 1834), 348.

the Standing Order. As stipulated in the Constitution of 1780, orthodox ministers' salaries depended on public taxation. Additionally, the clergy's continued conviction that humans were depraved convinced them that religion would not be supported voluntarily. Therefore, most orthodox ministers publicly defended the Standing Order as the only means to prop up religion. For their part, the Brahmins supported the preservation of the establishment for altogether different reasons. Their interest in the Standing Order proved largely political. Brahmins well knew that the privileged position of their Federalist party depended in no small measure on its continued endorsement by both Brahmin and orthodox Congregationalists. Stalwart support of the Standing Order, from which they as Bostonians gained no direct advantage, was the price they paid for united Congregational backing of Federalism. For the most part, Brahmins, who indirectly benefited from the establishment, let their orthodox colleagues, who had a more direct stake in its preservation, shoulder the bulk of its continued defense.

The year 1820 marked a turning point in the fate of the Standing Order. The Constitutional Convention of that year demonstrated the continued, albeit precarious, union of Brahmin and orthodox clergy in support of the Standing Order. Both parties managed to remain united just long enough to beat back a number of attempts to change Article 3 of the constitution of 1780, establishing the Congregational church. The convention concluded without proposing any significant alterations to the Standing Order, thereby ensuring continued state support of the Congregational clergy for the foreseeable future.

No sooner had the convention concluded its business than the orthodox and Brahmin wings of the Standing Order squared off for the final time. When Chief Justice Isaac Parker of the Massachusetts Supreme Court issued his *Baker v. Fales* ruling in February 1821, the Standing Order all but disintegrated. In what came to be called the Dedham decision, Parker confirmed the exclusive rights of the parish over the church in virtually all matters pertaining to the establishment, particularly those applying to church property. As a result, latitudinarian parishioners no longer felt obliged to compromise with orthodox church communicants. Left in a difficult position, communicants enjoyed a diminishing say in the operations of their parish church; nor could they secede to form new congregations without forgoing their rights to church property, which, according to Parker, was the sole possession of the parish. In essence, the Dedham decision declared that, as far as the state was concerned, the parish and not the church was the establishment. In Weberian terms, the state assumed a legalistic, as opposed to a corporatist, position in which the communicants possessed only an informal status, whatever the long-standing community practice. As a result, in the many churches that split along the same lines, Parker's Dedham decision threw the orthodox to the mercy of the Brahmins.

In many ways, the Dedham decision proved to be a grand irony. After all, for almost two decades the orthodox clergy had invested tremendous efforts in exposing and isolating the Brahmin apostates within the Standing Order. Now, with the stroke of a pen—a Brahmin one at that—all that struggle and sacrifice to purify the church, successful in large measure, had been for naught. Exposed and isolated, the Brahmins had become the establishment in the eyes of the state. This remarkable irony was completely lost on the orthodox because Parker's verdict promised to be such a complete and unqualified disaster for their cause. "We call the proceeding," the orthodox Enoch Pond declared on behalf of his brethren, "by the hard name of *plunder*."[2]

The Dedham decision removed the main material condition for orthodox support of the Standing Order. Not only could orthodox ministers no longer count on receiving tax support—for as soon as they broke from their parishes they ceased to be the oldest established church in their town—but also their tax money actually went to the support of their opponents from whom they had separated. The Dedham decision, in effect, put schismatic orthodox churches in an identical position vis-à-vis state taxation for the support of "Christian teachers" as that of the Baptists, Methodists, Universalists, and other dissenting sects. Such an anomalous condition necessitated some drastic changes for Massachusetts orthodoxy.[3]

At this moment of crisis, the orthodox secured the services of a promising new leader, Lyman Beecher of Connecticut. Beecher, as head of the Hanover Street Church in Boston, quickly displaced the vitriolic ministers

---

2. Enoch Pond, "Report on the Rights of the Congregational Churches of Massachusetts," *Congregational Quarterly* 5 (October 1863): 328.

3. In cases where incipient Unitarians split from an orthodox majority, the Dedham decision had similar results. Parker's pronouncement, by granting all legal right solely to the parishioners made compromise highly unlikely. Orthodox or no, in the wake of *Baker v. Fales*, communicants had virtually no chips with which to bargain with the parishioners.

who had been so instrumental in effecting the schism in the Standing Order. Out were the editors of the *Panoplist*, Jedidiah Morse, in particular, who by 1820 had tried the patience of his increasingly latitudinarian congregation at Charlestown.[4] Fresh from his fight over disestablishment in his home state of Connecticut, Beecher brought to the Bay State an intelligent and creative mind, as well as his seemingly inexhaustible fount of energy. His experience with disestablishment in Connecticut, which ran the gamut from despair to excitement, proved critical in leading orthodoxy in Massachusetts in a new and promising direction.[5] From the pulpit in his newly gathered Boston church, Beecher built on the fallout of the Dedham decision to bring his brethren to embrace voluntarism as the last, best hope for the future of Congregational orthodoxy. With fiery oratory and the adoption of revivalist techniques, Beecher and his colleagues rekindled orthodoxy at the very moment when the Standing Order was collapsing. By 1833, the termination of the religious establishment was welcomed by its former staunchest defenders.

As for the Brahmins, the Dedham decision confirmed, at least de jure, their long-held conviction that parishioners, not communicants, were the rightful heirs of the Standing Order. The verdict vindicated their position that Brahmin ministers and parishioners should not and could not be expelled from the Standing Order by orthodox zealots. But this vindication came at a price. As the orthodox gave up on the Standing Order, it became increasingly apparent that the Brahmins, shorn of their position as part of a large and diverse established church, albeit a feuding one, proved to be part of little more than an exclusive, predominantly eastern sect in an increasingly heterogeneous state. The formation of the American Unitarian Association in Boston in 1825 and the dedication the next year of Divinity Hall of the new divinity school at Harvard only confirmed the elitist nature of what came to be called Unitarianism. Its very exclusiveness, which became abundantly clear in the succeeding decades, proved its undoing, as the sect failed to grow much beyond the parochial confines of eastern Massachusetts. Like Laius and Jocasta, the Unitarians were eventually undone by their own children.[6]

---

4. See Joseph W. Phillips, *Jedidiah Morse and New England Congregationalism* (New Brunswick, N.J., 1983), 196–98.

5. See Barbara Cross, ed., *The Autobiography of Lyman Beecher* (New York, 1961), 1:251–60.

6. The harshest critics of "corpse-cold" Unitarians were the Transcendentalists like Theodore Parker and Ralph Waldo Emerson, the Brahmins' children.

In many ways, 1820 was an anomalous year in American history. It appeared to be an Era of Good Feelings; President Monroe ran unopposed for reelection, while Congress passed the Missouri Compromise, apparently placing the issue of slavery beyond partisan politics. Yet signs of uneasiness manifested themselves both in the splintering of the Republican party and in the promulgation of the antislavery Tallmadge Amendment. So, too, in Massachusetts, the year 1820 seemed to signal a compromise between the two feuding parties of the Standing Order. The successful preservation of the Standing Order in the constitutional convention in the face of numerous opponents reminded both factions of their mutual interest in its maintenance. This renewed union proved short lived, however, as the convention, called to confirm the separation of the free state of Maine, witnessed for the last time orthodox and Brahmins working together to preserve the Standing Order.

The separation of Maine from Massachusetts necessitated a constitutional convention, which met in Boston in the fall and winter of 1820–21. Many prominent citizens of the commonwealth attended, including John Adams, who was elected chairman but declined "on account of age and infirmity"; Daniel Webster; Joseph Story; Gov. Levi Lincoln; and Chief Justice Isaac Parker, who was about to decide the Dedham case.[7] With Parker serving as president, the convention convened on November 15, 1820. Many Federalists publicly expressed excitement in setting free their predominantly Republican neighbors to the north and turning Massachusetts into "a snug little Federalist state for the rest of their lives."[8] Nevertheless, many privately feared that calling a convention would provide their opponents with an opportunity to change the state constitution. While their fears were not realized in the main, the convention did take up several issues of the 1780 constitution, those of church and state paramount among them. The convention delegates created ten working committees, three of which examined the church establishment. The first reviewed the nature of Harvard's denominational affiliations; the second concerned itself with looking into changing the religious oath required of all state officers; and the third, and most important, committee critically scrutinized the Declaration of Rights, particularly as it pertained to establishing by taxation "public protestant teachers of morality."[9]

---

7. Alden Bradford, *History of Massachusetts from the Year 1790 to 1820* (Boston, 1829), 3:262.
8. Samuel Eliot Morison, *Life and Letters of Harrison Gray Otis* (Boston, 1913), 2:234.
9. *Journal of the Debates and Proceedings in the Convention of Delegates* (Boston, 1821), 1–11.

The great majority of the august gathering agreed with Judge Joseph Story "that the Constitution should be approached with great reverence, and that we should proceed with great caution."[10] With caution as the by-word and so many Federalist heavy hitters in attendance, the convention did indeed proceed slowly. The committee on Harvard, chaired by Josiah Quincy, who would soon become Harvard president, effectively beat back most challenges; calls for alteration came primarily from western delegates who had long resented Harvard's Brahmin character. One Republican critic went so far as to assert that Harvard, as "a spoiled child of the state," should be recognized as the private institution of a "particular denomination," and therefore ought to be stripped of all public funding.[11] In a response similar to his argument in the celebrated Dartmouth College case, Daniel Webster attempted to fend off in one grand flourish any alterations by contending that Harvard's "pre-existing corporate rights" precluded interference of any kind by the convention delegates.[12] Sensing the groundswell against the university, Webster and his allies made a tactical retreat, ultimately agreeing "that no injury would arise" to a minor change in that article of the constitution mandating that "the Clergymen, composing part of the Board of Overseers, are to be elected from Christians of a particular denomination."[13] The committee replaced it with the provision that Harvard's Board of Overseers "shall not hereafter be confined to any particular sect,"[14] a stipulation which met the overwhelming approval of Brahmin, orthodox, and dissenter alike.[15] The convention voted 227 to 44 in favor of the resolution.[16]

The second clash over the establishment focused on the oath taken by all state office holders, which amounted to an anachronistic religious test. Quakers and other dissenters argued that "swearing" anything, especially in a public ceremony, transgressed their rights; therefore, the provision

---

10. W. W. Story, *Life and Letters of Joseph Story* (Boston, 1851), 1:395.

11. *Journal of the Debates*, 43–47. For a fuller explication of Joseph Richardson's views as minister at Hingham, see his *An Oration Delivered in the South Parish, in Weymouth* (Hingham, Mass., 1828) in the Andover-Harvard Library.

12. "Report of the Committee to Inquire and Report upon the Constitutional Rights and Privileges of the Corporation of Harvard College," in *Journal of the Debates*, 245.

13. Ibid.

14. Ibid., 238–78.

15. The orthodox naturally supported this resolution. See chapter 4.

16. *Journal of the Debates*, 248.

should be stricken from the constitution. The committee, chaired by Webster, agreed on the whole with these criticisms and, sensing little risk, offered a provision by which Quakers could substitute "this I do under the pains and penalties of perjury" for "so help me God."[17] A few objections to this emendation were raised by the convention as a whole, the most strident coming from Boston merchant Samuel Hubbard. He argued that if citizens were "required to support the Christian religion, [was] it not wise to have Christian rulers?"[18] Hubbard went on to propose a substitute amendment, which left the oath intact, but it failed by a wide margin.[19] While the *Boston Recorder* worried over a decline of morality as a result of the new, relaxed oath,[20] the convention passed it without much debate, asserting that "the declaration of belief in the Christian religion ought not to be required . . . because it is implied, that every man who is selected for office, in this community, must have such sentiments of religious duty as relate to the firmness for the place to which he is called."[21] Like the resolution pertaining to Harvard, the proposed modification of the oath did not amount to much of an alteration.

Consideration of changing the Declaration of Rights engendered a great deal of interest, particularly amending Article 3 concerning public worship. Both within the committee charged to consider amendments and in the convention as a whole, proposed amendments varied from those that changed nothing to those virtually abolishing all ties between church and state. Expunging mandatory church attendance from the third article—a requirement that seemed to be a dead letter anyway—proved to be the only resolution upon which the majority agreed.[22] "The contest over the test oath and the corporation of Harvard University were minor skirmishes," wrote one historian, "compared with the battle over the Third Article of the Declaration of Rights."[23]

The real fight came when the convention began to debate the heart of Article 3: public support of the ministry. The first proposal, a rather mod-

---

17. Ibid., 65–66.
18. Ibid., 88.
19. Hubbard amendment voted down by 242 to 176. Ibid., 91–92.
20. See the *Boston Recorder*, May 13, 20, 27, 1820.
21. *Journal of the Debates*, 284.
22. Ibid., 161–63. The final vote as 296 to 29, the most lopsided vote in the convention.
23. Jacob Meyer, *Church and State in Massachusetts, 1740–1833* (New York, 1933), 192. This is the best book on the relation of church and state.

erate one, suggested incorporating, virtually verbatim, the 1811 Religious Freedom Act into the constitution.[24] Passed by a Republican legislature, this act effectively put unincorporated religious societies on even footing with incorporated ones by authorizing any taxpayer to have her or his religious taxes applied to any body of twenty persons or more that "have associated themselves together for the purpose of maintaining public worship."[25] Since the 1811 act had never been repealed, this resolution would only have written the status quo into the constitution. Significantly, alarmists on both sides immediately set out to defeat the resolution.

The Congregational position was set out by Leverett Saltonstall, a wealthy Unitarian of Salem. Saltonstall urged the committee to take no action at all: "it is not expedient to make any further amendment to the 3rd article," he declared, not so much for religious reasons, but on the most basic conservative grounds. "Corporate rights and privileges are sacred things," not to be tampered with lightly.[26] If the Religious Freedom Act of 1811 was effective, then the conservatives could see no reason to alter the fundamental constitution of the commonwealth.[27] The convention took little note of this argument, tabling Saltonstall's resolution by the vote of 159 to 110.[28]

The remainder of the debate centered around a resolution proposed by Henry Childs, maverick Congregational cleric of Pittsfield. Childs's proposal, by calling for each religious society, no matter what denomination, to raise its own funds, brought the debate into sharp focus.[29] The question was whether the people of Massachusetts should be compelled to support religious instruction or whether they would do so on a voluntary basis. Childs was answered by two Brahmin ministers from the Boston area, Joseph Tuckerman and Henry Ware. In an impassioned speech delivered a few days before Christmas, Tuckerman argued that "as no other state ever

---

24. This Republican-inspired act read: "All monies paid by any citizen of this Commonwealth to the support of public worship, or of public teachers of religion, shall, if such citizens require it, be uniformly applied to the support of the public teacher or teachers of his own sect or denomination, provided there be any on whose instructions he usually attends." See Edward Buck, *Massachusetts Ecclesiastical Law* (Boston, 1866), 44.

25. *Journal of the Debate,* 100–102.

26. Ibid.

27. Ibid., 163, 175–76.

28. Ibid., 161–90.

29. Ibid., 159.

did or can flourish without religion, any more than without a judiciary, it was quite as reasonable that every individual should be obliged to support religion in some form."[30] The establishment must be preserved; "not to do so would be pernicious."[31] A lay delegate from Boston may have elaborated the standpatters position best when he wrote that it was "the duty of the State to establish the Christian religion, because it aided the highest and best purposes of the State—its tendency was to make better subjects and better magistrates, better husbands, parents and children. It enforced the duties of imperfect obligations which human laws could not reach."[32] Ware and Tuckerman eventually prevailed. Childs's resolution went down to defeat by sixty votes.[33]

With both extremes defeated, the convention sought a compromise that would address the issue, but not go so far as to endorse the formal disestablishment of religion. Daniel Webster proposed the most interesting compromise, although it, too, was eventually rejected. Perhaps sensing the likely impact of the imminent Dedham decision, Webster submitted that orthodox and Brahmin be granted the same rights as dissenters in the Religious Freedom Act of 1811. Cognizant of the fact that the orthodox would not long support Brahmin churches from which they had split and vice versa, Webster wanted to make it possible for both sides to escape having their taxes go to any minister but their own. Remarkably, the vote on his plan resulted in a tie at 196 to 196 and so was tabled.[34] Any political recognition of the schism, many concluded, would spell the collapse of the Standing Order.

In the end, the only resolution amenable to the majority altered very little. In essence, it incorporated the basic thrust of the 1811 Religious Freedom Act into the constitution. The convention proposed that the religious stipulations of the Article 3 of the Declaration of Rights

> shall not be confined to Protestant teachers, but shall extend and be applied equally to all public Christian teachers of piety, religion and morality; and shall extend and be applied equally to all religious

---

30. Ibid., 165–66.
31. Ibid., 159–61.
32. Warren Dutton, as quoted in Richard Sykes, "Massachusetts Unitarianism and Social Change, 1780–1870" (Ph.D. diss., University of Minnesota, 1967), 168–69.
33. *Journal of the Debates,* 179.
34. Ibid.

societies, whether incorporated or unincorporated. . . . The clause
in the third article of the declaration of rights, which invests the
Legislature with authority to enjoin, on all the subjects of the Commonwealth, an attendance upon the instruction of public teachers,
shall be and hereby is annulled.[35]

The defeat of the Childs resolution and the substitution of this rather benign alternative signaled that, in the convention, at least, disestablishment
was impossible so long as both Brahmin and orthodox Congregationalists
remained united in championing the Standing Order, which they did for
the duration of the convention.

The Brahmins proved to be the most staunch defenders of the establishment at the 1820 convention, with the delegates from Suffolk and Essex
voting against the Childs resolution, the sole proposal for disestablishment,
by a margin of seventy to twenty-four.[36] That ministers like Tuckerman
and Ware backed the Standing Order at all requires some explanation, for
in many ways it seems anomalous to have Bostonians arguing that "providing for a system of moral instruction at public expense, as laying the only
sure foundation of free government."[37] After all, the provisions in the constitution establishing the Standing Order had no bearing on Boston. Boston, and Salem as well, had long enjoyed the privilege of voluntary support
of religion, a right that was reaffirmed in 1780, presumably on the basis
that Bostonians were more pious than their inland neighbors and therefore
needed no prodding to maintain their churches. Whatever the reasoning,
the fact remained that Massachusetts law had long since exempted Bostonians from any direct consequences of the very establishment they were
assiduously defending.

The Brahmin defense of the establishment at the convention stemmed
from several factors. The most obvious was that orthodox ministers, long
the most ardent defenders of the Standing Order even while attempting to
purge their erstwhile Brahmin colleagues, had barely any representation at
the convention. If the movement toward disestablishment was to be
thwarted, it was up to the Brahmins. For their part, the Brahmins were
motivated by a mixture of principles and politics. In an 1820 sermon entitled "Religion a Social Principle," William Ellery Channing warned the

---

35. Ibid., 101–2.
36. *Journal*, 252.
37. Dutton in Sykes, "Massachusetts Unitarianism," 169.

delegates that religion went hand in hand with civil law in that it "diminishes the necessity of publick restraints."[38] It would be unwise, Channing concluded, "for a community to leave to private discretion any great interest, in which safety is involved."[39] Similarly, Brahmins also understood that politics in Massachusetts had for years revolved in large measure around religion. The backbone of Federalist support, especially outside of Suffolk and Essex, rested with the great body of Congregationalists.[40] As Henry Adams observed, Federalism's "strength lay in the Congregational churches."[41] With the separation of Maine, Federalists hoped to inure themselves from Republican encroachment for years to come. Continued defense of public support of Congregational ministers, who outside the Boston area embraced orthodoxy, proved to be the price eastern Federalists paid for orthodox allegiance in the interior.

The sole Bostonian to back disestablishment openly and constantly proved to be none other than Joseph Story. Story took it upon himself to challenge a number of court decisions favoring establishment and publicly supported the Religious Freedom Act of 1811, which had marked the first legal setback for the Standing Order.[42] Critically important, however, to the judge's backing of this "anti-Federalist" measure as well as his push for disestablishment in the 1820 convention, was that Story was a Republican. With William Bentley, minister at Salem, Story was one of the few Brahmins to have chosen Jefferson over Adams and Republicanism over Federalism. Accordingly, he had no political interest in the maintenance of a church establishment. He had, in fact, quite the reverse.

The "cordial union between the clergy, the magistracy, the bench and bar," as Henry Adams styled it, was not lost upon other Republican leaders, who railed against this unholy alliance.[43] "It has been my lot," wrote one

---

38. William Ellery Channing, *Religion a Social Principle* (Boston, 1820).

39. Ibid.

40. James Banner, among others, makes this point, devoting an entire chapter to demonstrating it in his *To the Hartford Convention: The Federalists and the Origins of Party Politics in Massachusetts, 1789–1815* (New York, 1970). More recently, Ronald Formisano wrote that the "Congregational clergy were nine-tenths or more Federal." *The Transformation of Political Culture: Massachusetts Parties, 1790s–1840s* (New York, 1983), 156.

41. Henry Adams, *The History of the United States of America during the Administrations of Jefferson and Madison* (New York, 1921; reprint, Chicago, 1967), 59.

42. See Story, *Life of Story*, 1:394.

43. Adams, *History*, 58.

Republican, "to be opposed by the clergy, from whom I received the most abusive treatment I ever met with. . . . According to the best information I have, there is not so useless and hurtful a set of men in our country as the clergy. A man needs not a great share of knowledge to see that as a body of men they are professed enemies of our Republican government."[44] Disgust with the Federalist clergy was rampant among Republicans throughout the state, but nothing exceeded Republican contempt for the public support of these partisans. The ringing words of Isaac Backus were typical of the animosity displayed toward the establishment. "[T]he teachers and rulers of the uppermost party in Massachusetts," he declared, "are as earnest as ever Pharaoh was, to hold the church of Christ under the taxing power of the world, to support religious ministers."[45] Backus, Story, and the other Republicans knew that just as the Standing Order secured the domination of the "upper party," disestablishment would destroy Federalism in this, its last stronghold.

The failure of the 1820 convention to pass any amendments seriously challenging the Standing Order greatly encouraged the Congregationalists, who had feared calling the convention in the first place. When the amendments proposed by the convention went to the citizens of the state for ratification, the standpatters were even more animated. Ware went so far as to call the results of the election "the most gratifying, the most encouraging, and the most honorable, that could have been anticipated."[46] The populace rejected five of the fourteen amendments proposed by the convention, including those pertaining to Harvard and the Declaration of Rights. After so much vitriolic debate, the last amendment concerning church establishment went down to defeat by over 8,000 votes out of a total of 31,000 cast. Considering that the turnout was less than half of the eligible voters, the magnitude of the defeat was staggering.[47] Jacob Meyer attributes this defeat to chicanery on the part of the delegates, who, like Jeremiah Mason, feared "mischiefs to the Constitution."[48] They buried the

---

44. Elias Smith, *The Clergyman's Looking Glass: Or Ancient and Modern Things Contrasted* (Boston, 1804), 34.
45. Backus is quoted in William McLoughlin, *New England Dissent: 1630–1833* (Cambridge, Mass., 1971), 1:652.
46. Henry Ware, *1821 Election Sermon* (Boston, 1821), 11.
47. *Journal of the Debates*, 633.
48. Meyer, *Church and State*, 200.

religious provisions among the other proposed changes to the Declaration of Rights, which pertained not to religion but to criminal justice. As for the amendment concerning Harvard, the voters simply read the word Harvard, decided they must be against it, and voted negatively.[49] Whatever the reasons for the defeat of the amendments, the 1821 vote should not have cheered the defenders of the establishment, as it proved to be their last victory. The Dedham decision was about to explode the allegiance of the orthodox to the establishment and, in the process, precipitate the final crisis of the Standing Order.

The problems at the First Church of Dedham commenced when Joshua Bates, Dedham's minister since 1803, asked to be released from his pastorate in order to become the president of Middlebury College in Vermont. The year was 1818, and at least some part of Bates's decision to depart stemmed from the simmering tensions, so characteristic of many Massachusetts congregations, between Dedham's parishioners and orthodox communicants. The former faction, according to one contemporary, had long been exercised over Bates's consistently orthodox ministry. "Dr. Bates did so explain and enforce some of the christian doctrines," wrote Erastus Worthington in 1827, "that they always have excited doubts and controversy, and probably always will. This produced unfriendly criticism, which in turn exposed those who doubted, to the renewed charge of heresy and irreligious propensities."[50] Accordingly, the parish proceeded at once to secure a new pastor more to their liking. And, as with Dorchester, Princeton, and many other eastern towns, increasingly wealthy and influential parishioners were not about to brook much opposition from the shrinking body of church communicants. The next pastor would be their man.

In the first six months of 1818, the Dedham post was temporarily filled by Alvan Lamson, a recent Harvard graduate and "a scholar and a man of fair external character."[51] On the last day of August, upon the recommendation of a parish committee, Lamson was elected Dedham's new pastor by a vote of eighty-one to forty-four. The parish, "here voting as legal proprietors," comprised both church and non-church members and held col-

---

49. Ibid.

50. Erastus Worthington, *The History of Dedham from the Beginning of Its Settlement* (Boston, 1827), 111.

51. Samuel Haven, *Statement of the Proceedings in the First Parish and Church in Dedham, Respecting the Settlement of a Minister, 1818* (Cambridge, Mass., 1819), 9.

lectively "four fifths of the taxable property of the town."[52] In short, they were the wealthy. Problems started when the church voted not to assent to the parish choice by the narrow vote of seventeen to fifteen.[53] The parishioners, spoiling for a fight and exuding the confidence of a great numerical majority, sought to secure their man, the church's objections notwithstanding. They decided to convene an ordination council consisting of ministers and laymen from thirteen area churches, a veritable who's who of Massachusetts Brahminism including the likes of Ware, William Ellery Channing, and Harvard president John Thornton Kirkland.[54]

This distinguished group met on October 28 to ordain Lamson, but not before it was subjected to a lengthy harangue delivered by Samuel Haven of the Dedham church. Haven's speech, which was subsequently published as *A Statement of the Proceedings of the Church in the First Parish in Dedham,* remonstrated against a number of Brahmin assumptions. Haven emphatically declared that since the time of the Cambridge Platform, "church tradition and usage" demanded that only the church could ordain a minister, a position the orthodox steadfastly adhered to throughout the crisis. In ordaining Mr. Lamson the following day, the council rebuffed Haven, stating that the Brahmins "believe that this usage, founded on different circumstances of the Christian community, and on different laws of the commonwealth from those which now exist, is not to be considered universally necessary. In the present state of our religious societies, . . . we are bound to dispense with it."[55] The constitution of 1780 recognized the civic right, after all, of the parish to choose its "teacher." Whether the orthodox liked it or not, the parish majority was going to have its way in Dedham as it had in Dorchester and elsewhere.

None other than Henry Ware delivered Lamson's ordination sermon,

---

52. Enoch Pond quoted in George E. Ellis, "The Church and the Parish in Massachusetts: Usage and Law." Address delivered in Dedham, Massachusetts, November 19, 1888, as reprinted in *Unitarianism: Its Origin and History* (Boston, 1889), George E. Ellis, 148.
53. Worthington, *The History of Dedham,* 112.
54. Of Kirkland, Alvan Lamson once wrote: "I venerated and loved him, as I shall never venerate and love any other man." See letter from Lamson to William Sprague, reprinted in Sprague's *Annals of the American Pulpit* (New York, 1865), 8:273.
55. *Result of the Ecclesiastical Council, Convened at Dedham, October 28, 1818, to Assist at the Ordination of Rev. Alvan Lamson, over the First Parish in Dedham,* reprinted in Henry Ware, *A Sermon Delivered at the Ordination of the Reverend Alvan Lamson as the Minister of the First Church in Dedham* (Dedham, Mass., 1818), 36.

which, not surprisingly, echoed many long-standing Brahmin notions about toleration and catholicity of sentiment, a theme no doubt reflecting the gathering's uneasiness with their present actions. "It is not without much deliberation," Ware observed, "that the ordaining council have come to the determination to proceed to the ordination of the candidate, whom you have chosen in opposition to the opinion and wishes of so large and respectable portion of the church and religious society in this place."[56] Yet he acknowledged that the proceeding was "an unavoidable evil," whose cause was the lack of charity displayed by that "respectable portion" of communicants who failed to come to terms with the "diversity of taste, opinion, and views in the members of a christian society."[57] Ware and his colleagues reluctantly resolved: "Whereas cases may exist, in which a majority of a church do not concur with the religious society in the call of a minister, *Voted,* as the sense of this council, that such cases may still be so urgent, as to authorize an ecclesiastical council to proceed to the ordination of the candidate over said society."[58] While it was "a christian and a social duty not to inflict that disappointment willingly and unnecessarily," Ware concluded before the gathering that the council had no other choice but to sanction the parish's decision.[59] In short, that it had come to this was the orthodox communicants' own fault.

With Lamson duly ordained, the church communicants found themselves in a seemingly intractable dilemma. The majority of the communicants, together with the minority of the parish who were dissatisfied with Lamson's unorthodox ordination, hastily convened an ex parte council to consider its options. The clergy of the "churches in this association, which did not attend on a late session at the invitation of the parish" assembled in Dedham on November 18 for a two-day meeting.[60] Not surprisingly, the orthodox divines concluded that, in ordaining Lamson, the parish had usurped the privileges of the church. "In the settlement of a minister in the first church and parish," the report read, "the parish in opposition to the wishes of the church, have proceeded to settle a public teacher of religion and morality, not in accordance with the accustomed

---

56. Ware, *Sermon,* 22.
57. Ibid., 23.
58. *Result of the Ecclesiastical Council,* 34.
59. Ware, *Sermon,* 23.
60. Haven, *Statement of the Proceedings,* 84.

and pacific proceedings of congregational churches in New-England, nor in the judgment of this council, was this one of those cases of necessity, which in the opinion of some would justify such a procedure."[61] The assembled divines could do little more than confirm the prevailing "state of gloom and distress" and condemn the parish's outrageous proceedings.[62] The sole advice offered to the communicants, that they boycott Lamson and hold their own services, resulted in disaster. On November 15, 1818, at a meeting duly called for the purpose, Alvan Lamson was elected pastor by the assembled members of the First Church sympathetic to the parish. Those opposed to Lamson, having taken the advice of their ex parte council, declined to attend and otherwise ceased all relations with their opponents.

The seceding element of the First Church of Dedham, considering itself to be the true church insofar as it constituted the majority of the communicants, instituted a motion to regain possession of the meetinghouse and the rest of the church property. The members of the parish naturally responded in kind, instructing Eliphalet Baker, their newly elected deacon, to bring a legal motion against the seceding church and its nominal head, Deacon Fales. In consequence of these competing and mutually exclusive claims, "a law suit of great interest and importance arose, in which the first Parish, and the church connected with it, were one party, and the seceding members the other."[63] This was the case of *Baker v. Fales.*

The fissure between church and parish in Dedham that resulted in the protracted lawsuit was typical of the two-decade-old schism in the Standing Order. The orthodox church communicants attributed the turmoil to the parish's "want of such a spirit of condescension, as seems best adapted to produce and preserve unity."[64] As for the religious sentiments of parish, and of parishioners in the Bay State generally, the communicants and their sympathizers did not hold back any criticism. "We have said," the orthodox ex parte council noted with asperity and irony, "that a majority of the inhabitants of any town or parish may be deists or atheists, and not be chargeable with hypocrisy. We go further, and ask whether in many places

61. Quoted in Worthington, *The History of Dedham,* 113.
62. Haven, *Statement of the Proceedings,* 84.
63. Worthington, *The History of Dedham,* 113.
64. W. Greenough et al., "Result of the Council Convoked by the Church," in Haven, *Statement of the Proceedings,* 90.

it is not in fact the case that a majority neither believe nor disbelieve, and have neither knowledge or concern enough about the subject, to qualify them to select a minister."[65] Not only, then, did the traditional right to select a minister rest with the church, but so did the necessary spiritual qualifications, for only the communicants' religiosity was beyond reproach.

While the communicants railed about the decline of religion, the Dedham parishioners, echoing their Brahmin allies in Boston and beyond, attributed the controversy to the orthodox want of toleration. "Ministers of our holy religion, servants of the same master," Ware declared in his ordination sermon, "should allow no difference of opinion to impair their mutual esteem—to interrupt their christian fellowship," an obvious reference to the now universal practice of the orthodox to refuse exchanging pulpits with Brahmins.[66] The "diversity of taste, opinion, and views in the members of a christian society," was not to be lamented and contested, but celebrated, leaving final judgment of the religious nature of private citizens to "the great Head of the Church."[67] Peace could be attained so easily, if only the orthodox would practice toleration.

The one matter upon which both Brahmins and orthodox agreed was their mutual fear for the future. Coming at the end of a decade of disputation, the Dedham controversy portended poorly for the Standing Order. Ware admonished the Dedham parish in 1818 that the "Prospect before us is not that of unclouded serenity—your situation is not without its difficulties and trials, and dangers. There will be more than ordinary demand for wisdom and prudence, and fortitude, united with a spirit of conciliation."[68] With at least as much apprehension, Samuel Haven worried that the schisms and infighting among the Congregationalists "have so torn to pieces the Congregational charter, and scattered it to the winds, that they cannot put together its parts, nor hold anything under it."[69] As it quickly became apparent, both Haven and Ware had good reason to be fearful for the future.

Chief Justice Parker handed down his ruling during the March term of

---

65. Ibid., 93.
66. Ware, *Sermon,* 16–17
67. Ibid, 18, 23.
68. Ibid., 20.
69. Haven, *Statement of the Proceedings,* 87.

the 1821 Massachusetts Supreme Court session. The decision resolved two thorny issues concerning the relationship of church and parish in Massachusetts. The first dealt with the parish's election and ordination of Alvan Lamson, which the Dedham parish insisted was its prerogative, over the objections of the church. The second and more momentous issue was deciding precisely which group the state considered the legally incorporated First Religious Society of Dedham, a status both the parish and the church claimed. The latter issue proved important because all church property belonged to the legally recognized society. In both cases, Parker found for the parish.

Orthodox reaction to Parker's ruling, while not swift, proved to be acrimonious. Since Isaac Parker was a Harvard graduate, a Federalist, and a Bostonian—in short, the very embodiment of the Brahmin ideal—the Dedham church as well as orthodox Congregationalists from across the state ridiculed the decision as unfair and the chief justice as prejudiced and corrupt.[70] One member of the clergy, so outraged by the Supreme Court's endorsement of "plunder," passionately called upon the courts of Massachusetts "to revoke these unrighteous decisions, and put the Congregational churches of the State upon their original and rightful basis."[71] More recently, Conrad Wright has labeled Parker's decision "bad law based on a misreading of history," which needlessly and senselessly provoked the orthodox and their sympathizers.[72]

Parker reasoned in the Dedham case that the constitution of 1780, Article 3 of the Declaration of Rights in particular, designated the parish as the only legal—that is, incorporated—religious society recognized by the state. Accordingly, in all matters of the establishment in which the state recognized, invested with powers, or otherwise interacted with an incorporated body, that body must be the parish. Parker concluded, therefore, that in the Dedham case and throughout the Bay State "whenever a parish determines to assert its constitutional authority, there is no power in the state to oppose their claim."[73] Thus Dedham's first parish had been within its

---

70. The *Boston Recorder* printed the articles most greatly opposed to the decision. See *Recorder,* June 23, October 27, 1821.

71. Pond, "Report," 415.

72. Conrad Wright, "Institutional Reconstruction in the Unitarian Controversy," in *American Unitarianism, 1805–1865,* ed. Conrad Wright (Boston, 1989), 26.

73. *Baker v. Fales,* in Dudley Atkins Tying, *Reports of the Cases Argued and Determined in The Supreme Judicial Court of the Commonwealth of Massachusetts* 16 (Boston, 1811–23): 488–522.

rights to ordain the minister of its choice and, far more importantly, to claim its guardianship of all the property held in the name of the First Church of Dedham.

The orthodox communicants were confronted with a bitter pill. The fact was, they had left their own church, its meetinghouse, its silver, and its name. In short, they had seceded not as the First Church of Dedham but as individuals. As the decision made clear: "the secession of a whole church from a parish would be an extinction of the church, [so] it is competent to the members of the parish to institute a new church, or to engraft one upon the old stock if any of it should remain."[74] The church was only part of the parish, which constituted the official religious society. Faced with this result, communicants could either stay within the parish church or secede as individuals. The Dedham communicants, concluded Parker, had done the latter.

Whatever the merits of the case, whether it was "bad law" or a Solomonic decision, the Dedham case proved to be no more than the last in a series of controversies, most of which ended up in the courts, that reflected the weakening position of the traditional communicants vis-à-vis the parish. The secularizing trend that had initially manifested itself in the Brahmin churches of Boston had spread to surrounding towns, such as Dedham and Dorchester, and to centers of increasing commercialization, like Worcester. In each case, as fewer and fewer men of rank sought to become communicants, their status declined, particularly in comparison to that of the parishioners. As long as orthodox ministers were able to use the power of the Standing Order to browbeat their parishioners and to guarantee their own salaries, they had little to fear. But once the rift between Brahmin and orthodox became acute, and Harvard-educated ministers with tolerant demeanor and an easygoing literary style became available, communicants could do precious little as they witnessed wealthy parishioners exert their influence in virtually all church matters. Parishioners, no longer especially respectful of communicant status, inevitably demanded a position within their religious societies commensurate with that of their wealth, while simultaneously making it clear that their tax monies would support a ministry of their liking. The Dedham decision only confirmed the parish's right to put its mouth where its money was.

The Dedham case, "unsupported by reason, or the laws, and of fatal influences upon the liberties, if not the existence, of the churches," proved

---

74. Ibid., 415.

to be a watershed for orthodox Congregationalists.[75] As long as they constituted a minority within a given parish, which they generally did, the orthodox were essentially divested of all legally recognized rights. Their epic
struggle of the past two decades to split the Standing Order had been a
Pyrrhic victory, as virtually all the spoils of that bitter struggle went to
their enemies. The Dedham decision meant that the orthodox accrued no
material benefit from the Standing Order, as meetinghouse, communion
silver, and all other properties of the parish church belonged to the parish.
Thus, the State of Massachusetts put the orthodox in a position analogous
to that of a dissenting sect, forcing them to pay taxes to support Brahmin
pastors whose views they believed heterodox and whose services they refused to attend. The significance of Dedham, then, was to force the orthodox to reconsider in its entirety their position concerning a religious establishment. After 1821, the orthodox felt more of the burdens than
the benefits of established religion in Massachusetts. By the time Lyman
Beecher was settled as pastor of the new Hanover Street Church in Boston,
most ministers were ready to rid themselves of the last vestiges of the
Standing Order.

The Brahmins of the Standing Order had been able to grow consistently,
if modestly, despite the schism between themselves and the orthodox.[76] The
rising tensions over the establishment had actually helped them insofar as
most people perceived them as far more tolerant and open-minded about
the relation of church and state than the orthodox. The incipient Unitarianism of the Brahmins expanded outward from its base in Boston during
the second decade of the nineteenth century for several interrelated reasons. Having taken over Harvard and its divinity faculty, Brahmins were
able to supply educated, Harvard-trained ministers to fill numerous pastorates beyond Boston, while at the same time, many communities, enjoying the material prosperity of the period, came to shun the righteous-
ness and rigidity so characteristic of orthodox Congregationalism.[77]
Secularizing parishes, like those of Dorchester and Dedham, became intent

---

75. *Spirit of the Pilgrims* 1 (February 1828): 10.
76. The number of Unitarian parishes in 1830, just prior to disestablishment, totaled 107.
77. Liberal, or Unitarian, parishes sprang up in predominantly urban areas, where prosper-
    ity and secularization progressed most rapidly. For a discussion of social class and liber-
    alism, see Richard E. Sykes, "The Changing Class Structure of Unitarian Parishes in
    Massachusetts, 1780–1880," *Review of Religious Research* 12 (1970): 26–34.

on getting their say in the selection of their tax-supported "public Protestant teachers." At the same time, parishioners deferred less and less to communicants, as "owning the covenant" lost its once estimable prestige.[78] In short, the supply of Harvard-trained, Brahmin ministers and the demand for tolerant teachers of the Gospel proved a perfect fit in the increasingly latitudinarian climate of eastern Massachusetts. Parker's decision in the Dedham case only confirmed in law a trend almost two decades old.

The Dedham decision resulted in the acceleration of the Brahmin-inspired anti-orthodox movement in the towns of Massachusetts. In some instances, like Taunton and Groton, parish takeovers engendered bitter opposition, as the conflicts spilled over into the popular press and into the courts. In smaller towns, the disputes proved less acrimonious but the results were similar, with anti-orthodox parishes gaining control of their religious societies. By 1833, according to a study made by the orthodox General Association of Massachusetts Ministers that examined "the condition of those churches, which have been driven from their houses of worship by town or parish votes," Brahmin inroads proved truly staggering.[79] Prepared by Richard Storrs, orthodox minister at Brookline, the General Association report concluded that eighty-one churches had been "exiled" as a result of disputes with their parishes, with more than half of the splits resulting, like Dedham, from parishes settling a minister unacceptable to the orthodox communicants.[80] According to the Dedham decision, the expatriated orthodox churches, because they had departed as individuals as opposed to incorporated bodies, forfeited virtually all their financial assets, often totaling many thousands of dollars. One recent historian estimated that "orthodox Congregationalism lost a third of its church buildings, or about $600,000," while a contemporary appraised the value of property surrendered to be more than $750,000.[81] Whatever the exact figure, the conclusion was abundantly clear: the crisis of the Standing Order called for new measures by the orthodox.

---

78. George E. Ellis in a speech delivered in Dedham in 1888 accurately assessed the significance of the Dedham case of 1821: "it was whether the owning of a covenant and the partaking of an ordinance should secure in a parish the same exclusive right which it once had in citizenship." See Ellis, *Unitarianism*, 154.

79. *General Association of Massachusetts Congregational Ministers Records 1830–1854*, Congregational Library, Boston, 89.

80. This report was reprinted in the *Congregational Quarterly* 5 (1863): 212–60.

81. Sykes, "Massachusetts Unitarianism," 167.

The first proposal to address the legal situation of the orthodox Congregationalists came from Lyman Beecher, who had witnessed the disestablishment of the Congregational churches in his home state of Connecticut a decade earlier. As the pastor of the Hanover Street Church in Boston, Beecher articulated the first new approach to the establishment in "The Rights of the Congregational Churches of Massachusetts," published in 1826 in the wake of the controversy at Groton.[82] For Beecher, the problem was that the recent Brahmin construction of the constitution of 1780 was far too legalistic, neglecting the essential point of the relationship between church and parish. Each body had different and complementary authority, based on its essential nature. The important rights and privileges of the church, "enjoyed from the beginning," particularly pertaining to the settling of a suitable pastor, stemmed from the higher religious station of the communicants.[83] Only the reinvigoration of the traditional position of the communicants, therefore, would reverse the trend toward parish domination of the Congregational churches. Otherwise, the "safe, natural, and propitious alliance, between the church and the town, for the support of religion, consecrated by prayer, sanctioned by experience, and confirmed by the smiles of heaven," an alliance cherished by the orthodox, would be "destroyed."[84] Beecher concluded that the health of orthodoxy in Massachusetts should not depend on the courts or the state, which catered, so it seemed, to the Brahmins. "The experience of the past," Beecher warned his colleagues, "is beginning to produce a conviction in the minds of those who have been most forward to propagate their peculiar opinions by the aid of legislation, that in the end, more will be lost to their cause than gained by it."[85]

Persuading the orthodox clergy that the establishment was unnecessary proved to be a formidable task. Convinced of the public's natural depravity, as late as 1820 the official orthodox position was that, since "the State derives its strength from . . . our sacred institutions, then all classes of the community ought to submit cheerfully to the burden of maintaining

---

82. Lyman Beecher, *The Rights of the Congregational Churches of Massachusetts. The Results of an Ecclesiastical Council Convened at Groton, Massachusetts, July 17, 1826* (Boston, 1827).
83. Ibid., 31.
84. Ibid.
85. Ibid., 46.

them."[86] Yet, as Beecher had experienced in Connecticut, if a community submitted "cheerfully" to maintaining its churches, then it would do so voluntarily. Voluntarism had not ruined orthodoxy in Connecticut. Quite the contrary: "it was the best thing that ever happened to the State of Connecticut."[87] With the protracted and concerted efforts of the clergy, disestablishment would not destroy the Bay State churches either.

His Connecticut experience had taught Beecher that voluntarism was a great opportunity. He was convinced that the Bay State clergy would, in the end, respond similarly to its brethren to the south, who "thought they should be destroyed if the law should be taken away from under them. . . . But the effect, when it did come, was just the reverse of the expectation. Our fears had magnified the danger."[88] In fact, disestablishment had "freed its leaders for larger fields," and given them the opportunity to reconsider their role in inculcating and maintaining the vital piety of the flock.[89] "We were thrown on God and on ourselves," wrote Beecher, "and this created that moral coercion which makes men work. Before we had been standing on what our fathers had done, but now we were obliged to develop all our energy."[90] As in Connecticut, orthodoxy in Massachusetts would be saved by the new measures associated with the so-called Second Great Awakening. In the hands of the orthodox clergy, revivalism would bring people back to true religion voluntarily.

For years, revivals had been anathema to most Massachusetts Congregationalists, who considered them primitive and somehow beneath the dignity of a minister of the Standing Order. Even the orthodox had read Charles Chauncy's brutal condemnation of enthusiasm; they feared that revivals reeked of Methodism and democracy, while their results too often proved short lived, or so the Bay State clergy believed. Beecher sought to change his new colleagues' minds not by words but by deeds. Accordingly, within one month of his installation at Hanover Street on the first day of

86. *Boston Recorder,* September 16, 1820.
87. Cross, *Autobiography,* 1:252.
88. Lyman Beecher in *Autobiography, Correspondence, Etc. of Lyman Beecher, D.D.,* ed. Charles Beecher (New York, 1864), 1:451.
89. Sidney Mead, "Lyman Beecher and Connecticut Orthodoxy's Campaign against the Unitarians, 1819–1826," *Church History* 9 (1940): 221.
90. Cross, *Autobiography,* 1:336.

spring in 1826, Beecher commenced a revival resulting in the conversion of several hundred souls—virtually tripling his congregation—and in the creation of the Hanover Association of Young Men.[91] When a like number of conversions and similar associations came to pass at the Park Street and Old South congregations, Beecher was well on his way to demonstrating the efficacy of the revival method, even in the staid communities of eastern Massachusetts.[92] This newcomer from Connecticut was fast becoming the leader of the orthodox clergy.

The success of revivalism in Massachusetts was palpable. Within the first five years of Beecher's pastorate at Hanover Street, the very heart of Unitarian Boston boasted nine orthodox churches where a few years prior there had been but two.[93] That revivals were the cause of the great increase in orthodoxy seems doubtless, as Massachusetts experienced, according to the *Boston Recorder,* an astonishing 116 revivals in 1831 alone.[94] Beecher hardly needed better proof that the success of orthodoxy, far from depending on the establishment, hinged on the orthodox minister's ability to "talk to the conscience and make people feel."[95] Voluntarism breathed new life into the clergy and enhanced its "God-given" ability to save souls. Leonard Worthington, a colleague of Beecher, put it another way: "If religion cannot support itself, and must sink, we will sink with it."[96]

The logical progression from Jedidiah Morse and the *Panoplist* to Lyman Beecher and his *Spirit of the Pilgrims* is not hard to recognize. Entailing far more than their ringing critique of the Brahmin enemy, the orthodox position throughout the first third of the nineteenth century hinged on their adamant distinction between those possessing vital piety and those who did not. Ever fearful of the encroachment of the parishioners, especially the well-to-do, the orthodox clergy tirelessly sought to defend the rights and privileges of the communicants, who held fast to the true faith. It mattered less what precisely constituted this faith than how the commu-

91. Ibid., 108–10.

92. *Boston Recorder,* March 23, 1826.

93. Increase N. Tarbox, "The Congregational Churches of Boston since 1780," in *The Memorial History of Boston,* ed. Justin Winsor (Boston, 1881), 3:410–16. The new churches included Salem Street, Pine Street, Brighton, Dorchester Village, and Mariners' Church.

94. *Boston Recorder,* December 28, 1831.

95. Quoted in Mead, "Beecher," 231.

96. Leonard Withington, *Sermon Preached at the Annual Election, May 25, 1831* (Boston, 1831), 48.

nity was constituted. The communicants owned specific privileges and powers because they had come together solely on the basis of their ritual confession of faith. They were the true church; they were the defenders of God's true community, and they deserved power and status commensurate with that rank. Church communicants and their orthodox leaders in the ministry, by right and necessity, constituted the sacred community.

For three decades, the orthodox did battle with the erstwhile brethren. They refused to join them in fellowship, declined to exchange pulpits, and unceasingly sought to expose the great rift between themselves and their opponents. Morse, Jeremiah Evarts, Leonard Woods, John Codman, and subsequently Lyman Beecher were convinced that parishioners, no matter how prominent in civil society, must play a subsidiary role in religious society. Wealth and status simply did not translate from the secular to the religious world. The orthodox featured less affluence and culture than their counterparts, but they were more holy, and in church society that made all the difference. On account of their greater faith, they deserved—and demanded—greater power.

Once the orthodox jettisoned the old Calvinist conviction that humans would not attend to the church without compulsion, it was a short and logical step to embrace the revivalist techniques of the awakeners. As in the case of the church against the parish, revivals promised a means to differentiate the voluntary followers of Christ from fellow travelers, as it were. By emphasizing the emotional and personal aspects of their faith, evangelical ministers could renew that vital piety so central to defining a true religious community.

The Brahmins, especially in and around Boston, had come to a very different understanding. Deeply religious to be sure, they acted on the premise that religion was not necessarily the focal point of the community. In the increasingly complex society of the early republic, the church no longer dominated the Massachusetts landscape. The Brahmins differed fundamentally from the orthodox about many vital issues relating to the role of religion in society. In redefining the function of the minister, Brahmins rejected the "great stress" orthodox placed on "what is sometimes called the pastoral duty, on personal intercourse, that is to say, of the minister with his congregation."[97] In its place, the minister, leading more of a "life of thought" as William Ellery Channing stated, would serve as a moral

---

97. W. Henry Channing, *The Life of William Ellery Channing* (New York, 1880), 402.

and intellectual teacher and mentor for his congregation.[98] Brahmins consciously diminished the value of the "conversion experience," with the result that no more than a handful of male parishioners sought to become full church members. Similarly, Brahmins explicitly moved away from distinguishing between the formerly elevated status of church communicant and that of parishioner.

Ministers of what Ralph Waldo Emerson called "Boston religion" emphasized the relative importance of personal morality over doctrine and specific beliefs. To them, doctrinal conformity was a false idol; insistence on such conformity reflected nothing more than "dangerous delusions."[99] From the fight over the Hollis professorship in 1805 to the orthodox's maneuvering to create a presbyterian-like system a decade later, the demand for any specific doctrinal litmus test was nothing more than a tool in one party's "struggle to rise," to dominate the other.[100] Neither insisting on a creed nor stressing the value of becoming a communicant paved the way for the domination of the church by its parishioners whose power stemmed largely from their rank in civil society.

While the Brahmins did not move far afield from Boston and Cambridge, their systematic devaluation of communicant status served the interests of parishioners in their fight against church communicants throughout the state. Particularly in wake of the Dedham decision, parishioners and their liberal ministers undermined the authority of church communicants. By the end of the 1820s, most churches of the Standing Order had split apart, parishioners going one way and communicants another.

By the approach of formal disestablishment of church and state in Massachusetts, it is not surprising to find orthodox clerics like Parsons Cooke, minister from the town of Ware and orthodox propagandist, jettisoning any lingering hopes for the maintenance of the Standing Order. Enthusiastically embracing voluntarism, Cooke declared that it would be decidedly "favorable to the cause of truth," when "all laws requiring a tax for the support of the ministry will be repealed, and thus every sect will be left to

---

98. Ibid., 403.
99. William Bentley, *The Diary of William Bentley* (Salem, 1905–14), 1:161.
100. Ibid.

stand on its own merits."[101] Similarly, in a series of articles in *Spirit of the Pilgrims,* Beecher's orthodox periodical, one minister after another called for the termination of "the absolute civil dependence and vassalage" of the Congregational churches of Massachusetts.[102] When the orthodoxy clergy, who for years had tenaciously defended the establishment, so unequivocally called for its dismantling, the time had come for an end to the Standing Order.

The Brahmin party, too, had come to the conclusion that established religion in Massachusetts had little or no remaining value. With the demise of the Federalist party, the Brahmins could abandon all allegiance to the Standing Order, which for years they had supported as a sop to their orthodox brethren. "And it is a poor and false notion of religion," concluded Francis Greenwood of Boston's New South Church, "that she cannot stand as well without the support of the state as with it. I am persuaded that she stands much better without it, than with it."[103] With the formation of the American Unitarian Association in 1825, the Brahmins fully reconciled themselves to being just one denomination among many. So, as the eleventh amendment to the Massachusetts Constitution went into effect on January 1, 1834, Brahmin and orthodox alike had already bid the Standing Order adieu.

---

101. Parsons Cooke, *Unitarianism an Exclusive System, or the Bondage of the Churches That Were Planted by the Pilgrims* (Boston, 1828), 12.
102. *Spirit of the Pilgrims* 1 (January 1828): 120.
103. Francis Greenwood, "Installation Sermon for Mr Thompson," *Spirit of the Pilgrims* 5 (1832): 358.

Select Bibliography

Manuscript Collections

Adams, Hannah. Papers. Massachusetts Historical Society.

Allen, Joseph. Papers. Massachusetts Historical Society.

Allen-Ware Family. Papers. Massachusetts Historical Society.

Beecher, Lyman. Collection. Congregational Library, Boston.

Belknap, Jeremy. Papers. Massachusetts Historical Society.

Bond, George. Papers. Boston Public Library.

Boston Association of Congregational Ministers. Records: 1755–1836. Congregational Library, Boston.

Bulfinch, Charles. Papers. Massachusetts Historical Society.

Channing, William Ellery. Papers. Massachusetts Historical Society.

Coleman, Benjamin. Papers. Massachusetts Historical Society.

Dall, Caroline Healey. Papers. Massachusetts Historical Society.

Edes, H. H. Papers. Massachusetts Historical Society.

Emerson Collection. Massachusetts Historical Society.

Emerson Papers. Houghton Library, Harvard University.

Everett, Edward. Papers. Massachusetts Historical Society.

First Church of Boston. Records, 1790–1860. Boston. Massachusetts Historical Society.

Follen, Charles. Papers 2. Massachusetts Historical Society.

General Association of Massachusetts Congregational Ministers. Records. Congregational Library, Boston.

Harvard College Faculty Records, 1806–14. Harvard University Archives.

Harvard College Minutes. Harvard Corporation Records. Harvard University Archives.

King, Rufus. Papers. New York Historical Society.

Morse Family Papers. New York Public Library.

Morse Family Papers. Yale University Archives.

Morse, Jedidiah. Papers. Massachusetts Historical Society.

Morse, Samuel F. B. Papers. Library of Congress.
Parker, Theodore. Collections. Andover-Harvard Library.
Parker, Theodore. Collections. Boston Public Library.
Park Street Church. Archives. Boston.
Perry-Clarke Collection. Massachusetts Historical Society.
Pickering, Timothy. Papers. Massachusetts Historical Society.
Pierce, John. Collections. Massachusetts Historical Society.
Pierce, John. Papers. Massachusetts Historical Society.
Suffolk County Deed Registry. Park Street Church Archives. Boston.
Thacher, Peter. Papers. Massachusetts Historical Society.
Ware, Henry. Papers. Harvard University Archives. Cambridge, Massachusetts.
Ware Family Papers. Massachusetts Historical Society.
Wolcott, Oliver. Papers. Connecticut Historical Society.

Government Documents and Publications

Acts and Laws of the Commonwealth of Massachusetts. Boston, 1834.
Acts and Resolves, Public and Private, of the Province of Massachusetts Bay. Boston, 1869–1922.
Annotated Laws of Massachusetts. Boston, 1963.
Boston Directory, Containing the Names of the Inhabitants, Occupations, Place of Business and Dwelling Houses. Boston, 1798.
Ecclesiastical Constitution of the Congregational Churches of Massachusetts. Boston, 1816. Massachusetts Historical Society Collections, 1891.
Journal of the Convention for Framing a Constitution of Government for the State of Massachusetts Bay, from the Commencement of Their First Session, September 1, 1779, to the Close of Their Last Session, June 16, 1780. Boston, 1832.
Journal of the Debates and Proceedings in the Convention of Delegates. Boston, 1821.
Massachusetts Acts and Resolves. Boston, 1911.
Tabular View of Representation in the Commonwealth of Massachusetts, from 1780 to 1853. Edited by Ephraim M. Wright. Boston, 1854.

Newspapers and Periodicals

Boston Gazette
Boston Recorder
Christian Examiner
Chronicle (Boston)
Columbian Centinel
The Dial
General Repository and Review

Independent Chronicle (Boston)
Independent Ledger
Massachusetts Mercury
Monthly Anthology and Boston Review [Monthly Anthology]
New England Palladium
North American Review
Panoplist and Missionary Magazine [Panoplist]
Port Folio (Philadelphia)
Spirit of the Pilgrims

CONTEMPORARY PUBLICATIONS AND PRINTED DOCUMENTS

Ames, Fisher. *Works of Fisher Ames.* Edited by Seth Ames. 1854. Reprint, Indianapolis, 1983.

Backus, Isaac. *A History of New England with Particular Reference to the Baptists.* New York, 1871.

Bacon, Leonard. "An Historical Discourse." In *Contributions to the Ecclesiastical History of Connecticut.* New York, 1861.

Beecher, Lyman. *The Autobiography of Lyman Beecher.* Edited by Barbara Cross. New York, 1961.

———. *The Rights of the Congregational Churches of Massachusetts. The Results of an Ecclesiastical Council Convened at Groton, Massachusetts, July 17, 1826.* Boston, 1827.

Belknap, Jeremy. *A Sermon Delivered before the Convention of the Clergy of Massachusetts.* Boston, 1796.

———. *A Sermon, Preached at the Installation of Jedidiah Morse.* Boston, 1789.

Belknap Papers. *Collections of the Massachusetts Historical Society.* 5th ser., 23 (1877); 6th ser., 4 (1891).

Bentley, William. *A Charge Delivered before the Morning Star Lodge.* Worcester, Mass., 1798.

———. *The Diary of William Bentley.* 4 vols. Salem, 1905–14.

Blair, Hugh. *Lectures on Rhetoric and Belles Lettres.* London, 1785.

Boudinot, Elias. *Journey to Boston in 1809.* Edited by Milton H. Thomas. Princeton, 1955.

Bowen, Francis. *Principles of Metaphysics and Ethical Science.* Boston, 1826.

Bradford, Alden. *An Oration, Pronounced at Wiscasset, on the 4th of July, 1804.* Boston, 1805.

Buckminster, Joseph Stevens. *Works.* 2 vols. Boston, 1839.

Channing, William Ellery. *Religion a Social Principle.* Boston, 1820.

———. *A Sermon Delivered at the Ordination of Rev. John Codman.* Boston, 1808.

———. *The Works of William Ellery Channing.* 6 vols. Boston, 1888.

Chauncy, Charles. *Seasonable Thoughts on the State of Religion in New England.* Boston, 1743.

Cooke, Parsons. *Recollections of Dr. Griffin*. Boston, 1855.

———. *Unitarianism an Exclusive System, or the Bondage of the Churches That Were Planted by the Pilgrims*. Boston, 1828.

Dwight, Timothy. *Travels in New England and New York*. 4 vols. New Haven, Conn., 1821–22.

Eckley, Joseph. *A Discourse before the Society for Propagating the Gospel among the Indians and Others in North America*. Boston, 1806.

———. *A Discourse, Delivered before the Members of the Boston Female Asylum*. Boston, 1802.

Eliot, Ephraim. *Historic Notes of the New North Religious Society in the Town of Boston*. Boston, 1822.

Emerson, William. *A Sermon on the Decease of the Rev. Peter Thacher, D.D.* Boston, 1803.

Evarts, Jeremiah. *Review of American Unitarianism*. Boston, 1815.

"The Exiled Churches of Massachusetts." Reprinted in *Congregational Quarterly* 5 (July 1863): 216–40.

Facts and Documents, Exhibiting a Summary View of the Ecclesiastical Affairs, Lately Transacted in Fitchburg; Together with Some Strictures on the Result of a Late Party Council, In Said Town, and General Observations: The Whole Designed to Vindicate the Rights of the Churches, and to Illustrate the Subject, and Enforce the Importance, of Church Discipline. Boston, 1802.

"First Church of Boston Records." Edited by Richard Pierce. *Publications of the Colonial Society of Massachusetts* 40 (1961): 589–603.

Gardiner, John Sylvester John. *Fast Day Sermon Preached at Trinity Church, in Boston, April 7, 1808*. Boston, 1808.

Griffin, Edward Dorr. *A Sermon Preached, 1-10-1810*. Boston, 1810.

———. "Christian Boldness." *The American Pulpit*. Edinburgh, 1852.

Grund, Francis J. *Aristocracy in America: From the Sketchbook of a German Nobleman*. 1839. Reprint, New York, 1959.

Hale, Enoch. *Extracts from the Minutes of the General Association of Massachusetts Proper*. Boston, 1811.

Harris, Thaddeus M. "An Oration on Learned Associations." 1790 Phi Beta Kappa Address at Harvard. Pierce Collections. Massachusetts Historical Society.

Haven, Samuel. *Statement of the Proceedings in the First Parish and Church in Dedham, Respecting the Settlement of a Minister, 1818*. Cambridge, Mass., 1819.

Hawley, Joseph. "Protest to the Constitutional Convention of 1780." In *Smith College Studies in History*, edited by Mary Catherine Clune, 30–49. Northampton, Massachusetts, 1917–18.

Hayward, Silvanus. "Creeds as a Test of Fellowship Among Christians." *Congregational Quarterly* 8 (October 1866): 382–87.

Historical Register of Harvard University. Cambridge, Mass., 1937.

Howard, Simeon. *A Sermon Preached before the Honorable House of Representatives of the State of Massachusetts.* Boston, 1780.

Howe, M. A. DeWolfe, ed. *Journal of the Proceedings of the Society Which Conducts the Monthly Anthology and the Boston Review (October 3, 1805–July 2, 1811).* Boston, 1910.

Kirkland, John Thornton. *A Sermon Delivered at the Interment of the Rev. Jeremy Belknap.* Boston, 1798.

Lathrop, John. *A Discourse Delivered in the Church in Hollis Street, April 13, 1808.*

———. *A Discourse Delivered on the Lord's Day, 17 May, 1812.* Boston, 1812.

———. *A Sermon Delivered at the Interment of the Rev. Joseph Eckley.* Boston, 1811.

Lawrence, E. A. "Review of the Career of Leonard Woods." *Congregational Quarterly* 1 (April 1859): 109–19.

Lowell, John. *An Inquiry into the Right to Change the Ecclesiastical Constitution of the Congregational Churches of Massachusetts.* Boston, 1816.

Mather, Cotton. *Ratio Disciplinae Fratum Nov-Angolorum.* Boston, 1726.

Mayhew, John. *Observations of the Charter and Conduct of the Society for the Propagation of the Gospel.* Boston, 1763.

Memorial of the Proprietors of the New South Meeting-House in Dorchester to the Ministers of the Boston Association. Boston, 1813.

Memorial of the Semi-centennial Celebration of the Founding of the Theological Seminary at Andover. Andover, 1859.

Morse, Jedidiah. *An Address Inaugurating the Charlestown Association for the Reforming of Morals.* Boston, 1813.

———. *Annual Convention Sermon.* Boston, 1812.

———. *An Appeal to the Public on the Controversy Respecting the Revolution in Harvard College.* Charlestown, Mass., 1814.

———. *Sermon Delivered at the Ordination of Joshua Huntington.* Boston, 1808.

———. *A Sermon, Exhibiting the Present Dangers, and Consequent Duties of the Citizens of the United States of America.* Charlestown, Mass., 1799.

———. *Sermon on the National Fast, May 9, 1798.* Boston, 1798.

———. *Thomas Belsham's "American Unitarianism: Or a Brief History of the Progress and Present State of the Unitarian Churches in America."* Boston, 1814.

———. *The True Reasons on Which the Election of a Hollis Professor of Divinity in Harvard College was Opposed at the Board of Overseers, Feb. 14, 1805.* Charlestown, Mass., 1805.

Narrative of the Conduct of the Corporation of Harvard College Relative to the Late Disorders Perpetrated by the Students. Cambridge, Mass., 1807.

Norton, Andrews. "A Contrast Between Calvinists and Hopkinsians." *General Repository and Review* 3 (April 1813).

Oliver, Peter. *Origins and Progress of the American Revolution: Tory View.* Edited by Douglas Adair and John A. Shutz. New York, 1961.

Palfrey, John G. *A Discourse on the Life and Character of the Rev. John Thornton Kirkland.* Cambridge, Mass., 1840.

Payson, Phillips. *A Sermon Delivered before the Honorable Council of the State of Massachusetts.* Boston, 1778.

Pearson, Eliphalet. "Intended Publication Relative to Choice of Professor of Divinity." Harvard University Archives.

———. "Pearson Resignation Letter." Harvard Corporation Records. Harvard University Archives.

Pond, Enoch. "Report on the Rights of the Congregational Churches of Massachusetts." *Congregational Quarterly* 5 (October 1863).

Proceedings of the (Park Street) Business Meetings, 1809–1834. Boston, 1834.

Proceedings of the Second Church and Parish in Dorchester. Boston, 1812.

Quincy, Josiah. *Biographical Sketches.* Cambridge, Mass., 1851.

———. *The History of the Boston Athenaeum With Biographical Notices of Its Deceased Founders.* Cambridge, Mass., 1851.

———. *The History of Harvard University.* 2 vols. Cambridge, Mass., 1840.

Reed, John. "Annual Sermon of 1807." In *Annual Sermons Delivered to the Massachusetts Convention of Congregational Ministers.* Boston, 1807.

Report of the Committee of the West Parish Association on the State of Religion. Boston, 1825.

The Result of an Ecclesiastical Council, Convened at Groton, Massachusetts, July 17, 1826. Boston, 1827.

Richardson, Joseph. *An Oration Delivered in the South Parish, in Weymouth.* Hingham, Mass., 1828.

Sargent, Winthrop. *Boston: A Poem.* Boston, 1803.

Smith, Elias. *The Clergyman's Looking Glass: Or Ancient and Modern Things Contrasted.* Boston, 1804.

Sprague, William. *Annals of the American Pulpit.* 9 vols. New York, 1857–1869.

———. *The Life of Jedidiah Morse.* New York, 1874.

———. *Memoir of the Rev. Edward D. Griffin, D.D.* New York, 1839.

Stearns, Charles. *A Sermon Delivered before the Convention of Congregational Ministers in Massachusetts, at their Annual Meeting in Boston, June 1, 1815.* Boston, 1815.

Stuart, Moses, "On the Study of the German Language." *Christian Review* 6 (1841).

Thacher, Samuel Cooper. "Memoir of the Life and Character of the Late Rev. William Ellery." *Collections of the Massachusetts Historical Society,* 2d ser., 1 (1812): 254–58.

Tracy, Ebenezer C. *Memoir of the Life of Jeremiah Evarts, Esquire.* Boston, 1845.

Tuckerman, Joseph. *The Principles and Results of the Ministry at Large, in Boston.* Boston, 1838.

Tudor, William, Jr. *Miscellanies.* Boston, 1821.

Wansey, Henry. "An Excursion to the United States of North America in the Summer of 1794." In *America through British Eyes,* edited by Allan Nevins. New York, 1948.

Ware, Henry. *1821 Election Sermon*. Boston, 1821.

———. *Result of the Ecclesiastical Council, Convened at Dedham, October 28, 1818, to Assist at the Ordination of Rev. Alvan Lamson, over the First Parish in Dedham*. Dedham, Mass., 1818.

———. *A Sermon Delivered at the Ordination of the Reverend Alvan Lamson as the Minister of the First Church in Dedham*. Dedham, Mass., 1818.

Ware, Henry, Jr. *Sober Thoughts on the State of the Times*. Boston, 1835.

Ware, William, ed. *American Unitarian Biography*. Boston, 1850.

Willard, Sidney. *Memories of Youth and Manhood*. 2 vols. Cambridge, Mass., 1855.

Withington, Leonard. *Contributions to the Ecclesiastical History of Essex County, Massachusetts*. Boston, 1865.

———. *Sermon Preached at the Annual Election, May 25, 1831*. Boston, 1831.

Wood, Leonard. *History of the Andover Theological Seminary*. Boston, 1885.

Worthington, Erastus. *The History of Dedham from the Beginning of Its Settlement*. Boston, 1827.

BOOKS

Adams, Henry. *The Education of Henry Adams*. Boston, 1918.

———. *The History of the United States of America during the Administrations of Jefferson and Madison*. New York, 1921. Reprint, Chicago, 1967.

Adams, James Truslow. *New England in the Republic, 1776–1860*. New York, 1926.

Ahlstrom, Sidney. *A Religious History of the American People*. New Haven, Conn., 1972.

Ahlstrom, Sidney, and C. H. Carey, eds. *An American Reformation: A Documentary of Unitarian History*. Middletown, Conn., 1985.

Akers, Charles W. *Called Unto Liberty: A Life of Jonathan Mayhew*. Cambridge, Mass., 1964.

———. *The Divine Politician: Samuel Cooper and the American Revolution in Boston*. Boston, 1982.

Alexander, J. W. *Life of Archibald Alexander*. New York, 1894.

Allen, Joseph A. *Our Liberal Movement in Theology*. Boston, 1882.

Allen, Joseph, and Richard Eddy. *History of Unitarians and Universalists in the United States*. New York, 1894.

Allen, William. *Memoir of John Codman, D.D.* Boston, 1853.

Allmedinger, David. *Paupers and Scholars*. New York, 1975.

Amory, Cleveland. *The Proper Bostonians*. New York, 1947.

Amory, Thomas. *Life and Times of James Sullivan*. Boston, 1859.

Andrew, John A., III. *From Revivals to Removal: Jeremiah Evarts, the Cherokee Nation, and the Search for the Soul of America*. Athens, Ga., 1992.

Atkins, Glen G., and Frederick L. Fagley. *History of American Congregationalism*. Boston, 1942.

Ayer, Hannah P. *A Legacy of New England*. Minneapolis, 1950.

Bacon, Leonard. "An Historical Discourse." In *Contributions to the Ecclesiastical History of Connecticut*. New York, 1861.

Bailyn, Bernard. *The New England Merchants in the Seventeenth Century*. Cambridge, Mass., 1979.

Baldwin, Alice. *The New England Clergy and the American Revolution*. Durham, N. C., 1928.

Banner, James. *To the Hartford Convention: The Federalists and the Origins of Party Politics in Massachusetts, 1789–1815*. New York, 1970.

Baritz, Loren. *City on a Hill: A History of Ideas and Myths in America*. New York, 1964.

Batchelder, Samuel F. *Bits of Harvard History*. Cambridge, Mass., 1924.

Bates, Joshua. *Reminiscences of John Codman, D.D.* Boston, 1853.

Beecher, Charles, ed. *Autobiography, Correspondence, Etc. of Lyman Beecher, D.D.* New York, 1864.

Bender, Thomas. *New York Intellect*. Baltimore, 1987.

Berk, Stephen E. *Calvinism versus Democracy: Timothy Dwight and the Origins of American Evangelical Orthodoxy*. Hamden, Conn., 1974.

Bilhartz, Terry. *Urban Religion and the Second Great Awakening*. New York, 1986.

Bloom, Harold. *The American Religion: The Emergence of the Post-Christian Nation*. New York, 1992.

Bode, Carl. *The American Lyceum: Town Meeting of the Mind*. New York, 1956.

Bolton, Charles K., ed. *Athenaeum Centenary*. Boston, 1907.

Bonomi, Patricia U. *Under the Cope of Heaven: Religion, Society, and Politics in Colonial America*. New York, 1986.

Booth, John N. *The Story of the Second Church in Boston*. Boston, 1960.

Bradford, Alden. *History of Massachusetts from the Year 1790 to 1820*. 3 vols. Boston, 1822–29.

Brauer, Kinley. *Cotton versus Conscience*. New York, 1967.

Brooke, John L. *The Heart of the Commonwealth: Society and Political Culture in Worcester County, Massachusetts, 1713–1861*. New York, 1989.

Brooks, Van Wyck. *The Flowering of New England: 1815–1865*. New York, 1936.

Brown, E. F. *Joseph Hawley*. New York, 1931.

Brown, Jerry Wayne. *The Rise of Biblical Criticism in America, 1800–1870: The New England Scholars*. Middletown, Conn., 1969.

Brown, Richard. *Knowledge Is Power: The Diffusion of Information in Early America, 1700–1865*. New York, 1989.

Buck, Edward. *Massachusetts Ecclesiastical Law*. Boston, 1866.

Budington, William I. *History of the First Church, Charlestown*. Boston, 1845.

Buell, Lawrence. *New England Literary Culture: From the Revolution to the Renaissance*. New York, 1984.

Bullock, Steven C. *Revolutionary Brotherhood: Freemasonry and the Transformation of the American Social Order, 1730–1840*. Chapel Hill, 1996.

Bushman, Richard. *From Puritan to Yankee: Character and Social Order in Connecticut, 1690–1765.* New York, 1967.

Butler, Jon. *Awash in a Sea of Faith: Christianizing the American People.* Cambridge, Mass., 1990.

Calhoun, Daniel. *Professional Lives in America: Structure and Aspiration, 1750–1850.* Cambridge, Mass., 1965.

Cayton, Mary Kupiec. *Emerson's Emergence: Self and Society in the Transformation of New England, 1800–1845.* Chapel Hill, 1989.

Channing, William Henry. *The Life of William Ellery Channing.* New York, 1880.

Charvat, William. *Literary Publishing in America.* New York, 1959.

———. *The Origins of American Critical Thought, 1810–1835.* Philadelphia, 1936.

Clark, Joseph Sylvester. *A Historical Sketch of the Congregational Churches in Massachusetts.* Boston, 1858.

Clifford, Deborah Pickman. *Crusader for Freedom: A Life of Lydia Maria Child.* Boston, 1992.

Cole, Charles C. *The Social Ideas of the Northern Evangelists, 1829–1860.* New York, 1954.

Conforti, Joseph A. *Samuel Hopkins and the New Divinity Movement: Calvinism, the Congregational Ministry, and Reform in New England between the Great Awakenings.* Grand Rapids, Mich., 1981.

Cooke, George Willis. *Unitarianism in America.* Boston, 1902.

Commager, Henry S. *The Era of Reform, 1800–1860.* Princeton, 1960.

Cozort, Deborah, et al. *Guide to Archives of King's Chapel.* Boston, 1980.

Crawford, Mary C. *Romantic Days in Old Boston.* Boston, 1922.

Curtis, George. *A Memorial of Wendell Phillips from the City of Boston.* Boston, 1884.

Cushing, Henry. *Government in Massachusetts.* New York, 1896.

Delbanco, Andrew. *William Ellery Channing: An Essay on the Liberal Spirit in America.* Cambridge, Mass., 1981.

Dexter, Henry M. *Congregationalism: How Congregationalism Works.* Boston, 1871.

Djilas, Milovan. *The New Class: An Analysis of the Communist System.* New York, 1957.

Doherty, Robert. *Society and Power, Five New England Towns, 1800–1860.* Amherst, Mass., 1977.

Douglas, Ann. *The Feminization of American Culture.* New York, 1977.

Edes, Henry. *History of the Harvard Church in Charlestown, Mass., 1815–1870.* Boston, 1879.

Eidsmoe, John. *Christianity and the Constitution: The Faith of Our Founding Fathers.* Grand Rapids, Mich., 1987.

Eliot, Samuel. *Sketches of the History of Harvard College.* Boston, 1848.

Elkins, Stanley. *Slavery: A Problem in American Institutional and Intellectual Life.* New York, 1959.

Ellis, Arthur B. *History of the First Church in Boston.* Boston, 1881.

Ellis, George, ed. *Unitarianism: Its Origin and History.* Boston, 1889.

Englizian, H. Crosby. *Brimstone Corner: A History of Park Street Church.* Chicago, 1968.

Fagley, Frederick L. *The Congregational Churches.* New York, 1925.

Fenn, William. *A Religious History of New England—The King's Chapel Lectures.* Cambridge, Mass., 1917.

Fischer, David Hackett. *The Revolution of American Conservatism: Federalist Party in Jeffersonian Democracy.* New York, 1965.

Foote, Henry W. *Annals of King's Chapel.* 2 vols. Boston, 1881–96.

Formisano, Ronald. *The Transformation of Political Culture: Massachusetts Parties, 1790s–1840s.* New York, 1983.

Foster, Frank Hugh. *A Genetic History of New England Theology.* New York, 1963.

Frederickson, George. *The Inner Civil War: Northern Intellectuals and the Crisis of the Union.* New York, 1965.

Frothingham, Paul R. *Edward Everett, Orator and Statesman.* Boston, 1925.

Frothingham, Octavius Brooks. *Boston Unitarianism.* New York, 1890.

———. *Transcendentalism in New England.* Boston, 1875.

Gannett, William C. *Ezra Stiles Gannett; Unitarian Minister in Boston, 1824–71.* New York, 1875.

Garrison, Francis J. *Ann Phillips: Wife of Wendell Phillips, A Memorial Sketch.* Boston, 1886.

Gatell, Frank O. *John Gorham Palfrey and the New England Conscience.* Cambridge, Mass., 1963.

Gausted, Edwin S. *Faith of Our Fathers: Religion and the New Nation.* San Francisco, 1987.

———. *The Great Awakening in New England.* New York, 1957.

Gawalt, Gerard. *The Promise of Power: The Emergence of the Legal Profession in Massachusetts, 1760–1840.* Westport, Conn., 1979.

Gibbs, George. *Memoirs of the Washington and Adams Administrations, Edited from the Papers of Oliver Walcott, Secretary of the Treasury.* 2 vols. New York, 1846.

Gilmore, Michael T. *Romanticism and the Marketplace.* Chicago, 1985.

Glover, Willis. *Evangelical Nonconformists and Higher Criticism in the Nineteenth Century.* New York, 1955.

Goen, C. C. *Revivalism and Separatism in New England, 1740–1800: Strict Congregationalists and Separate Baptists in the Great Awakening.* New Haven, Conn., 1962.

Gonnaud, Maurice. *An Uneasy Solitude: Individual and Society in Work of Ralph Waldo Emerson.* Paris, 1964.

Goodman, Paul. *Towards a Christian Republic: Antimasonry and the Great Transition in New England.* Oxford, 1988.

Gouldner, Alvin. *The Dialectic of Ideology and Technology: The Origins, Grammar and Future of Ideology.* New York, 1976.

———. *The Future of Intellectuals and the Rise of the New Class.* New York, 1979.

———. *The Two Marxisms: Contradictions and Anomalies in the Development of Theory.* New York, 1980.

Gramsci, Antonio. *The Modern Prince and Other Writings.* New York, 1957.

Green, Martin. *The Problem of Boston.* New York, 1966.

Greenslet, Ferris. *The Lowells and Their Seven Worlds.* Boston, 1946.

Griffin, Clifford S. *Their Brothers' Keepers: Moral Stewardship in the United States, 1800–1865.* New Brunswick, N.J., 1960.

Griffin, Edward G. *Old Brick: Charles Chauncy of Boston, 1705–1787.* Minneapolis, 1980.

Hall, David. *The Faithful Shepherd: A History of the New England Ministry in the Seventeenth Century.* New York, 1972.

Harding, Vincent. *A Certain Magnificence: Lyman Beecher and the Transformation of American Protestantism, 1775–1863.* Brooklyn, 1991.

Haroutunian, Joseph. *Piety versus Moralism: The Passing of New England Theology.* New York, 1932.

Harris, Neil. *The Artist in American Society, 1740–1860.* New York, 1966.

Hatch, Nathan O. *The Democratization of American Christianity.* New Haven, Conn., 1989.

———. *The Sacred Cause of Liberty: Republican Thought and the Millennium in Revolutionary New England.* New Haven, Conn., 1977.

Hazen, Henry. *History of Billerica.* Boston, 1883.

Heimert, Alan. *Religion and the American Mind: From the Awakening through the Revolution.* New York, 1966.

Herbert, Jerry S., ed. *American, Christian or Secular? Readings in American Christian History and Civil Religion.* Portland, Ore., 1984.

Hersh, Blanche. *The Slavery of Sex: Feminist Abolitionists in America.* Urbana, 1978.

Higginson, Thomas Wentworth. *Cheerful Yesterdays.* Boston, 1896.

Higham, John. *From Boundlessness to Consolidation: The Transformation of American Culture, 1848–60.* Baltimore, 1969.

Hill, Hamilton. *History of the Old South Church.* 2 vols. Boston, 1889.

Hovey, Alvah. *Memoir of the Life and Times of Rev. Isaac Backus, A.M.* Boston, 1859.

Howe, Daniel Walker. *The Unitarian Conscience: Harvard Moral Philosophy, 1805–1861.* Cambridge, Mass., 1970.

Howe, M. A. DeWolfe. *Boston: The Place and the People.* New York, 1903.

Hunt, Freeman. *Worth and Wealth.* New York, 1857.

Hutchinson, William R. *The Transcendental Ministers: Church Reform in the New England Renaissance.* New Haven, Conn., 1959.

Jaher, Frederic Cople. *The Urban Establishment.* Urbana, 1982.

Jedrey, Christopher M. *The World of John Cleaveland: Family and Community in Eighteenth-Century New England.* New York, 1979.

Johnson, Paul. *A Shopkeeper's Millennium.* New York, 1978.

Kerber, Linda. *Federalists in Dissent: Imagery and Ideology in Jeffersonian America.* Ithaca, 1971.

Kirsh, George. *Life of Jeremy Belknap.* New York, 1972.

Knight, Janice. *Orthodoxies in Massachusetts: Rereading American Puritanism.* Cambridge, Mass., 1994.

Konrad, George, and Ivan Szelenyi. *The Intellectuals on the Road to Class Power: A Sociological Study of the Role of the Intelligentsia in Socialism.* New York, 1979.

Kuehne, Dale S. *Massachusetts Congregationalist Political Thought, 1760–1790: The Design of Heaven.* Columbia, Mo., 1996.

Lader, Lawrence. *The Bold Brahmins: New England's War against Slavery, 1831–1860.* New York, 1961.

Lauer, Paul E. *Church and State in New England.* Baltimore, 1892.

Lee, Eliza Buckminster. *Memoirs of Rev. Joseph Buckminster, D.D., and of His Son, Rev. Joseph Stevens Buckminster.* 2d ed. Boston, 1851.

Livermore, Shaw. *The Twilight of Federalism.* Princeton, 1962.

Lodge, Henry Cabot, ed. *Life and Letters of George Cabot.* Boston, 1877.

Loring, James Spear. *The Hundred Boston Orators.* 3d ed. Boston, 1854.

Lothrop, S. K. *The History of the Brattle Street Church.* Boston, 1851.

Lukács, Georg. *History and Class Consciousness: Studies in Marxist Dialectics.* Cambridge, Mass., 1971.

Lyon, William H. *Charles Chauncy.* Boston, 1903.

Marcon, Jane Belknap. *Life of Jeremy Belknap.* New York, 1847.

Mathews, Jean. *Toward a New Society: American Thought and Culture, 1800–1830.* Boston, 1991.

McCaughey, Robert. *Josiah Quincy: The Urbane Federalist.* Cambridge, Mass., 1974.

McColgan, Daniel T. *Joseph Tuckerman: Pioneer in American Social Work.* Washington, 1940.

McLoughlin, William G. *New England Dissent: 1630–1833.* Cambridge, Mass., 1971.

Meyer, Jacob. *Church and State in Massachusetts, 1740–1833.* New York, 1933.

Miller, Perry. *Life of the Mind in America from the Revolution through the Civil War.* New York, 1965.

Miller, William Lee. *The First Liberty: Religion and the American Republic.* New York, 1986.

Morgan, Edmund. *Visible Saints: History of a Religious Idea.* Boston, 1965.

Morison, Samuel Eliot. *Harrison Gray Otis, 1765–1848: The Urbane Federalist.* Boston, 1969.

———. *Life and Letters of Harrison Gray Otis.* Boston, 1913.

———. *A Maritime History of Massachusetts, 1783–1860.* Boston, 1921.

———. *Three Centuries of Harvard.* Cambridge, Mass., 1936.

Morse, James K. *Jedidiah Morse: A Champion of New England Orthodoxy.* New York, 1939.

Moss, Richard J. *The Life of Jedidiah Morse: A Station of Peculiar Exposure.* Knoxville, 1995.

Mott, Frank Luther. *History of American Magazines, 1741–1850*. New York, 1930.

Murdock, Virgil E. *Institutional History of the American Unitarian Association*. Minneapolis, 1975.

Nettels, Curtis. *The Emergence of a National Economy, 1775–1815*. New York, 1962.

Nye, Russel. *Fettered Freedoms: Civil Liberties and the Slavery Controversy, 1830–1860*. East Lansing, Mich., 1949.

O'Connor, Thomas. *Lords of the Loom: Cotton Whigs and the Coming of the Civil War*. New York, 1968.

Parrington, Vernon L. *Main Currents in American Thought*. 2 vols. 1927. Reprint, New York, 1954.

Perry, Bliss, ed. *Historical Collections*. Boston, 1911.

Perry, Lewis. *Radical Abolitionism: Anarchy and the Government of God in Anti-Slavery Thought*. New York, 1973.

Phillips, Joseph W. *Jedidiah Morse and New England Congregationalism*. New Brunswick, N.J., 1983.

Pocock, J. G. A. *The Machiavellian Moment: Florentine Political Thought and the Atlantic Republican Tradition*. Princeton, 1975.

Quincy, Josiah N. *Figures of the Past, from the Leaves of Old Journals*. 1883. Reprint, Boston, 1926.

Quine, Willard Van Orman. *The Roots of Reference*. La Salle, Ill., 1974.

Riegler, Gordon. *Socialization of the New England Clergy*. New York, 1945.

Robbins, Chandler. *History of the Second Church or Old North in Boston*. Boston, 1852.

Robinson, David. *The Unitarians and the Universalists*. Westport, Conn., 1985.

Robinson, William A. *Jeffersonian Democracy in New England*. New Haven, Conn., 1916.

Robson, David W. *Educating Republicans: The College in the Era of the Revolution, 1750–1800*. Westport, Conn., 1985.

Rose, Ann. *Transcendentalism as a Social Movement, 1830–1850*. New Haven, Conn., 1981.

Rowe, Henry K. *History of Andover Theological Seminary*. 9 vols. Newton, Mass., 1933.

Rusk, Ralph L. *The Letters of Ralph Waldo Emerson*. New York, 1939.

Rutman, Darrett. *Winthrop's Boston: A Portrait of a Puritan Town, 1630–1649*. Durham, N. C., 1965.

Schlesinger, Arthur. *The American as Reformer*. Cambridge, Mass., 1957.

Schneider, Herbert. *The Puritan Mind*. Ann Arbor, 1930.

Scott, Donald. *From Office to Profession: The New England Ministry, 1750–1850*. Philadelphia, 1978.

———. *Pastors and Providence: Ministerial Styles in 19th Century America*. New York, 1976.

Shama, Simon. *Dead Certainties (Unwarranted Speculations)*. New York, 1991.

Simpson, Lewis P. *The Brazen Face of History: Studies in Literary Consciousness*. Baton Rouge, 1980.

————. *The Man of Letters in New England and the South.* Baton Rouge, 1973.

————, ed. *The Federalist Literary Mind: Selections from the* Monthly Anthology and Boston Review, *1803–1811.* Baton Rouge, 1962.

Sinnott, Edward W. *Meetinghouse and Church in Early New England.* New York, 1963.

Smith, Timothy L. *Revivalism and Social Reform: American Protestants on the Eve of the Civil War.* New York, 1957.

Smith, Wilson. *Professors and Public Ethics: Studies of Northern Moral Philosophers before the Civil War.* New York, 1956.

Spiller, Robert A., ed. *The American Literary Revolution.* New York, 1967.

Staloff, Darren Marcus. *The Making of an American Thinking Class: Intellectuals and Intelligentsia in Seventeenth-Century Massachusetts.* New York, 1997.

Stauffer, Vernon. *New England and the Bavarian Illuminati.* New York, 1918.

Steele, Jeffrey. *The Representation of the Self in the American Renaissance.* Chapel Hill, 1987.

Stevens, Bruce M. *God's Last Metaphor: The Doctrine of the Trinity in New England Theology.* Berkeley, 1981.

Stevenson, Louise L. *Scholarly Means to Evangelical Ends: The New Haven Scholars and the Transformation of Higher Learning in America, 1830–1890.* Baltimore, 1986.

Stewart, James. *Holy Warriors: The Abolitionists and American Slavery.* New York, 1976.

Story, Ronald. *Harvard and the Boston Upper Class: The Forging of an Aristocracy, 1800–1870.* Middletown, Conn., 1980.

Story, W. W. *Life and Letters of Joseph Story.* Boston, 1851.

Stout, Harry S. *The New England Soul: Preaching and Religious Culture in Colonial New England.* New York, 1986.

Sweet, William Warren. *Religion in the Development of American Culture, 1765–1840.* New York, 1952.

Taylor, Robert J., ed. *Massachusetts, Colony to Commonwealth, Documents on the Formation of the Constitution, 1775–1780.* Chapel Hill, 1961.

Thomas, George M. *Revivalism and Social Change.* Chicago, 1989.

Thompson, John. *Ideology and Modern Culture.* Berkeley, 1984.

————. *Studies in the Theory of Ideology.* Stanford, 1990.

Thornton, Tamara Plakins. *Cultivating Gentlemen: The Meaning of Country Life among the Boston Elite, 1785–1860.* New Haven, Conn., 1989.

Tracy, Patricia J. *Jonathan Edwards, Pastor: Religion and Society in Eighteenth-Century Northampton.* New York, 1979.

Turner, James. *Without God, without Creed: The Origins of Unbelief in America.* Baltimore, 1985.

Tyack, David. *George Ticknor and the Boston Brahmins.* Cambridge, Mass., 1967.

Tying, Dudley Atkins. *Reports of Cases Argued and Determined in the Supreme Judicial Court of the Commonwealth of Massachusetts.* 16 vols. Boston, 1811–23.

Walker, George Leon. *Some Aspects of the Religious Life of New England with Special Reference to the Congregationalists.* Boston, 1897.

Walker, Peter. *Moral Choices: Memory, Desire and Imagination in Nineteenth Century American Abolitionism.* Baton Rouge, 1978.

Walker, Williston. *A History of the Christian Church.* 1919. Rev. ed. New York, 1959.

———. *Ten New England Leaders.* Boston, 1901.

Walters, Kerry. *The American Deists: Voices of Reason and Dissent in the Early Republic.* Lawrence, Kans., 1992.

Weber, Donald. *Rhetoric and History in Revolutionary New England.* New York, 1988.

Weber, Max. *Economy and Society.* 2 vols. Berkeley, 1978.

Wells, William V. *Life and Public Service of Samuel Adams.* New York, 1888.

Wertenbaker, Thomas J. *Puritan Oligarchy.* New York, 1947.

Whitehead, John S. *The Separation of College and State, Columbia, Dartmouth, Harvard, and Yale: 1776–1876.* New Haven, Conn., 1973.

Wiecek, William. *The Sources of Anti-Slavery Constitutionalism in America, 1760–1848.* New York, 1977.

Wilbur, Earl M. *A History of Unitarianism in Transylvania, England, and America.* 2 vols. Cambridge, Mass., 1952.

Williams, Daniel Day. *The Andover Liberals.* New York, 1941.

Williams, George H., ed. *The Harvard Divinity School: Its Place in Harvard University and in American Culture.* Boston, 1954.

Williams, Peter. *Popular Religion in America: Symbolic Change and the Modernization Process in Historical Perspective.* Chicago, 1989.

Wilson, John F. *Church and State in American History.* Boston, 1965.

Wilson, Robert J., III. *The Benevolent Deity: Ebenezer Gay and the Rise of Rational Religion in New England, 1696–1787.* Philadelphia, 1894.

Winsor, Justin, ed. *The Memorial History of Boston.* 4 vols. Boston, 1881.

Wisner, Benjamin B. *The History of the Old South Church in Boston.* Boston, 1830.

Worthley, Harold F. *Inventory of the Records of the Particular (Congregational) Churches of Mass to 1805.* Cambridge, Mass., 1970.

Wright, Conrad. *The Beginnings of Unitarianism in America.* Boston, 1955.

———. *The Liberal Christians: Essays on American Unitarian History.* Boston, 1970.

———, ed. *American Unitarianism, 1805–1865.* Boston, 1989.

———, ed. *A Stream of Light: A Sesquicentennial History of American Unitarianism.* Boston, 1975.

Wright, Conrad Edick. *The Transformation of Charity in Revolutionary New England.* Boston, 1992.

Yacavone, Donald. *Samuel Joseph May and the Dilemmas of the Liberal Persuasion.* Philadelphia, 1991.

Young, Alexander. *Discourses on the Life and Character of John Thornton Kirkland.* Boston, 1840.

ARTICLES

Amory, Cleveland. "Boston's Old Guard." *Harper's,* October 1947, 320–26.

Anderson, Fred. "A People's Army: Provincial Military Service in Massachusetts during the Seven Years' War." *William and Mary Quarterly,* 3d ser., 40 (1983): 501–27.

———. "Why Did Colonial New Englanders Make Bad Soldiers? Contractual Principles and Military Conduct during the Seven Years' War." *William and Mary Quarterly,* 3d ser., 38 (1981): 395–417.

Banner, Lois. "Religious Benevolence and Social Control: A Critique of an Interpretation." *Journal of American History* 60 (1973): 23–41.

Birdsall, Richard. "The Second Great Awakening and the New England Social Order." *Church History* 39 (1970): 345–64.

Bolton, Charles K. "Social Libraries in Boston." *Publications of the Colonial Society of Massachusetts* 12 (1908–1909): 332–38.

Breitenbach, William. "The Consistent Calvinism of the New Divinity Movement." *William and Mary Quarterly,* 3d ser., 41 (1984): 241–64.

Brown, Ralph. "The American Geographies of Jedidiah Morse." *Annals of the Association of American Geographers* 31 (1941): 145–212.

Brown, Richard D. "Spreading the Word: Rural Clergymen and the Communitarian Network of Eighteenth-Century New England." *Proceedings of the Massachusetts Historical Society* 94 (1984): 1–14.

———. "Who Should Rule at Home? The Establishment of the Brahmin Upper Class." *Reviews in American History* 9 (March 1981): 55–61.

Buell, Lawrence. "Identification of Contributors to the *Monthly Anthology and Boston Review,* 1804–1811." *ESQ* 23 (1977): 99–105.

———. "J. S. Buckminster: The Making of a New England Saint." *Canadian Review of American Studies* 10 (Spring 1979): 1–29.

———. "The Unitarian Movement and the Art of Preaching." *American Quarterly* 24 (1972): 166–90.

Bumstead, J. M. "Religion, Finance, and Democracy in Massachusetts: The Town of Norton as a Case Study." *Journal of American History* 57 (1971): 817–31.

Carwardine, Richard. "The Second Great Awakening in the Urban Centers: An Examination of Methodism and the 'New Measures.'" *Journal of American History* 59 (1972): 327–40.

Cayton, Mary Kupiec. "The Making of an American Prophet: Emerson, His Audiences, and the Rise of the Culture Industry in Nineteenth-Century America." *American Historical Review* 92 (1987): 597–620.

Chipley, Louise. "'The Best Instruction of the People': William Bentley on the Congregational Clergy and the Republic, 1783–1819." *Essex Institute Historical Collections* 127 (1991): 194–210.

————. "Consociation and the Unitarian Controversy in Connecticut." *Proceedings of the Unitarian Universalist Historical Association* 21 (1987): 13–27.

Cushing, John D. "Notes on Disestablishment in Massachusetts." *William and Mary Quarterly*, 3d ser., 26 (1969): 169–90.

Danto, Arthur. "Deep Interpretation." *Journal of Philosophy* 78 (November 1981): 691–706.

Donald, David Herbert. "Toward a Reconsideration of the Abolitionists." In *Lincoln Reconsidered: Essays on the Civil War Era*, edited by David Donald. New York, 1989.

Downs, Lenthiel. "Emerson and Dr. Channing: Two Men from Boston." *New England Quarterly* 20 (1947): 516–34.

Eliot, Samuel. "The Charities of Boston." *North American Review* 91 (July 1860): 144–67.

Ellis, George E. "The Church and Parish in Mass: Usage and Law." In *Unitarianism: Its Origins and History*. Boston, 1889.

Faust, C. H. "The Background of the Unitarian Opposition to Transcendentalism." *Modern Philology* 35 (1938): 297–324.

Fenn, William W. "How the Schism Came." *The Proceedings of the Unitarian Historical Society* 1 (1925): 3–21.

————. "The Revolt against the Standing Order." In *A Religious History of New England—The King's Chapel Lectures*. Cambridge, Mass., 1917.

Forman, Charles. "'Elected Now By Time': The Unitarian Controversy, 1805–1835." In *A Stream of Light: A Sesquicentennial History of American Unitarianism*, edited by Conrad Wright. Boston, 1975.

Gillette, E. H. "History and Literature of the Unitarian Controversy." *Historical Magazine*, 2d ser., 9 (1871).

Giltner, John H. "The Fragmentation of New England Congregationalism and the Founding of Andover." *Journal of Religious Thought* 20 (1964): 27–42.

Goodheart, Lawrence, and Robert O. Curry. "The Trinitarian Indictment of Unitarianism: The Letters of Elizur Wright, Jr., 1826–27." *Journal of the Early Republic* 3 (fall 1983): 281–96.

Goodman, Paul. "Ethics and Enterprise: The Values of a Boston Elite, 1800–1860." *American Quarterly* 18 (1966): 437–51.

Goodwin, Gerald. "The Myth of Arminian-Calvinism in Eighteenth Century New England." *New England Quarterly* 41 (1968): 213–37.

Green, Samuel S. "Voluntary System in the Maintenance of Ministers." *Proceedings of the American Antiquarian Society* 4 (1886): 86–126.

Griffin, C. S. "Religious Benevolence as Social Control." *Mississippi Valley Historical Review* 44 (1957): 423–44.

Gross, Robert A. "Printing, Politics, and the People." *Proceedings of the American Antiquarian Society* 99 (1989): 375–97.

Hall, David D. "The Victorian Connection." *American Quarterly* 27 (1975): 561–74.

Howe, Daniel Walker. "The Decline of Calvinism: An Approach to Its Study." *Comparative Studies in Society and History* 14 (1972): 306–27.

———. "Political Culture in the North during the Second Party System." *Journal of American History* 77 (1991): 1216–39.

Jaher, Frederic Cople. "Nineteenth-Century Elites in Boston and New York." *Journal of Social History* 6 (1973): 32–77.

Johnson, Harriet E. "The Early History of the Arlington Street Church." *Unitarian-Universalist Historical Society Proceedings* 5 (1937): pt. 2, 30–33.

Kulikoff, Allan. "The Progress of Inequality in Revolutionary Boston." *William and Mary Quarterly,* 3d ser., 28 (1971): 374–412.

Krutz, Ernest, and William Hutchinson. "Boston Area Resources for the Study of Religion." *Religious and Theological Resources* 2 (October 1971): 190–212.

Lee, Robert Edson. "Timothy Dwight and the *Boston Palladium." New England Quarterly* 35 (1962): 229–46.

Lewis, W. David. "The Reformer as Conservative: Protestant Counter-Subversion in the Early Republic." In *The Development of American Culture,* edited by Stanley Cobin and Lorman Ratner. Englewood Cliffs, N.J., 1970.

Lippy, Charles. "The 1780 Massachusetts Constitution: Religious Establishment or Civil Religion?" *Journal of Church and State* 20 (1978): 533–49.

———. "Trans-Atlantic Dissent and the Revolution: Richard Price and Charles Chauncy." *Eighteenth-Century Life* 4 (1977): 31–37.

Lord, Arthur. "Some Objections to the Constitution, 1780." *Publications of the Massachusetts Historical Society* 50 (1917): 54–88.

Mathews, Don. "The Second Great Awakening as an Organizing Process, 1780–1830: An Hypothesis." *American Quarterly* 21 (1969): 23–43.

McGovern, James R. "The Student Rebellion in Harvard College, 1807–1808." *Harvard Library Bulletin* 19 (1971): 341–55.

McLoughlin, William G. "The Role of Religion in the Revolution: Liberty of Conscience and Cultural Cohesion in the New Nation." In *Essays on the American Revolution,* edited by Stephen G. Kurtz and James H. Hutson. Chapel Hill, 1973.

Mead, Sidney. "Lyman Beecher and Connecticut Orthodoxy's Campaign against the Unitarians, 1819–1826." *Church History* 9 (1940): 218–34.

———. "The Rise of the Evangelical Conception of the Ministry in America." In *The Ministry in Historical Perspective,* edited by Richard Neibuhr and Dan Williams. New York, 1958.

Miller, Perry. "Emersonian Genius and the American Democracy." *New England Quarterly* 26 (1953): 27–44.

———. "Jonathan Edwards' Sociology of the Great Awakening." *New England Quarterly* 21 (1948): 50–77.

———. "Jonathan Edwards to Emerson." *New England Quarterly* 13 (1940): 589–617.

Morison, Samuel Eliot. "The Great Rebellion in Harvard College and the Resignation of President Kirkland." *Publications of the Colonial Society of Massachusetts* 27 (1928): 54–112.

———. "The Struggle over the Ratification of the Constitution of 1780." *Publications of the Massachusetts Historical Society* 50 (1917): 356–91.

Peabody, Andrew P. "The Unitarians in Boston." In *The Memorial History of Boston,* edited by Justin Winsor, 468–79. Boston, 1881.

Pease, Jane H. "Can This Old Union Be Restored? Some Questions About Social and Intellectual History." *Journal of the Early Republic* (spring 1991): 1–18.

Pease, William. "Doctrine and Fellowship: William Channing Gannett and the Unitarian Creedal Issue." *Church History* 25 (1956): 3–31.

Pierce, Richard, ed. "A Historical Introduction to the Records of the First Church of Boston." *Publications of the Colonial Society of Massachusetts Collections* 39 (1961).

Prince, Carl. "The Passing of the Aristocracy: Jefferson's Removal of the Federalists, 1801–1805." *Journal of American History* 52 (1966): 563–75.

Quint, Alonzo. "Ministerial Associations in Massachusetts." *Congregational Quarterly* 5 (October 1863): 261–95.

Randolph, Edward. "The Present State of New England." In *Historical Collections,* edited by Bliss Perry. Boston, 1911.

Rich, Robert. "A Wilderness of Whigs: Wealthy Men of Boston." *Journal of Social History* 4 (spring 1971): 263–76.

Robinson, David. "The Legacy of Channing: Culture as a Religious Category in New England Thought." *Harvard Theological Review* 74 (1981): 221–39.

———. "The Road Not Taken: From Edwards, through Chauncy, to Emerson." *Arizona Quarterly* 48 (1992): 45–61.

Rose, Anne C. "Social Sources of Denominationalism Reconsidered: Post-Revolutionary Boston as a Case Study." *American Quarterly* 38 (1986): 243–64.

Schmotter, James. "The Irony of Clerical Professionalism: New England's Congregational Ministers and the Great Awakening." *American Quarterly* 31 (1979): 148–68.

Scott, Donald. "The Popular Lecture and the Creation of a Public in Mid–19th Century." *Journal of American History* 66 (1980): 791–809.

Seaburg, Alan. "Some Unitarians' Manuscripts at Harvard." *Harvard Library Bulletin* 26 (1978): 112–20.

Shiels, Richard D. "The Scope of the Second Great Awakening: Andover, Mass." *Journal of the Early Republic* 5 (1985).

Simpson, Lewis P. "Federalism and the Crisis of Literary Order." *American Literature* 32 (1960): 253–66.

———. "The Intercommunity of the Learned: Boston and Cambridge in 1800." *New England Quarterly* 23 (1950): 491–503.

———. "A Literary Adventure of the Early Republic, the Anthology Society, and the *Monthly Anthology.*" *New England Quarterly* 27 (1954): 168–90.

————. "'The Literary Miscellany' and the 'General Repository.'" *Library Chronicle* (University of Texas) 3 (1950): 177–90.

Smith, Henry Nash. "Emerson's Problem of Vocation: A Note on the 'American Scholar.'" *New England Quarterly* 12 (1939): 52–67.

Smith, Philip C. F. "William Bentley on Trade and Marine Artificers." *Essex Institute Historical Collections* 113 (1977): 204–15.

Staloff, Darren Marcus. "Intellectual History Naturalized." *William and Mary Quarterly,* 3d ser., 50 (1993): 406–17.

Stewart, Robert C. "Reading Dr. Bentley: A Literary Approach to a Historical Diary." *Essex Institute Historical Collections* 113 (1977): 147–62.

Story, Ronald. "Class and Culture in Boston: The Athenaeum, 1807–1860." *American Quarterly* 27 (1975): 178–99.

————. "Harvard and the Boston Brahmins: A Study in Institutional and Class Development, 1800–1865." *Journal of Social History* 8 (1975): 99–112.

Strange, Douglas. "Abolitionism as Treason: The Unitarian Elite Defends Law, Order and the Union." *Harvard Library Bulletin* 28 (1980): 152–70.

Stout, Harry. "Rhetoric and Reality in the Early Republic: The Case of the Federalist Clergy." In *Religion and American Politics,* edited by Mark A. Noll, 62–76. New York, 1990.

Swift, Lindsay. "The Massachusetts Election Sermons." *Colonial Society of Massachusetts Collections* 1 (1894): 388–450.

Sykes, Richard E. "The Changing Class Structure of Unitarian Parishes in Massachusetts, 1780–1880." *Review of Religious Research* 12 (1970): 26–34.

Tarbox, Increase N. "The Congregational Churches of Boston since 1780." In *The Memorial History of Boston,* edited by Justin Winsor, 401–17. Boston, 1881.

Thompson, J. Earl, Jr. "An 'Unnecessary, Unjust, and Inexpedient' War: Congregational Clergy Dissent against the War of 1812." *Andover Newton Quarterly* 11 (1970): 35–47.

Vella, Michael W. "Theology, Genre, and Gender: The Precarious Place of Hannah Adams in American Literary History." *Early American Literature* 28 (1993): 21–41.

Wach, Howard M. "Unitarian Philanthropy and Cultural Hegemony in Comparative Perspective: Manchester and Boston, 1827–1848." *Journal of Social History* 26 (1992–93): 539–57.

White, Eugene E. "Decline of the Great Awakening in New England, 1741–1746." *New England Quarterly* 24 (1951): 21–54.

Whitehill, Walter Muir. "Three Letters of John Quincy Adams." *Athenaeum Items* 62 (July 1955).

Wood, Gordon. "Rhetoric and Reality in the American Revolution." *William and Mary Quarterly,* 3d ser., 23 (1966): 3–32.

Worthley, Harold Field. "A Historical Essay: The Massachusetts Convention of Congregational Ministers." *Proceedings of the Unitarian Universalist Historical Society* 12 (1958): 49–63.

Wright, Conrad. "The Controversial Career of Jedidiah Morse." *Harvard Library Bulletin* 31 (1983): 64–87.

———. "The Election of Henry Ware: Two Contemporary Accounts." *Harvard Library Bulletin* 17 (1969): 245–78.

———. "In Search of a Usable Past." *Collegium Proceedings* 1 (1979): 115–36.

———. "Piety, Morality, and the Commonwealth." *Crane Review* 9 (1967): 90–106.

———. "The Rediscovery of Channing: Some Comments on Recent Scholarship." *Proceedings of the Unitarian Historical Society* 12, (1958): 8–25.

———. "Unitarian Beginnings in Western Mass." *Proceedings of the Unitarian-Universalist Association* 21 (1989): 27–41.

Wyatt-Brown, Bertram. "Prelude to Abolitionism: Sabbatarian Politics and the Rise of the Second Party System." *Journal of American History* 58 (1971): 316–41.

Unpublished Dissertations and Papers

Alliman, Kirk Gilbert. "The Incorporation of Massachusetts Congregational Churches, 1692–1833: The Preservation of Religious Autonomy." Ph.D. diss., University of Iowa, 1970.

Beasley, James Roland. "The Success of the Cambridge Platform: Interchurch Communion in Early Massachusetts." Ph.D. diss., Tufts University, 1980.

Cadova, Eduardo. "Nature's Politics: Emerson and the Institution of American Letters." Ph.D. diss., University of California, Irvine, 1988.

Denton, Charles Richard. "American Unitarians, 1830–1865: A Study of Religious Opinion on War, Slavery and the Union." Ph.D. diss., Michigan State University, 1968.

Duran, Juan Batista. "The Theological Anthropology of Leonard Woods." Ph.D. diss., Drew University, 1983.

Farrior, John E. "A Study of the 'North American Review': The First Twenty Years." Ph.D. diss., University of North Carolina, Chapel Hill, 1954.

French, Roderick. "The Trials of Abner Kneeland." Ph.D. diss., George Washington University, 1971.

Gilmore, William J. "Orestes Brownson and New England Religious Culture." Ph.D. diss., University of Virginia, 1971.

Giltner, John H. "Moses Stuart, 1780–1852." Ph.D. diss., Yale University, 1956.

Greene, Sue N. "Contribution of the *Monthly Anthology* to American Letters." Ph.D. diss., Michigan State University, 1964.

Hanson, Debra. "Bluestockings and Bluenoses: Gender, Class and Conflict in the Boston Female Anti-Slavery Society, 1833–1840." Ph.D. diss., University of California, Irvine, 1980.

Harrington, Richard Parker. "The *Monthly Anthology:* Literary Excellence as Interpreted by a 'Society of Gentlemen.'" Ph.D. diss., University of Texas, 1964.

John, Richard. "Managing the Mails: The U.S. Postal System in National Politics." Ph.D. diss., Harvard University, 1989.

Johnson, Jane. "Through Change and through Storms: Federalist Unitarian Thought, 1800–1860." Ph.D. diss., Radcliffe, Harvard University, 1958.

Katz, Seymour. "The Unitarian Ministers of Boston." Ph.D. diss., Harvard University, 1961.

Kohr, Russell Vernon. "Early History and Influence of Hollis Professorship." Master's thesis, Western Michigan University, 1981.

Lang, Amy Schrager. "The Antinomian Strain in American Culture." Ph.D. diss., Columbia University, 1980.

Lazarow, Jama. "A Good Time Coming: Religion and the Emergence of Labor Activism in Antebellum New England." Ph.D. diss., Brandeis University, 1983.

McGill, Robert A. "Emerson and His Audience." Ph.D. diss., University of Pennsylvania, 1959.

Minnis, John H. "Joseph Stevens Buckminster: A Critical Study." Ph.D. diss., University of Pennsylvania, 1963.

Myers, John L. "The Agency System of the Antislavery System, 1832–37; and Its Antecedents in Other Benevolent and Reform Societies." Ph.D. diss., University of Michigan, 1961.

Phillips, Joseph W. "Jedidiah Morse: An Intellectual Biography." Ph.D. diss., University of California, Berkeley, 1978.

Rich, Robert Stanley. "Politics and Pedigrees: The Wealthy Men of Boston, 1798–1852." Ph.D. diss., University of California, Los Angeles, 1975.

Senior, Robert. "New England Congregationalism and the Antislavery Movement, 1830–1860." Ph.D. diss., Yale University, 1964.

Staloff, Darren Marcus. "The Making of an American Thinking Class: Intellectuals and Intelligentsia in Seventeenth-Century Massachusetts." Columbia University, 1991.

Streeter, Robert. "Critical Thought in the 'North American Review,' 1815–1856." Ph.D. diss., Northwestern University, 1943.

Sykes, Richard E. "Massachusetts Unitarianism and Social Change, 1780–1870." Ph.D. diss., University of Minnesota, 1967.

Thompson, J. Earl. "A Perilous Experiment: New England Clergy and American Destiny, 1796–1826." Ph.D. diss., Princeton University, 1968.

Vanderpool, Harold Young. "The Andover Conservatives: Apologetics, Biblical Criticism, and Theological Change at the Andover Theological Seminary, 1808–1880." Ph.D. diss., Harvard University, 1971.

Wagner, Marta. "The American Scholar in the Early National Period: College Education, 1782–1837." Ph.D. diss., Yale University, 1983.

Walsh, Evelyn Marie. "The Effects of the Revolution on Boston." Ph.D. diss., Brown University, 1964.

Wilson, Byron. "Activities of the New England Transcendentalists in the Dissemination of Culture." Ph.D. diss., University of North Carolina, 1941.

Wright, Conrad Edick. "Christian Compassion and Corporate Beneficence: Charity in New England, 1750–1840." Ph.D. diss., Brown University, 1980.

Index